# ORCOP

The Story of a Herefordshire Village

from Pre-history to Present Times

# ORCOP

## The Story of a Herefordshire Village

## from Pre-history to Present Times

Delphine Coleman

Delphine Coleman

Published in 1992 by
The S. P. A. Ltd
Units 7/10 Hanley Workshops
Hanley Swan, Worcs.

in conjunction with
DELPHINE COLEMAN



*Front Cover. Harvest Scene. Herefordshire harvest scene painted by George Robert Lewis circa 1815 by kind permission of the Tate Gallery.*

British Library Cataloguing in Publication Data

A catalogue record for this book is available from the
The British Library

ISBN 1 85421 194 3

Designed and produced by Images Design & Print Ltd., Hanley Swan, Worcs.
Printed and bound in Great Britain by Hartnolls Ltd, Bodmin, Cornwall.

# Dedication

***For Robin who tickled the trout,***
***and Ruth who picked kingcups, in the Garron.***

# CONTENTS


| | | Page No. |
|---|---|---|
| | Author's Notes | 10 |
| | Acknowledgements | 11 |
| | "Testimonial" by Harold Vinal | 13 |
| | Frontispiece | 14 |
| | Introduction | 15 |
| 1 | Geographical Location | 16 |
| 2 | Prehistoric Period | 24 |
| 3 | The Period before Domesday | 30 |
| 4 | The Hundred of Wormelow and Archenfield | 35 |
| 5 | Orcop – Origins of Name | 44 |
| 6 | The Descent of the Manor | 47 |
| 7 | The Pye Family | 60 |
| 8 | Aspects of Life in the Manor of Orcop in the 17th, 18th, and 19th Centuries | 76 |
| 9 | The Old Mills | 112 |
| 10 | The Parish Church | 123 |
| 11 | The Parish Church – Its development | 131 |
| 12 | Parish Life | 140 |
| 13 | Charities and the Poor Law | 153 |
| 14 | Aspects of Agriculture | 171 |
| | A Selection of Photographs of Farmhouses, cottages, Farm Implements and Country Crafts relating to this chapter | 200 |
| 15 | Orcop Hill Baptist Chapel | 226 |
| 16 | Garway Hill Primitive Methodist Chapel | 233 |
| 17 | The Village School | 239 |
| 18 | The Village Hall | 269 |
| 19 | Folk Lore and Superstition | 276 |
| 20 | The Village In 1967 | 281 |
| 21 | Postscript 1992 | 288 |
| | Orcop map showing locations in text. | 291 |
| | Glossary of Terms | 292 |
| | Bibliography | 294 |
| | Periodicals and Trade Directories | 300 |
| | List of Photographs, Illustrations and Maps. | 301 |

# Author's Notes

Included in this book are some photographs from the portfolio of the late Sandra James, who died in 1990 aged 29. She was born at Garway Hill, and spent nearly all her life in the parish of Orcop.

I would like to thank the following for their assistance in the final preparation of the story.

Dr. G.E. Aylmer, Rev. S. Ashton, Mrs. M. Fletcher, Mrs. M. Gardiner, Mr. R.J.H. Hill, Reference Librarian, Hereford City Library, Miss S. Hubbard and the staff of Hereford County Record Office, Mr. R. Humphreys, Major M. Munthe, Mrs C. Peill, Mr. and Mrs. J. Porter, Mr. N. Reeves, Mrs. J. Reynolds, The Royal Commission on the Historical Monuments of England, Mrs. D. Ruck, The Tate Gallery, Mr. and Mrs. G. Thomas, Mr. A. Twiston-Davies, Mr. Donovan C. Wilson.

The staff of the S. P. A. for their guidance and courtesy throughout.

Summer 1992.

# Acknowledgments

I wish to record my grateful thanks to the following who have assisted me in the preparation of this story by way of advice, information, access to documents, old deeds and photographs and allowed me to enter their homes for the purpose of photography.

Dr G.E. Aylmer.
Rev D. Acott.
The British Museum.
The Baptist Union.
Mr and Mrs C. Davies.
Mr and Mrs E. Davies.
Mr Godfrey Davies.
Mrs K. Davies.
Mr and Mrs S. Davies.
Miss G. Dredge.
Rev W. Evans.
Mr and Mrs D. Gatfield.
Mrs F. Gatfield.
Mr and Mrs J. George.
Mr and Mrs A.S. Griffiths
Mr F.H. Greening.
Hereford Diocesan Records Office, (Mrs Whiting).
Mr J. Hillaby and the History Department of Hereford College of Education.
Miss C. Isherwood.
Miss E.M. Jancey and staff of Hereford County Records Office and Library.
Mrs W. Jenkins.
Miss L.B.I.M. Lawrence.
Mr and Mrs Lomax.
Rev D. Lunt.
The Archivist of Llandaff Cathedral.
Commander J.E.H. Lucas-Scudamore.
The Archivist of the Methodist Central Office.
Mr and Mrs F. Meadmore.

Mr and Mrs G. Meadmore.

Mr and Mrs A. Morgan.

Mr A.J. Morgan.

Mr F.C. Morgan, Hereford Cathedral Archives.

Miss P. Morgan, Hereford Cathedral Archives.

The staff of the National Library of Wales, Aberystwyth.

The National Society.

Mr K. Nuttall.

Mr R.J. Philips, Education Department of Hereford College of Education.

Post Office Telephones Manager, Shrewsbury.

Post Office Archives, London.

Public Record Office

Mr and Mrs J. Panniers.

Mr L. Stockwell.

Mr R. Stewart.

Mr and Mrs L.G. Sayce.

Mrs L. Sayce.

Mr and Mrs T. Smith.

Mr F. Sharpe.

Mr R.P. Shaw,

Mr and Mrs A.H. Thomas.

Mr and Mrs W.A. Twiston-Davies.

Mr L. Williams.

Miss A. Williams.

Mr and Mrs J. Williams.

Mr B.J. Whitehouse and the staff of Hereford City Reference Library.

Rev F. Wilcock.

I offer my thanks to my husband for his guidance in the illustrations, and to my son for printing and developing almost all the black and white photographs. Thanks are also due to my many friends, the other inhabitants of Orcop, for their kind hospitality, their reminiscences and the enthusiastic interest they have shown in this story.

# Testimonial

For those who gave their strength and hope to the earth,
For the plough-driver and the seed-sower, this song
In memory of their greatness and their honour.

For those with calloused hands and bent backs
Who drove horses in the July sun,
For the stackers of hay on hot afternoons,
Who knew autumn could be ominous and the heat a scourge.

For those who walked the cornfields, and heard song ripple
out of the grass like a scythe,
Who lay on the slopes and watched twilight make love to the land.

For those who went forth at morning with a handful of seeds,
And came back at evening, their bodies fragrant with loam
from the foothills,
This obituary in memory of their fortitude and their honour.

The earth was a saga they told with their hands,
And they consoled their minds with dreams
Under the eaves of winter with the snow banked at the doors
And the owl's cry in their ears.

They chewed spring in their mouths, and their food was the wind,
They twisted the ropes of dead corn in their hands
And gave us bread out of the vast green oven of the land.

The grass will write their names, though their graves are forgotten,
The wind will sing their praise forever,
The myrtle will bloom where they sleep.

Harold Vinal. "Modern Narrative Poetry".

*View from Garway Hill,*
*Sandra James.*

# Introduction

I first came to Orcop on a warm September evening in 1954.

The reason was to "look it over" when my husband, a teacher, thought it might have some promise, as the headship of the village school was due to fall vacant at Christmas. No main water supply, no electricity, no bathroom, nothing in fact, that we had been used to, or expected to have, was to be found there, but it attracted us from the start.

From more than eighty applicants, my husband was appointed, and we moved in on Maundy Thursday 1955. We were to live there until 1966.

From the very beginning, we became part of Orcop, and Orcop became part of us. Now, I live there no more; Orcop much maligned and butt of many an unkind joke, is no longer my village, yet I shall always be able to say, not with humility, but with pride, "I am an Orcopian."

***Spring 1967.***

# Chapter One

## GEOGRAPHICAL LOCATION

Herefordshire is in what an American would call "The Middle West". In the south western corner of the county lies the Hundred of Wormelow, which is that part of Herefordshire which lies between the River Wye on the east, and the Rivers Worme and Monnow on the west and south west, from Haywood on the north, down to the confines of Dixton parish in Monmouthshire on the south. With the Hundred of Ewyas Lacy, adjoining Wormelow on the north west, this region constitutes the Welsh portion of Herefordshire.[1]

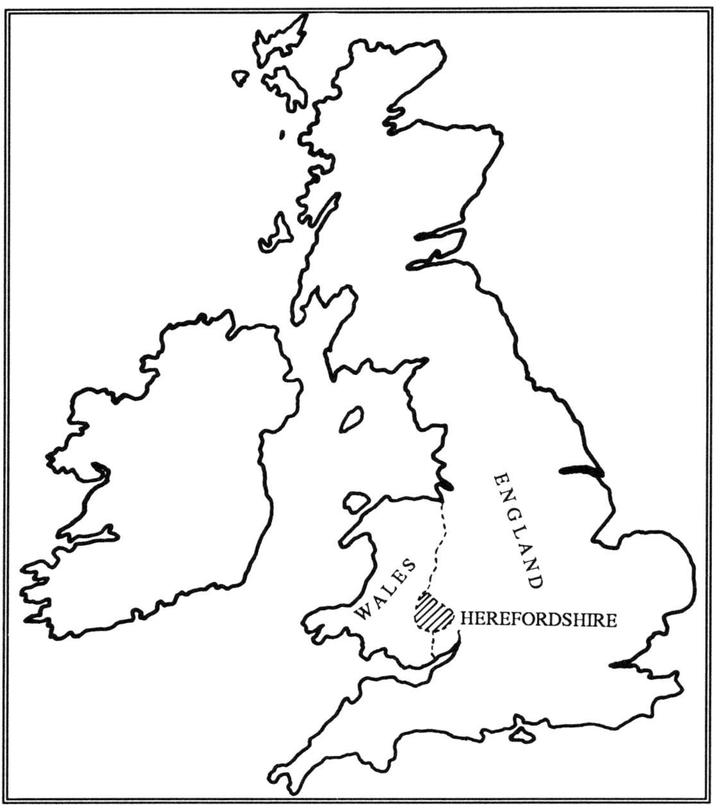


***Map to show position of the county of Herefordshire in relation to England and Wales. Note how the Welsh border and Herefordshire's western border are common.***

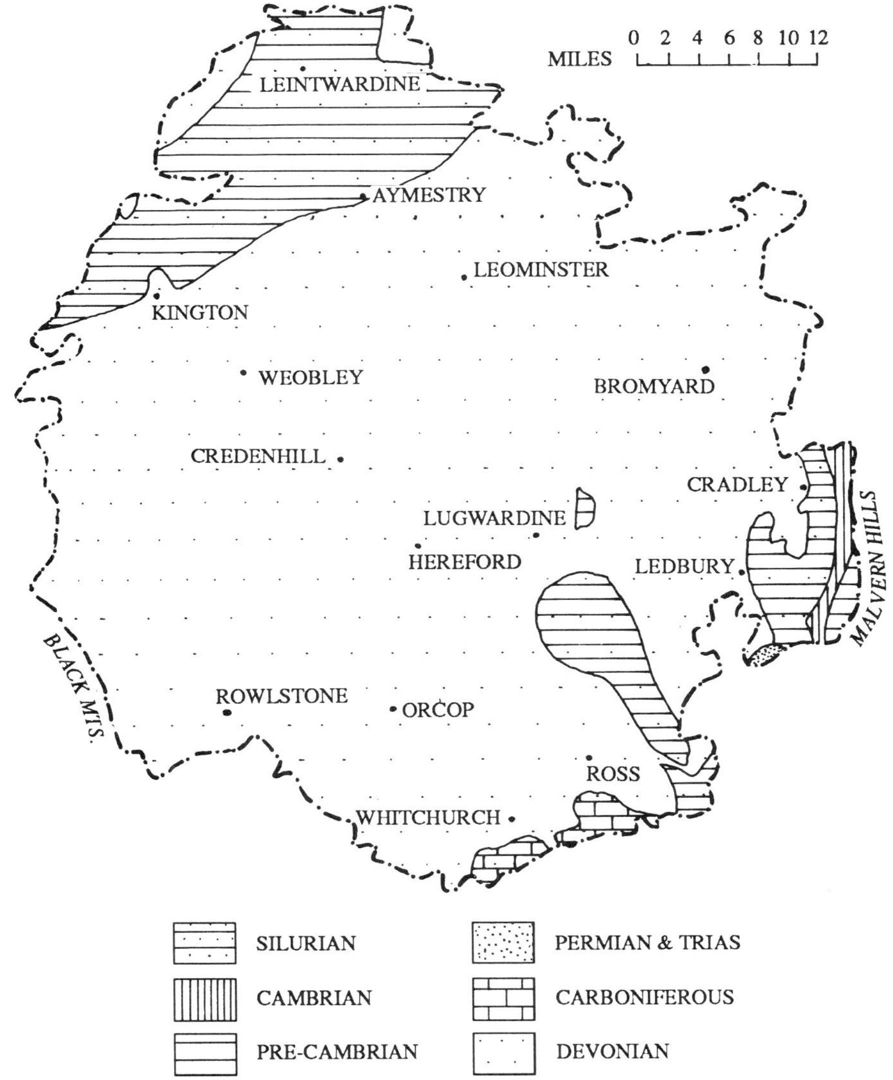


***Geological Map of Herefordshire,***
***(reproduced from Jakeman and Carver's Trade Directory of 1941).***

John Hobson Matthews in his preface to "The Hundred of Wormelow" written in 1912 states,

*"No part of England or Wales is more remote from what is commonly termed 'civilisation' than Wormelow.*

***Map of Herefordshire showing the position of Orcop in Archenfield.***

Wormelow takes its name from the river Worme, which is called Guormui. This in Welsh would be *Gywrmwy,* meaning "the winding river". The root of the word is allied to Latin *vermis,* (what winds about), a worm. The latter half of the place-name is the Saxon "low", a division of territory. Hence the whole word signifies the territory watered by the Gywrmwy or River Worme. The Worme, however, does not run through the Hundred of Wormelow, but only bounds it for a short distance on the north west.[2]

With the exception of the parishes of Callow, Saint Devereux, Holme Lacy and Kenderchurch, which are in the Hundred of Webtree, the Hundred of Wormelow corresponds to the Deanery of Archenfield, which is practically the ancient British-Welsh province of Ergyng.

The village of ORCOP, regarded as the most isolated parish in the Wormelow Hundred, is situated 11 miles equidistant from Ross-on-Wye, Monmouth and Hereford. It lies in a basin, drained by the river Garren (or Garron) which begins life as a spring on the eastern slope of Garway Hill, and is surrounded by hills; the Saddlebow and Coles Tump on the north, Garway Hill on the west, the Old Hall Wood terminating at "the Banky" on the south, and Little Hill on the East. What remains of the medieval village, is 2½ miles south west of the main Hereford to Monmouth road, and 5 miles due east of the main Hereford to Abergavenny road. Lying, as it does, off the main transport routes, its history is little documented, and its way of life has remained feudal in character until just after the turn of the twentieth century.

William Cobbett, in his travels through Herefordshire, while staying with the Palmer family at Old Hall, Pencoyd, some 4 miles away, was taken hare hunting to Orcop on the 16th November 1821, and describes the area thus: [3]

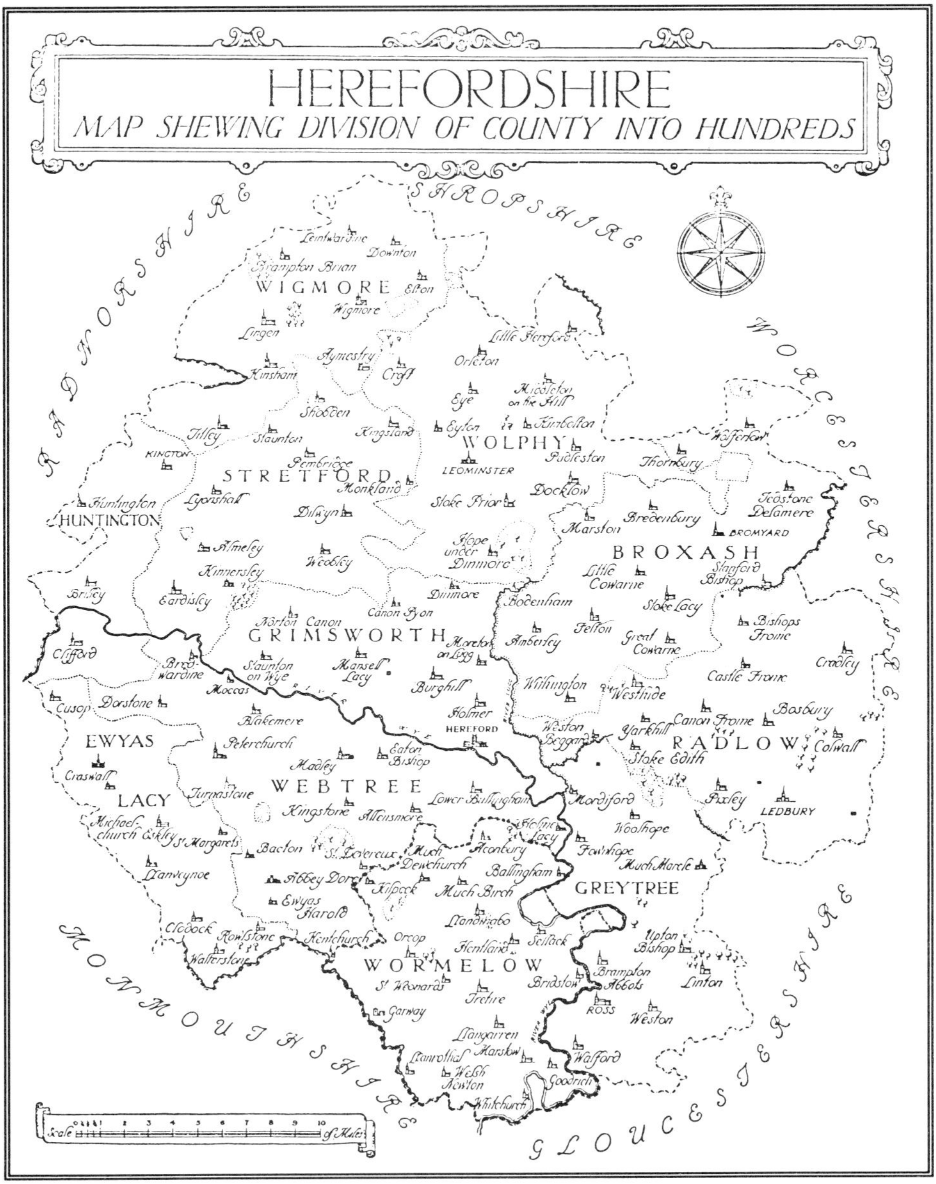


*From Royal Commission on Historical Monuments. Herefordshire South West.*

*"A steep and naked ridge, lying between two flat valleys, having a mixture of pretty large fields and small woods, formed our ground. The hares crossed the ridge forward and backward, and gave us numerous views and very fine sport. I never rode on such steep ground before; and, really, in going up and down some of the craggy places, where the rains had washed the earth from the rocks, I did think once or twice of my neck".*

Another description, from an old manuscript containing information gathered for the purpose of compiling a history of the parishes of the Wormelow Hundred, gives the following information. From the names which are known of occupiers of farms, this document could be reasonably accurately dated as belonging to the last decade of the eighteenth century.[4]

*"The land is cold and bare, and was probably cultivated but in a small degree a few centuries ago, being almost secluded from the rest of the world by high hills surrounding it on all sides and on which cultivation seems to have been making a slow and laboured progress since it first commenced in the vale. There is very little coppice or meadow, and the latter is very inferior. The soil is a stiff reddish clay, and wheat the best adapted grain. No family of consequence, nor any material or particular information are to be met with in this Parish at any period".*

Happily, for the purpose of this story, and for Orcop, the Lordship of the Manor remained vested for three hundred years in the adjoining parish of Much Dewchurch, and in 1950 the Clive family who then owned it, presented a large collection of documents relating to the Mynde Estate of Much Dewchurch, to the National Library of Wales at Aberystwyth. As a result of numerous visits to this fine library, I have been able to gain much useful information which had hitherto been unknown, and uncatalogued, which relates directly to Orcop. When commencing the preparation of this story in its final form in March 1967, I traced a further collection of documents from the Mynde Estate, among which were copies and one original of 25 Court Rolls dating from 1737 to 1808. Also in this collection were rent books, cottage and farm agreements, Estate accounts and details of maintenance work carried out on the farms owned by the Estate in the late nineteenth and twentieth centuries.

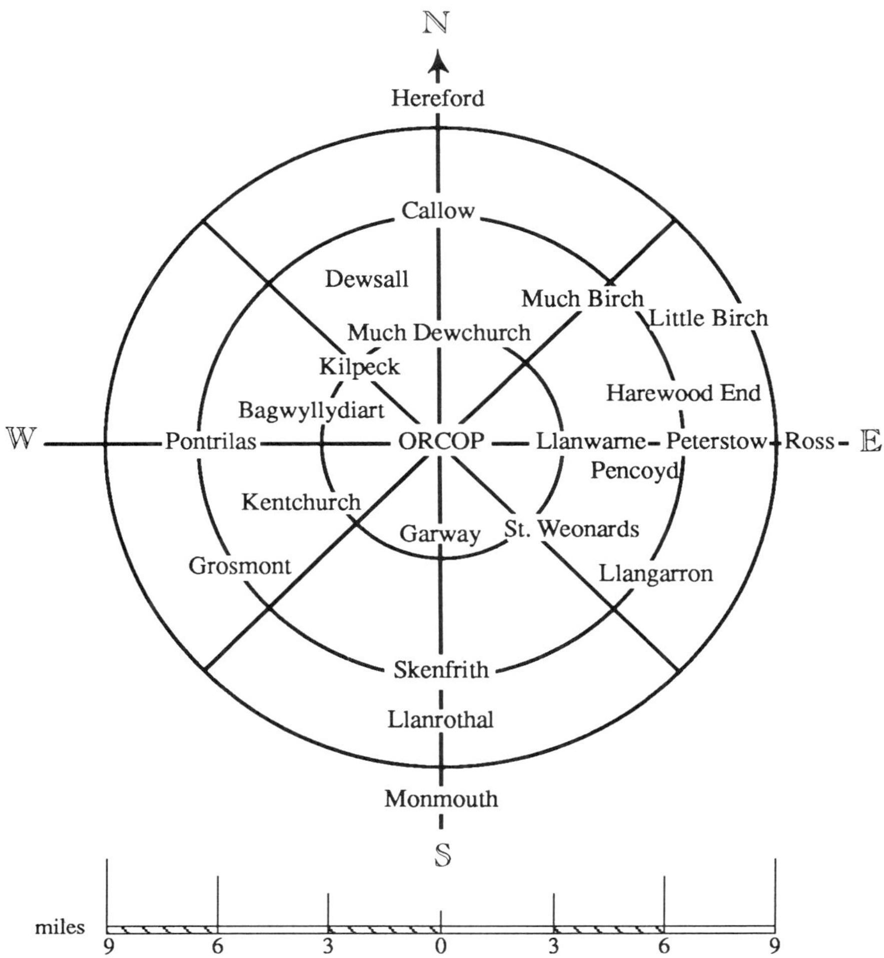


***The position of Orcop, distance and direction, in relation to other villages in the neighbourhood. All measurements are approximate.***

*A view of Orcop from Stars' Pitch.*

***Sam Ashton***

# Chapter 1

## REFERENCES


| | | |
|---|---|---|
| 1. | J. H. Matthews | Collections towards the History and Antiquities of the County of Hereford in continuation of Duncumb's History.*Hundred of Wormelow, Upper Division, Part 1.*Hereford, 1912. Volume V. Preface. |
| 2. | Matthews | p.1. |
| 3. | W. Cobbett | *Rural Rides,* First Edition 1830. |
| 4. | M.S.S. | *Wormelow 2.* Hereford City Library. Reference Department. |

# Chapter Two

## Prehistoric Period

Herefordshire, with the rest of Britain north of a line roughly from the Severn to the Wash, was covered by ice during the last three principal glacial periods when evidence of Palaeolithic (Old Stone Age) man is represented in Europe. Material remains of Mesolithic or Middle Stone Age settlers have been found in King Arthur's Cave, near Ganarew. Their economy was based on hunting, fishing and gathering, and their most characteristic flint form was a small blade, or microlith, employed singly as the tip of an arrow or collectively as the barbs in a bone fish spear.

In the Neolithic period or New Stone Age, the heavy clay soils of the county gave rise to thick oak forests which presented many problems to the first farmers, and necessitated the clearing of large tracts of woodland for their crops and herds. In the area nearest to Orcop there is a Megalithic tomb known as Arthur's Stone at Dorstone, seventeen miles away, a cist grave at Llangarron, six miles away, and a Bronze Age round barrow at St Weonards, which adjoins the village of Orcop. There are remains of Iron Age camps at Eaton Bishop, Walterstone, Aconbury, Dinedor and Little Doward.

In Orcop itself, the Historic Monuments Commission list Coles Tump at the west end of Orcop Hill as an earthwork. This consists of a series of round and rectangular mounds. At the west end is a natural tump crowned by a round enclosure about 19 yards in diameter with a slight ditch and sunk top. Immediately against the ditch on the north east is a rectangular sinking; 320 yards to the east is a circular mound 34 yards in diameter and 2 feet high, crossed by a slight scarp making the south half higher than the north half. Between these two earthworks are 7 rectangular "pillow mounds" and one round mound. The pillow mounds vary from 12 to 24 yards in length, from 4 to 6 yards in width and from 2½ to 4 feet in height. The Commission comment that in type it is precisely similar to a so-called barrow in the camp at Midsummer Hill in the Malverns, but some authorities, according to the Commission, consider this series of mounds to be artificial rabbit warrens of no great age. There is no order of alignment, and near to the middle of the group is the round mound, about 8 yards in diameter and 2½ feet high. Nothing else has been written about the origin of this earthwork. When the great agricultural drive took place during the war years in 1939-1945, local people say the mounds were levelled as a result of ploughing to quite an extent, but there are still distinct signs of some of the mounds, particularly the round enclosure which bears a close resemblance to a disc barrow.

The Woolhope Club of Hereford have made certain conjectures about its later use as a probable sanctuary of the Silures. These people who inhabited South

Wales and the Welsh Marches for at least one thousand years before the Romans landed in Britain, though a Welsh speaking people, were not of Celtic origin. The Roman historian, Tacitus, tells us they were exactly like the Iberi in Spain, and the Iberi, were originally immigrants from Libya, the desert west of the Nile. These Libyans, like their descendants, the Basques, the fellow countrymen of Saint Ignatius Loyala, founder of the Jesuits, were brave and fanatically religious soldiers, who professed a religion which was not unlike that of the Babylonians and Canaanites of the Old Testament. Most of their rites were connected with human sacrifice, and to these customs and to the worship of the supreme deities in high places, the Silures remained faithful after their settlement in Britain.[2]

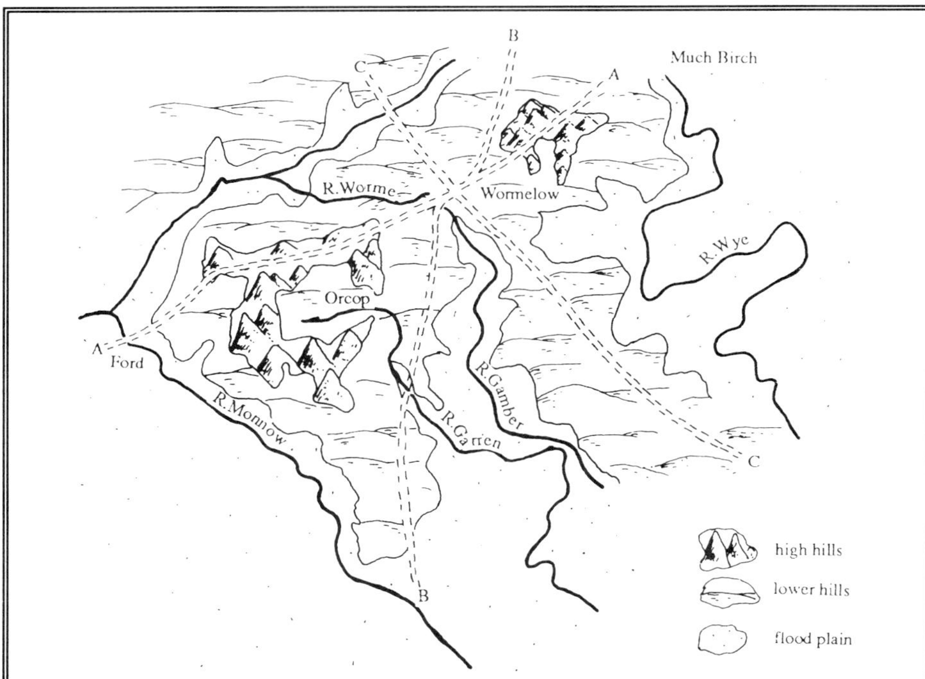


***Map of the "gap" at Wormelow, between the rivers Worme and Gamber, and the high ground of Orcop and Much Birch, showing how the ancient way crossed from hill to hill (AA) avoiding the rivers. The later road from Hereford to Monmouth (BB) avoided the rivers and the hills, and passed through the gap. Road (CC) runs from Hay in the West to Ross-on-Wye in the East crossing over the Roman road from Hereford to Abergavenny. The ford crosses the Monnow at Corras in the parish of Kentchurch.***

Orcop Hill is one of the highest points in the chain of hills which form a horse-shoe separating the basins of the Gamber and Garren from those of the Worme and the Monnow, and extends from the Wye at Ballingham to the Monnow at Kentchurch. At Wormelow the chain is interrupted by a gap which lies on the watershed between the Worme and the Gamber, and is traversed by the roads which lead from Hereford to Ross and Monmouth, and by Skenfrith to Abergavenny. For centuries these roads formed the easiest passage from the Midlands and the North into South Wales, and was especially important in the days when the principal seat of the iron industry in England was in the neighbourhood of the Forest of Dean. At Wormelow it is crossed by a greenway and field track coming from Much Birch, which, passing through Bryngwyn Wood, runs south-westwards over Orcop and Garway Hills to the ford over the Monnow at Great Corras Farm at Kentchurch, (see diagram p.25). This trackway formed part of the ancient British road from the Midlands to the Bristol Channel, which crossed the Severn below Worcester, traversed the Malverns, and after crossing the Wye, reached the Usk at Charlestown facing Caerleon, where the ancient British stronghold of Belinstock stood. Hubert Reade in his paper to the Woolhope Club (2 above), suggested that Orcop Hill, easily accessible as it was from the chief seats of the Silures, was chosen at a very early date as a "high place" in which they celebrated their solemn festivals. The name "Butters Court", (a secluded or remote spot) which is a farm near Orcop Hill, but in the next parish of Much Dewchurch, and Coles Tump bear this out. He suggests Coles Tump may take its name from a British word meaning "Light". As both Butters Court Tump and Coles Tump are grassy summits, they stand out in the light of the rising and setting sun, (e.g. see photograph below). Such places might well have been taken to be sanctuaries of the Sun Gods.

***Coles Tump taken by Mr. Alfred Watkins in 1925 showing Skirrid, Sugar Loaf and Black Mountains.***

The sacrifices always took place in a sacred grove, usually well watered, which adjoined their meeting place, and if either Butters Court or Coles Tump was a sanctuary for the Silures it must have necessarily have had such a grove near it. Near to both spots is the grove known locally by the names of "Poor Man's Wood", (a poor man is a well known euphemism in Old English for the Devil), or "Fairy Ring". In this wood are the springs from which the whole of the large

Mynde Estate of Much Dewchurch is kept constantly supplied with water, and many are the superstitions which have attached to it through the years. These will be mentioned in a later chapter on Folk Lore and Superstition.

Alfred Watkins also points out that these high points often coincided with ancient trackways, and that Scotch firs are almost certain signs either of the line of an ancient track, or more particularly, its sighting points.[3] He noted that on a Woolhope Club outing several members pointed out that Coles Tump was in direct alignment to a sighting cutting at Marstow, which in turn aligned with others. Coles Tump commands views of other mountain points for twenty miles, and half the trees are Scotch firs, the others being beeches. The origins of Coles Tump have proved of interest to several noted Hereford scholars, but nothing has been done to further these conjectures.

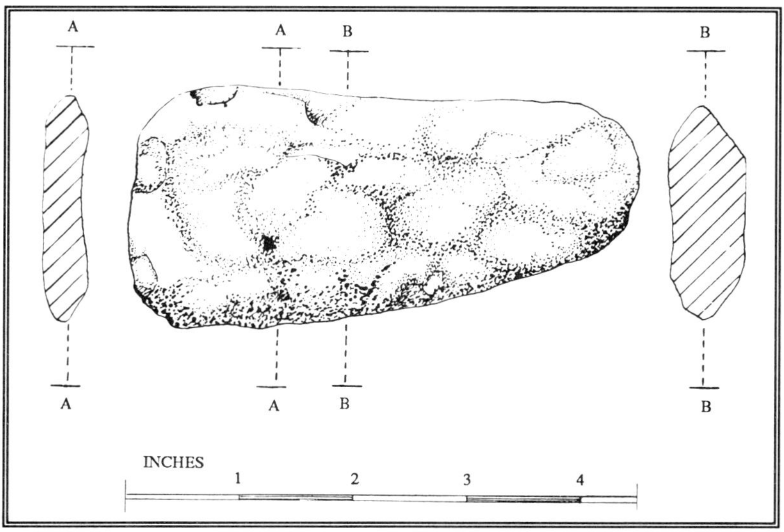


***Late Neolithic Axe. Found in the Garren Brook, and given by Stephen Williams, Garway House, Garway Hill. Length 123 mm, width 59mm, thickness 19mm. A weakly shaped implement which has been partially ground at the blade and butt; the blade half of one face shows dark brown staining consistent with partial exposure in the bed of the stream. "The poor quality of the implement makes me believe that the rock is not from a very distant source, and certainly more likely to be Welsh than to be from the Lake District." (Professor Shotton). The rock is a fine siliceous ash with spongy patches of sphene (leucoxene), and is certainly to be included in Group VIII, though Professor Shotton thinks that is a group of multiple origin. The possibility of multiple origin arises from the finding of a solitary flake assignable to group VIII among the quantities of debris at the Group VI axe factory site at Pike of Stickle, Westmorland, suggesting an additional outcrop of the parent rock. An origin in the Lower Llanvirnian of South West Wales has been postulated for Group VIII, and it is significant that of the 14 items assigned to this Group and published to date 12 have been found between Pembrokeshire and Hampshire. A number of others from Wales and Herefordshire await publication. Woolhope Club 1963 part III.***

The only prehistoric finds in the village are a Bronze Age, dark grey, flint, rounded thumbscraper which was found in the school playground in 1956, and more recently in 1963, a late Neolithic axe head which was found in the Garren Brook. Both these implements were given to the Hereford Museum. The axe head is shown, together with descriptive details on the previous page.

# Chapter Two

## REFERENCES


| | | |
|---|---|---|
| 1. | – | Royal Commission on the Historical Monuments of England. Herefordshire. Vol. 1. South-West. H.M.S.O. London, 1931. Page 52 |
| 2. | H. Reade | Transactions of the Woolhope Naturalists' Field Club. "Ghosts of Much Dewchurch". 26th July 1928. Page 156 ff. |
| 3. | A. Watkins | The Old Straight Track. London. 1st Edition 1925. Pages 62 and 189. |

# Chapter Three

## The Period Before Domesday

As already stated the Hundred of Wormelow corresponded to the ancient British kingdom of Ergyng or Urging, later to become known as Erchenfield, Urchenfield, Irchenfield, and finally the Deanery of Archenfield. At the time of the Roman invasions, Ergyng formed part of Britannia Secunda or Siluria, the region inhabited by the Silures. The Silures put up a strong resistance, and Tacitus tells of the last desperate battle of the Wye. Where the Great Doward, near Whitchurch, slopes down to the right bank of the Wye, the spot is called "The Slaughter". In the final struggle the Silures were led by Caractacus, who, after fighting many battles against the Romans, had taken refuge with the western tribes. Before the year 78 A.D. Frontinus had crushed the Silures, and the important town of Ariconium at Weston-under-Penyard, 3 miles from Ross-on-Wye, was the headquarters of the Roman force which policed the whole district from the Forest of Dean to the banks of the Usk.

Two Roman roads pass through the district of Archenfield; that from Kenchester, the Roman fort of Magna, to Abergavenny, a distance of approximately 25 miles, which is a spur off Watling Street, and the road from Hereford to Monmouth, West Watling street. Traces of the Kenchester to Abergavenny road were discovered at Abbeydore, some 7 miles from Orcop, when the Golden Valley Railway was being constructed.[1] It is assumed that the road followed the course of the present main road, but there is also the possibility that it followed a ridgeway route running parallel to the main road, through Llangua towards Skirrid Fawr, and so into Abergavenny.[2]

With regard to the road from Hereford to Monmouth, this formed part of the base road to connect Chester, Caerleon and Gloucester, which were the fortresses responsible for the control of Wales. West Watling Street ran from Chester, through Wroxeter, Hereford and Monmouth, to the southcoast road at Chepstow, with connections to Caerleon and Gloucester.[3] Although there are no traces of the road from Hereford to Monmouth, it followed the only course possible along the ridges until some 3 miles before Monmouth, when it drops down through the villages of Welsh Newton and Buckholt to reach its destination. This is the course of the present main road which passes within 1½ miles of one end of the village of Orcop. There are, however, no traces of Roman occupation or contact with Roman civilisation to be found in the village. Iron ashes have been found in the parishes of Bridstow, Hentland, Ganarew, Goodrich, Llangarron, Peterstow and St. Weonards, which indicate Roman penetration in the near vicinity, but no doubt the surrounding hills and woods of the area did not attract settlement. Roman coins have also been found at Bishopswood and Lydbrook, both villages which border on the Forest of Dean, and one of the most interesting memorials, a Roman altar, is to be found in the Church of Tretire. A well-known Herefordshire antiquary, the Rev. John Webb who was a former Rector of Tretire, found the altar in the possession of a village doctress who had been using part of it as a mortar.[4]

After the departure of the Roman legions early in the 5th century, the Dark Ages intervene, and much of the country's history remains obscured. The Angles penetrated into Ergyng, and by 586 A.D. the area had submitted together with the rest of the county, thus becoming part of the Kingdom of Mercia, later to become the greatest and largest principality of the Anglo- Saxon Heptarchy. The author of "The Hundred of Wormelow" believes that the population of Ergyng were never wholly subdued, and that the Anglo-Saxons contracted military alliances with the Welshmen of the district. Right down the Middle Ages this pattern persisted with the Welsh of Ergyng fighting under the standard of the English King against their kinsfolk over the border. The district must have been a veritable "cockpit" of the continuous strife which took place in the Marches between English and Welsh. Welsh was spoken in this district up to the end of the 19th century. Attention is also drawn to the preponderance of Welsh names on the right or west bank of the Wye, the side of the Wormelow Hundred, while the place names of the left or east bank are Teutonic or English. This indicates that a great deal of self-government was granted to the people of Ergyng, and that the district was never completely colonised by the Saxon invaders. The people in this district were in possession of superior privileges, and mention is made in old manuscripts of their great courage. The Book of Llandaff or Liber Landavensis is the oldest document available for the history of the Welsh Marches, and from it the following pedigree of the Kings of Ergyng can be traced.[5] No more definite date can be given for this pedigree than the early part of the 6th century.

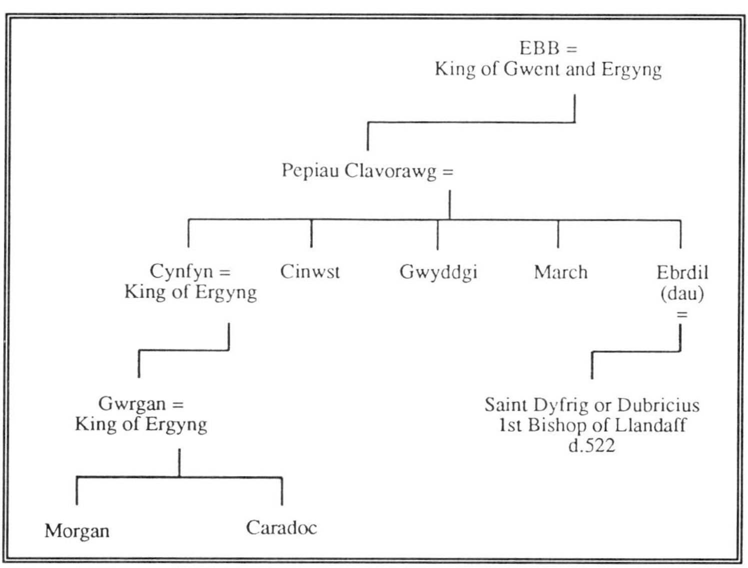

The connection with Ergyng of St. Dyfrig or Dubricius can be seen by the fact that four churches in the district were dedicated to him, namely, those at Ballingham, Hentland, St. Devereux and Whitchurch. Tradition also has it that St. David restored the sight of one of the Kings of Ergyng, and his name is also perpetuated in the churches of Much and Little Dewchurch, Dewsall, and formerly, Kilpeck. The whole of the Deanery of Archenfield was in the diocese of Llandaff up to 1133, and the jurisdiction of the Bishop of St. Davids extended to part of Herefordshire as late as 1852.

Mercian supremacy waned after the death of Offa (758-796 A.D.) but the district of Archenfield still seems to have been an area of some consequence since in 918 the Bishop was taken prisoner by a Danish raiding party, and held to ransom for a considerable sum. A translation of the Anglo-Saxon Chronicle gives the following information.[6]

> *"918. Here in this year a great ship host of the enemy came over hither from the south from Brittany, and with it two Earls Othot and Hroald and they fared west till they arrived within the mouth of the Severn, and they harried in Wales everywhere by the sea coast where they pleased, and they seized Cameleae, Bishop in Archenfield, and led him with them to their ships, and then King Edward ransomed him again with forty pounds. Then after that the whole host landed, and would still plunder towards Archenfield. Then met them the men of Hereford and of Gloucester and of the nearest fortresses and fought against them, and put them to flight and slew Earl Hroald and a brother of the other Earl Othot and many of the host and drove them into an enclosure and there beset them, until they deliver hostages to them on the condition that they would depart from King Edward's dominions".*

The first half of the tenth century saw the gradual establishment of West Saxon rule over all England. By the time of the Norman Conquest, the old Kingdom of Ergyng appears to have become the Hundred of Wormelow. Prior to this administrative problems and law cases were dealt with by a folk moot which was an assembly of the head men. This probably met at Wormelow which was ideally situated as a meeting place, situated at an important crossroads, (e.g. see diagram on page 25). These meetings took place in the open, often at some prominent landmark, which later gave its name to the Hundred. One version of the name Wormelow is "the low or hill near the Worme", and the names of the village inn at the crossroads together with the whole of the immediate vicinity, are "The Tump Inn" and Wormelow Tump.[7]

The first reference to Wormelow is in Domesday Book; the name Archenfield is suggested by both Prebendary Seaton and J.H. Matthews (4 and 5), to be a derivation of the Latin, Ariconium, the name of the old Roman town near the present-day Weston-under-Penyard. Another spelling is Urchenefled, as instanced in the "Testa de Nevill" of 1243 which is interesting in view of a comment in the undated "Wormelow" manuscript in the Hereford City Library, that this is "the land of the hedgehogs". An old English word for the hedgehog, is an "urchin", and in an old Church wardens' Account of Orcop dated 1746, money was paid for 4 urchins. In the past it was common for money to be paid by the Church wardens for the killing of vermin, and the hedgehog was considered to be vermin because people believed they suckled the udders of the cows lying down in the fields.

References to Archenfield in the Anglo-Saxon Chronicle of 915 give three different spellings, Ircingafeldes, Yrcingafeld, Iercingafeld, which can be phonetically connected with Ariconium, though the element "inga" is more indicative of a Saxon derivation.[8] The word appears in more than a dozen forms in Liber Landavensis.

At the time of Domesday the district was referred to as the Hundred of Wormelow and Irchenfield. Up to this time there is no documented evidence that the village of Orcop existed. Since, in later times, the Manor of Orcop came under certain authority of the Manor of Wormelow, it will be worthwhile to devote a short chapter to the customs and documentary evidence that relate to the Hundred of Wormelow and Irchenfield. Since the latter has so many different spellings, as do many other places in my story I shall use the spellings as used in my sources.

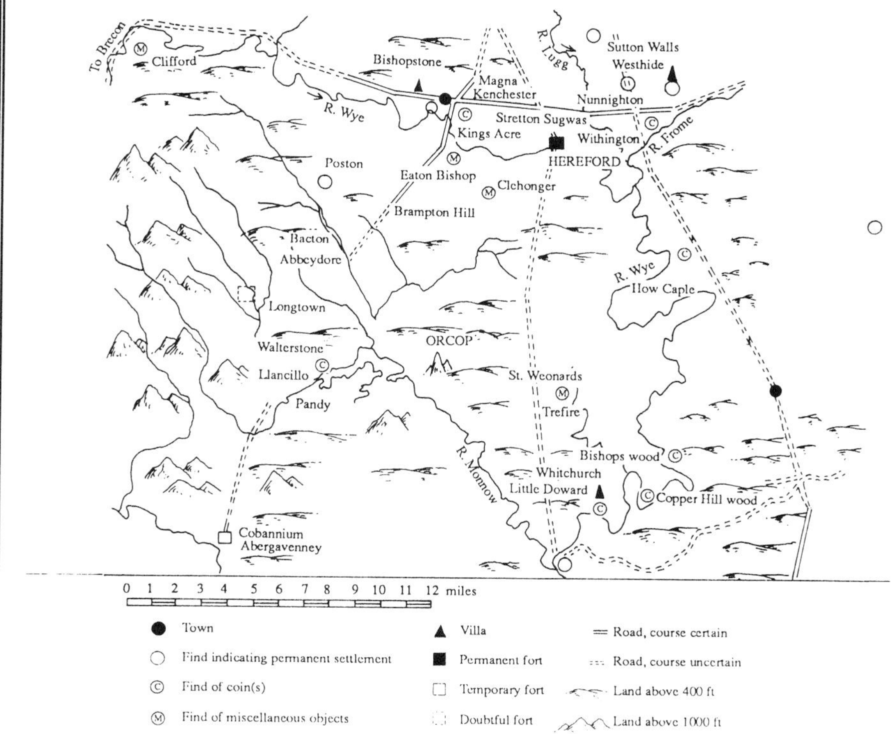


*The Roman Occupation in the vicinity of Orcop.*

# Chapter Three

## REFERENCES


| | | |
|---|---|---|
| 1. | A.T. Bannister. | The History of Ewias Harold. Hereford. 1902. p. 98. |
| 2. | I.D. Margary. | Roman Roads in Britain. London. 1957. Volume 11. p. 75. |
| 3. | I.D. Margary. | Volume 11, p. 49. |
| 4. | Rev. Preb. J. Seaton. | History of the Deanery of Archenfield. Hereford 1903. p. 1 and 2. |
| 5. | J. H. Matthews. | Preface. |
| 6. | – | Anglo Saxon Chronicle. Translated by E.E.C. Gomme. 1909. |
| 7. | A.T. Bannister. | Place-names of Herefordshire, Cambridge. 1916. p. 214. |
| 8. | A.T. Bannister. | Place-names of Herefordshire. p. 6. |

# Chapter Four

## THE HUNDRED OF WORMELOW AND ARCHENFIELD

Wormelow is first documented in the Domesday Book of 1086. The following is a translation.[1]

*"In Hereford city in the time of King Edward there were 103 men dwelling within and without the wall, and they had these underwritten customs . . . He who had a horse, thrice in the year rode with the Sheriff to the Pleas and to the Hundred of Vrmelauia". (Wormelow).*

The Hundred of Wormelow has only one entry in Domesday as under –[2]

*"In Wermelav Hundred. St. Peter of Gloucester holds Wesvode, the chief of this manor. King Edward held there 6 hides. One of these hath Welsh customs and the others English . . ."*

It is thought that Westvode was Gillow Manor, near Hentland. This entry indicates that Wormelow was also identified as a Manor. A hide was a unit of land, the measurement of which varied in different parts of the country, usually from 80 to 120 acres.

Archenefelde, however, appears to be of considerably more importance. The following translation of the entries in Domesday relate to the Welsh holders of land there.[3]

*"If any one of them die, the King has 20 shillings from him by custom.*

*If any Welshman steal man or woman, horse, ox or cow, he restores upon conviction thereof, first the property stolen and gives 20 shillings forfeit. For a stolen sheep, however, or a bundle of sheaves of corn, he pays 2 shillings compensation.*

*If any one kill one of the King's vassals and commit heinfare (the going away of a man from his Lord) he gives the King 20 shillings in payment for the man and 100 shillings forfeit. If he shall slay the vassal of any thane he gives 10 shillings to the dead man's Lord.*

*If a Welshman shall slay a Welshman, the relations of the slain meet together, and plunder the slayer and his kinsmen, and burn their houses until about noon on the morrow, when the dead man's body may be buried. Of this plunder the King has a third, but of all the rest they are quit.*

*So, also, whoever shall set fire to a house and be thereof accused, shall defend himself by 40 men. The which if he be unable to do, he shall pay 20 shillings to the King.*

*If anyone shall conceal from custom a sextary of honey, upon proof thereof, for one sextary he shall return five, if he hold as much land as ought to give it.*

*If the Sheriff call them out to a shire-mote, six or seven of the best among them to go with him. Whoever, after having been called, does not go, gives 2 shillings or an ox to the King, and whoever remains away from the Hundred pays as much.*

*He pays in like manner, who, being commanded by the Sheriff to go with him into Wales, does not do so. For if the Sheriff does not go, not one of them will.*

*When the army marches against the enemy, they form by custom the vanguard, and on its return the rearguard.*

*These were the customs of the Welsh in the time of King Edward in Archenefelde".*

These customs lasted, with slight modifications, for two centuries or more after the Norman Conquest. From an entry in the "Testa de Nevill" dated 1243, we learn that "Urchenefeld in Wallia" was held from the King in sergeantry (a particular kind of knight service) by a community of Welshmen living according to "the customs of Urchenefeld". The community was bound to furnish, once a year when the King required them to join the army in Wales, 50 men for 15 days service, at their own expense. If the King required them for a longer period, he had to provide them with necessaries. If he wished them to serve in England, they must serve at their own expense for one day and one night, and if he wished to have them in England for a longer period, he must provide them with necessaries as above. And they were bound to render to the King 19 marks a year, and did not owe any other service except only suit of the Hundred, according to the custom of Urchenefeld. The term "suit" meant attendance at the Hundred Court.

Another Domesday mention of Archenefelde states:-[4]

*"In Archenefelde the King hath 100 men, less 4, who have 73 ploughlands with their men, and give of custom 41 pints of honey and 20 shillings for all the things that they were wont to give, and 10 shillings for fumage (hearth tax) and they do not give gelds (tribute) or other custom, save that they go forth in the King's army if they are commanded".*

*"If a free man there dies, the King shall have his horse with the arms (the original heriot). From the vill, when he dies, the King shall have 1 ox. King Griffin and Blein (Griffith ap Llewelyn, King of Wales) laid waste this land in the time of King Edward, and therefore it is not known of what kind it was at this time".*

A heriot was a fine in kind or cash payable to the Lord of the Manor on the decease of the owner or land holder or vassal. The word comes from the Anglo Saxon "heregeatu", meaning military accoutrements. From the foregoing it can be seen that the King's Court of his Hundred of Wormelow was held before the Sheriff of Hereford, who was attended by citizens on horseback.

The district is known variously as the Hundred of Wormelow and Irchenfield, and sometimes the names are given separately to Hundreds which makes it very confusing, but it seems safe to assume that they were one and same. The area had many ancient customs, and these are listed below in chronological order. Much of this information has been taken from Wormelow Court Rolls which were quoted in the "Wormelow 1 and 2" in the Hereford City Library. I have endeavoured to trace these Court Rolls, but according to the Manorial Registers of the Historical Manuscripts Commission the only Court Rolls that exist are at the National Library of Wales, Aberstwyth, (1 extract, torn and in Latin), and the Public Record Office in London, (1574-75), and those of the Courts Leet held between 1806-1905 in the Hereford County Records Office. The dates of these do not agree with the dates listed in the manuscript, and I feel that possibly there may be Court Rolls in the hands of a private collector which stem from the holder of the Lordship of Wormelow. This said Lordship devolved for several generations on the Hoskyns family of Harewood, near Ross-on-Wye, and much of the information in the manuscripts seems to have been culled from there.

***Undated.***

*"The principal possessions most necessary for the heir of a freeholder within the Lordship of Irchenfield to have after the death of his father, with the assent of the Doomesmen (judges) and suitors.*

*The best horse and harness, if any.*
*The best ox.*
*The best wayne (wagon).*
*The best standard bruche (spit) and andiron.*
*The best charger. (a large dish).*
*The best standard grate.*
*The best quern mill.*
*The great iron bar to hang the pot on.*
*The great standard coffer. (a large chest).*
*The best brass pot or pan.*

*The best spoon.*
*The best salt cellar.*
*A standing vase if any be.*
*If there be 2 beds, the heir to have the best which is a down bed.*
*A great table board and tressles.*

***Coram Rege***

***Pleas 1225.***

*The men of the Hundred of Irchinfeld from time immemorial have pleaded, and had their pleas of all pleas which pertain to the Crown, or of appeals or trespasses against the King's peace, only before the Sheriff of Hereford, and not before any Justices. Therefore, the appeal is sent back into the Hundred aforesaid".*

This was to prove of great importance in the later disputes between the Manors of Orcop and Wormelow for possession of cottages on the waste of Orcop.

***Undated.***

*"A certificate of exemption and priviliges belonging to tenants holding of Wormelow Manor.*

*These persons are to certify to all persons to whom it may concern that T.J. ... of St. Weonards in the manor of Archenfield and the Hundred of Wormelow, farmer, is a tenant and inhabitant of the manor which is ancient demesne having a right to be toll free in every market, town or city throughout England for all goods, chattles and cattle which he shall buy or sell within the same realm of England, and hath a right to be quit of portage, murage and passage, and is entitled to all other immunities and priviliges which of right belong to the tenants and inhabitants of the said manor or hundred under the King's Great Seal now in my custody".*

Murage was the term for money used for keeping the walls of a town in repair. Portage was the term for the price of carrying.

***1584.***

*"At an enquiry at the Booth Hall, Hereford, in 1584, touching the descent of lands and customs, it was stated by witnesses that partition of land was in accordance with gavelkind , namely, land of ancient demesne had to be divided among the brethren of a family. It was also stated that all Archenfield is exempted from the authority of the Sheriff of the City of Hereford.*

***1589***

*"It is stated that any person who has for himself any enclosure out of common, field or pasture must enclose it with his own hedge and not make his neighbour's hedge serve."*

***1637***

*Jurors found that all trees growing on waste land belonged to the Lord unless custom or presentation proved to the contrary.*

*August, being the harvest month, was to be free from courts. It is recorded that because a court must not be kept in harvest time, Walter Gwatkin was amerced (fined) £5 for striking the book out of the Bailiff's hand when he should have been sworn on the jury."*

The Gwatkin family were living in Orcop at this time, and served the Mynde Estate in later years.

***1637.***

*"A distress must be prized and if the owner comes not in 3 days, it is to be sold and the debt satisfied and the overplus to be returned.*

***1639.***

*We find that tenants of the said manor have free fishing within the rivers of Wye and Garron for themselves and their own household servants only, of every parish and township within the said manor that is adjoining the said rivers except exempted places where other subjects have free fishing by the King's grant.*

*We find that every tenant within the said manor that hath free fishing within the river of Wye if he take any salmon or salmons within the same river, and have a purpose the same to sell, that they ought to bring them to the Fish Board at Hoarwithy, and offer the same there to be sold (by quarters or otherwise) as the Board and seller can agree, and if the buyer will bestow 4d or 6d the seller is to furnish him accordingly by the space of 2 hours, before they bring the same to any market town, and we further say that the custom of the said manor be, is and hath been; and we further present that no persons can have the privilige or benefit of fishing in the said river, unless he be the freeholder within the said manor, and they have to fish with such nets and engines as are allowed by the laws and statute of this realm of England".*

The manuscript states that on the 5th May 1569 Richard Beare of Kings Caple was presented because after he had taken one salmon from the Wye, and brought it to the Fish Board, he refused to sell the same to the tenants, or to cut the salmon or suffer the same to be cut. At this same Court in 1569, Edward and Thomas Gunter were summoned for fishing, and taking salmon not being tenants. Gunter was a name very common in Orcop in later years. At the Court Leet of 1639 where this right of fishing was re-affirmed, Thomas Jones of Orcop was one of the Jury. The purpose of the fish being taken to the Board at Hoarwithy was to enable the poor people to have an opportunity of buying the fish cheaply in small portions. After two hours the seller was at liberty to take his catch to the market.

The right of free fishing in the Wye and Garron is again reiterated in the following extract from a Court Baron held on the 23rd May, 1905.[5]

> *"The Jurors present that the Fishboards at Hoarwithy have been allowed to decay, and should be renewed to enable the Freeholders within the district of the Free Fishery of this Manor or Hundred to expose for sale thereon the salmon or salmons caught in the Rivers Wye and Garron in accordance with the ancient custom of this Manor or Hundred. And they further present that the freeholders' rights in the free fishing of the rivers aforesaid should be enquired into and maintained".*

This free fishing lasted until 1911 when two fishermen had a case brought against them which they eventually lost, after several appeals, in 1911 by a majority of 1 vote, the case having been heard in the House of Lords.

*1717.*

> *"It is certified that William Lambert of ye parish of Orcop, yeoman, a tenant and resident in Irchinfeld in ye manor or Hundred of Wormelow, hath the right to enjoy all the rights, priviliges and amenities of an ancient demesne, tenant of Wormelow aforesaid, according to the laws of England, and the several Charters under the Great Seal of England now in my custody granted for the confirmation of the rights, liberties, franchises, and priviliges of the ancient demesne, tenant of the manor of Irchenfield and Wormelow".*

The Lordship of Wormelow is described by Leland about 1538 thus –

> *"It is a great lordship belonging to the Earl of Shrewsbury and lieth between Monmouth and Hereford about 2 miles from each of them. It is very full of enclosures of corn and wood. Gentlemen called Minos be great possessors of it".*

The "Minos" referred to are the Mynors family who have owned Treago Castle, a fortified mansion in St. Weonards, for many centuries. Their descendants are still in occupation. The Manor of Wormelow was a large one, and in 1589 there were 37 parishes or single suits that owed Suit and Doom to the Manor Court of Wormelow; these included the village of Orcop. A perambulation of the Manor (see page 42) dated 1639 shows that the bounds stretched from Llanrothall near Monmouth, through Garway and Kentchurch, along the Saddlebow Hill in Orcop and through Much Dewchurch to Dewsall, Haywood and Aconbury. Villages to the east of Wormelow owing suit and service included Hentland, Bolstone, Kings Caple, Little Dewchurch and Much Birch.

The Hundred of Wormelow and Irchenfeld was granted by Henry 111 in 1227 to Hubert de Burgh.[6] In 1252 the men of Irchenfeud obtained from the King the de-forestation of that lordship. This meant that the inhabitants were no longer subject to Norman forest laws, which allowed the deer to roam through their lands without hindrance or redress. In 1330 Edward 111 committed the custody of the Hundred of Wormelowe in Irchenfeld to John de Bradeston, and to Henry de Pembrugg the custody of Irchenfeld. This latter grant appears to separate the two districts whereas previously they had been known under one title. By 1346 the Hundred of Irchingfeld and the Hundred of Wormelowe were possessed by Richard Talbot, Elizabeth, his wife, and their heirs. The Talbots, later Earls of Shrewsbury, continued to hold the Wormelow Hundred for several generations and by 1604 it was styled "Wormelow Court of Gilbert, Earl of Shrewsbury". The Hundred was next held by Henry, Earl of Kent, Stephen Ashby and Richard Clark (see chapter VIII pages 87 and 88.) until the latter half of the 18th century when it was bought by Sir Hungerford Hoskyns of Harewood in whose family it remained until 1892 when it was sold to Major Henry Harrison Parry. At the Court Leet held on the 23rd May 1905, the Lord of the Manor or Hundred of Wormelow was Joseph Harrison Parry, and the last known Lord of Wormelow was Joseph Henry Parry in 1909.[7]

J.H. Matthews says that "after the death of Henry de Grey, Duke of Kent, 5th June 1740, the Hundred of Wormelow, together with the lordships of Goodrich Castle and Wilton, which were all held by him, were sold under the direction of Trustees to different purchasers. Goodrich Castle was bought by Admiral Thomas Griffin of Hadnock, and the Manor or Hundred of Wormelow by Sir Hungerford Hoskyns of Harewood, bart. . . ." This must be incorrect since John Symons of the Mynde fought two cases against the Lord of Wormelow regarding the possession of cottages on the waste of Orcop in 1736 and again in 1746 when Stephen Ashby and Richard Clarke were named as Lords of Wormelow.

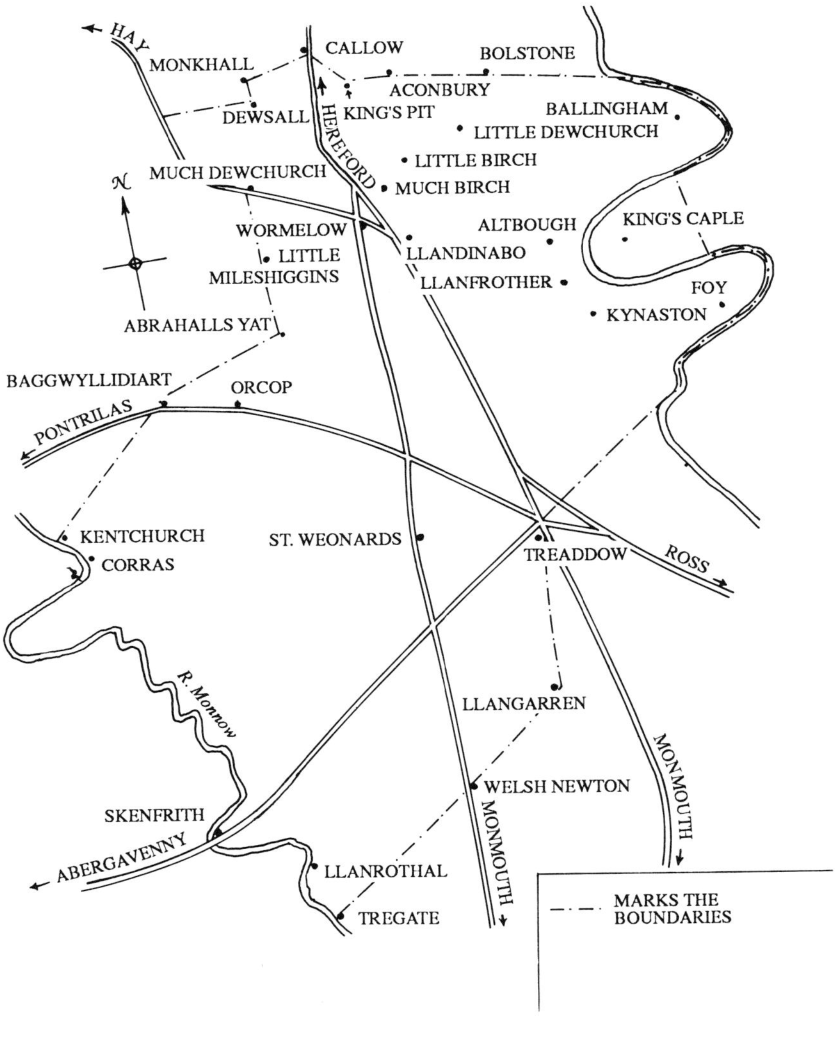


***Plan of the Manor of Wormelow in 1639,***
***drawn from an original perambulation in Hereford County Record Office.***

# Chapter Four

## References


| | | |
|---|---|---|
| 1. | V.H. Galbraith and J. Tait (eds) | Herefordshire Domesday. Pipe Roll Society. London. 1950. p.1. |
| 2. | V.H. Galbraith. and J. Tait (eds) | Herefordshire Domesday. p. 20. |
| 3. | A.T. Bannister. | The History of Ewias Harold. Hereford. 1902. Private Subscription. p.102. |
| 4. | V.H. Galbraith. and J. Tait (eds) | Herefordshire Domesday. p.19. |
| 5. | – | Rolls of Courts Baron and Courts Leet, Wormelow Hundred and Manor. 1806-1905. M.S.S. Hereford County Record Office. |
| 6. | J.H. Matthews. | p. 17. |
| 7. | – | Rolls of Courts Baron and Courts Leet. As 5 above. |


Court Rolls.

All the extracts quoted in this chapter have been taken from the two books of M.S.S. notes entitled Wormelow 1 and 2 in the City Library, Hereford. The notes are not indexed, and are interspersed between notes on the various parishes in the Wormelow Hundred. It is mentioned in one place that the Court Rolls were preserved at Harewood; this can only mean Harewood House, Herefordshire, which was razed many years ago. I understand that the Parry family moved to Lancashire.

# Chapter Five

## ORCOP – ORIGINS OF NAME

Orcop is not mentioned in the Domesday Survey, although this distinction was claimed for it by Prebendary Seaton, who added that it was styled Hir Cop (long hill) in the Survey. The entry by which he was misled is as follows:[1]

> *"The land of Osbern, son of Richard, in Hezetree Hundred. . . The same Osbern holds and held HERCOPE as half a hide".*

The Hezetree Hundred was situated in the north of the county, part of it in present-day Radnorshire. Its boundaries are still not clearly defined since it became joined to the Hundred of Wigmore in later years. Orcop lies at the opposite end, in the south west of Herefordshire, and more recent research by Lord Rennell of Rodd, has now identified Hercope with the village of Lower Harpton near Old Radnor.[2] I also note that in a copy of notes used in the trial of 1736 (see page 88) putting the case for the defence against the Lord of Wormelow Manor, the following states [3]

> *"We have a copy of Doomsday book which shows that* Hercopp *in the Marches of Wales was then a manor, but as Hezitree Hundred is there mentioned at the top, it is doubtful whether Hercopp is not a different manor from ours, and therefore not proper to produce this copy".*

Orcop is first mentioned in an Ancient Charter of 1138.[4] The Domesday Survey states that on the border of Archenfield there were nine waste manors, and in Archenfield itself "King Grifin and Blein laid waste this land in the reign of King Edward", so very little is known of the settlements in this area. Orcop could well have been in this waste area, but no documented mention of it comes to light until 1138. This refers to "nominati in nemore de Orcop"; "mentioned as in the grove of Orcop". A further note in the same Charter states –

> *"This is one place, along with others in Herefordshire and Gloucestershire which were confirmed to Roger, son of Miles of Gloster, and to Cecily his wife, of all the land which her father, Payn FitzJohn, had inherited or acquired together with her own marriage portion".*

The origin of the name is stated in the Concise Oxford Dictionary of English Place Names (Ekwall), Place Names of Herefordshire (Bannister), and English Place Name Elements (Smith), to be Old English or Anglo-Saxon. The village is situated on the borders of Wales in the ancient kingdom of Mercia which was an old English dialect region, but the Celtic influence was also strong in this part of Herefordshire. The Liber Landavensis of 1132 shows that there were Welsh settlements at Kilpeck and Callow to the north of the Aconbury to Garway line of hills, and Welshmen and hides of Welsh land were recorded as having been on the west bank of the Wye at Ewyas Harold, Bacton and Llanwarne, all within 7 miles of Orcop. Celtic settlements have been located on hill tops, St. Weonards being one such example, this within 2 miles of Orcop. Two old Celtic routes of travel are mentioned by J.N.Jackson in the region, one of which travels along the ridge crest of the Saddlebow and Orcop Hills.[5] Both Llanwarne and Kilpeck are stated to be Old Welsh names, but the name Orcop still remains obscure in its origins. The local pronunciation has been, and still is, "Arcop", and Matthews suggests that although Welsh was the vernacular in the village at the end of the 19th century, the "A" sound given to the initial letter could be due to West Saxon influences.[6] The oldest records always show the name spelt with an "O". The village would seem to be named through its topography; the following definitions are taken from the Welsh-English Dictionary:[7] Or = margin or border, ridge, bank, edge; Copa or Copp = summit, top, tuft, peak, mound, ridge. Many of the farms in the village have Welsh names, and the Visitation of 1397 (see page 140) mentions that the villagers of Garway, which adjoins Orcop, complained that their priest could not speak Welsh and since there were few that could speak English, he was unable to perform his parish duties in a proper manner.

The name varies in certain documents, some that I have found are:-

| | | |
|---|---|---|
| ***1173*** | *Horcop* | *Charter Rolls.* |
| ***1244*** | *Orcope* | *Inquisition on death of Walter de Baskerville.* |
| ***1291*** | *Orcoppe* | *Taxation of Pope Nicholas IV* |
| ***1398*** | *Orcupusmor* | *Old Lease in Mynde Collection.* |
| ***1417*** | *Orcoppesmore* | *Old Lease in Mynde Collection.* |
| ***1538*** | *Arcoppe* | *Valor Ecclesiasticum* |
| ***1610*** | *Arcopp* | *John Speede's Map.* |
| ***1679*** | *Orcobs* | *Marriage Licence, Cathedral Archives.* |
| ***1680*** | *Horcopp* | *Visitation. Cathedral Archives.* |

In later maps by Richard Blome and others, the name remains the same as Speede's version which would suggest that these were mostly faithful copies.

# Chapter Five

## REFERENCES


| | | |
|---|---|---|
| 1. | Rev. Prebendary Seaton. | p. 74. |
| 2. | Lord Rennell of Rodd. | Centenary Volume, Woolhope Club Transactions. Gloucester, 1954. p.145. |
| 3. | – | M.S.S. Copy of notes for the defence in case Stephen Ashby Plaintiff, and William Abrahall, Defendant. Mynde Collection, 2996-3012. |
| 4. | – | Ancient Charters prior to 1200. Edited by Pipe Roll Society, 1888. |
| 5. | J.N. Jackson. | Centenary Volume. Woolhope Club Transactions. Gloucester, 1954. p.186. |
| 6. | J.H. Matthews | p.108. |
| 7. | – | Geiriadur Mawr. Welsh-English Dictionary. Aberystwyth. 1958. p. 97 and 350. |

# Chapter Six

## THE DESCENT OF THE MANOR

The earliest mention of the Lordship comes from the Llyfr Baglan which states that Sir Rhydderch Legros, knight, was of "Arcope", and had a daughter Nest who was married to Cradoc, great grandson, in the male line of Ynyr, King of Gwent.[1] Legros must have lived in the early 12th century, possibly in the Castle and J.M. Matthews states he was probably the original Norman grantee of the lordship which was afterwards held by the Baskerville family. I think it is more likely that he was a descendant of the original Norman knight who probably accompanied the Conqueror in 1066, and married into a Welsh family since the name Rhydderch is Welsh, its English equivalent being Roderick, although the surname is Norman. It is also written as Sir Rothes Le Gros, (Baskerville family tree).

The Baskervilles came from Basqueville, about 10 miles south-west of Dieppe, where they resided prior to the Conquest, some members of the family accompanying the Duke of Normandy at the time of the Conquest. The name appears on the roll of honour in Battle Abbey. By the time of Henry I they were established at Eardisley in North Herefordshire. Sir Roger Baskerville married Ann, a daughter of Rhydderch Legros, and presumably Orcop was part of her dowry.

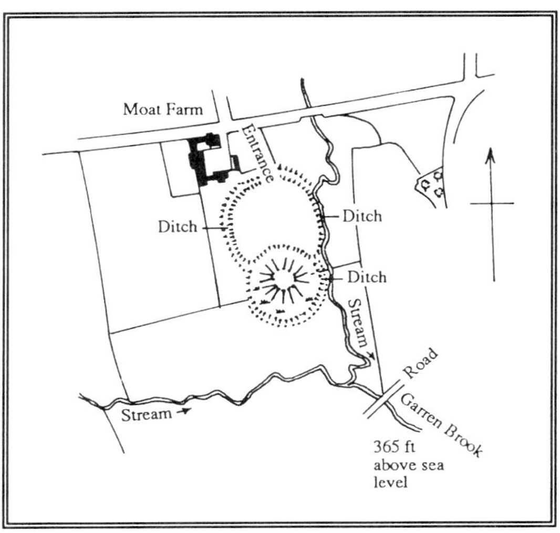


***Orcop Castle Mound***

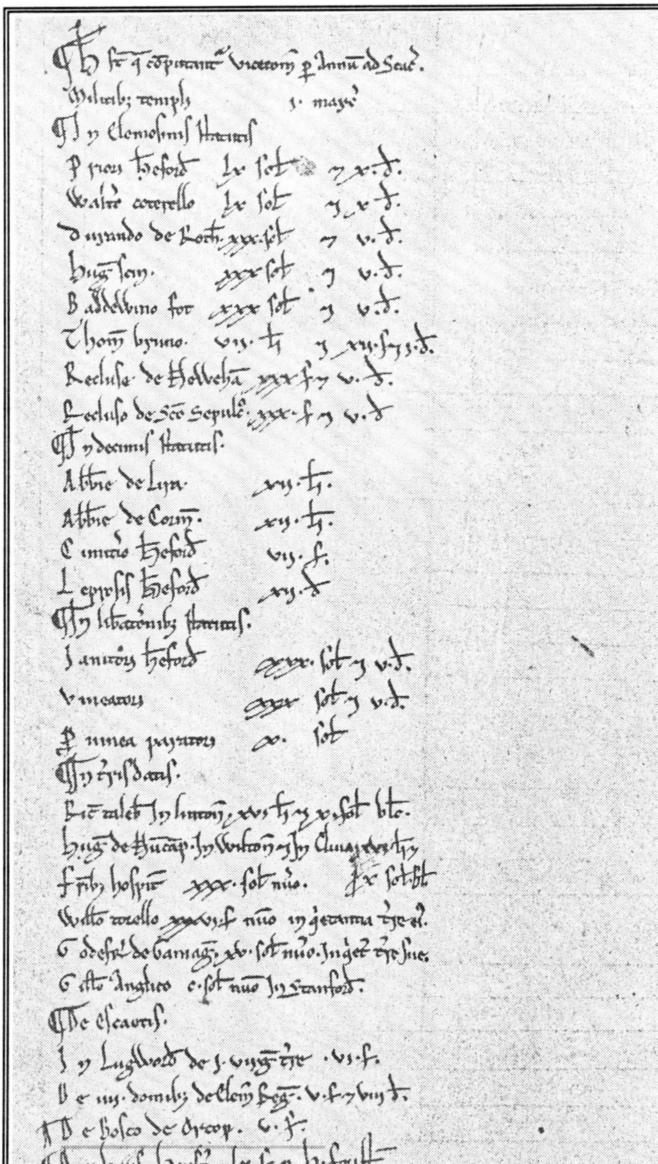

***Copy of Sheriff's Account dated 1172 showing the wood of Orcop to be assessed at five shillings.***

***(Herefordshire Domesday. p.80.)***

From 1168 to 1614 the lordship of Orcop remained in the possession of the Baskervilles, apart from a short change of ownership, firstly between 1211 and 1222, and again in 1278 when lands in Erdesle and Orcop appear to have been in the hands of Roger de Clyfford.[2]

The Manor of Orcop was shown as belonging to Walter de Bascheruille in 1168 for which he rendered account of five shillings "of the cense of the wood of Orcop".[3] This same entry appears in the Rolls for several subsequent years. An addition to the work done by V.H. Galbraith on the Herefordshire portion of Domesday Book is a Sheriff's Account specifying the sums contributed by the City of Hereford, five royal manors, and the Anglo-Welsh district of Archenfield. The total sum was £164.16.5. of which £21.0.0 came from Archenfield. Orcop's contribution is noted thus: "De Bosco de Orcope v solidos". (see page 48).[4]

Robert de Baskerville was Lord of Orcop in 1173, and Ralph de Baskervile in 1176. In the year 1211 the Red Book of the Exchequer shows that the manor had increased in value, since by this time, Walter de Baskeruile held Orcop in Irchenefeld of the King in chief, for 60 shillings.[5]

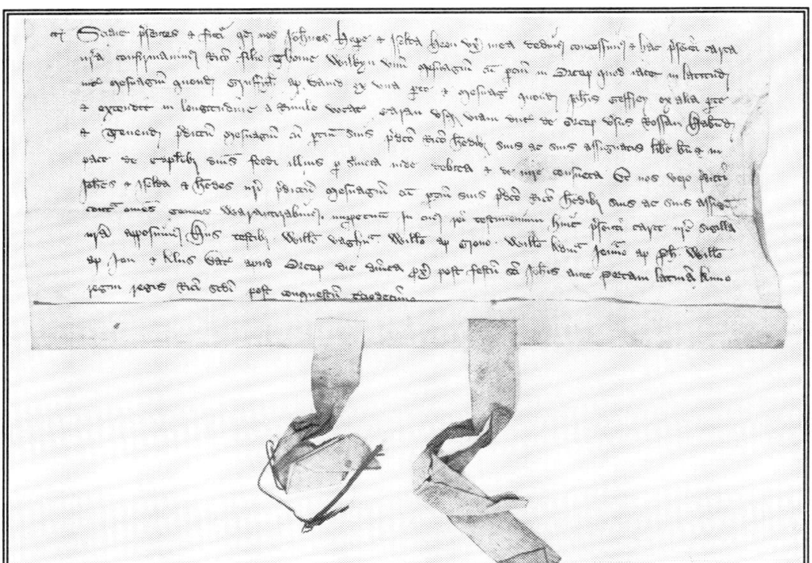

***Mynde 88. 1390. Sunday next after feast of St John ante Portam Latinam.***

***1. John Hopere and Isolda Heen, his wife.***

***2. Thomas Wilkyn.***

***Grant of a messuage in Orcop which lies in breadth between the messuage formerly of Gruffyth ap David and the messuage formerly of John Geffrey and extending from the river called Garan as far as the way leading from Orcop towards Rosse. Witnesses, William Vaghan, William ap Grono, William Adam, Ievan ap Phillip, William ap Jon. Dated at Orcop.***

On the death of Walter de Baskeruile in 1244, an Inquisition was taken, and it is interesting to note that of the 12 jurymen, only one was not a Welshman.[6] Their findings were that –

> *"Sir Walter de Baskeruile held of the King in chief the manor of Orcope with the appurtenances, in Urchenefeld in free socage in the law of Urchenefeld at the yearly rent of 60 shillings for finding two men for the Manor of Orcope, and two men for the aforesaid appurtenances, to go in the service of our Lord the King towards Wales, 15 days at their cost, and one day and one night towards England. The manor is worth 7 pounds a year. Walter de Baskeruile, his son, is his next heir".*

This Walter in 1253 obtained a charter of free warren in Orcop.[7]

The Recovery of lands from Roger de Clyfford by the Edict of Kenilworth of 1278 shows the Baskervilles back in possession of the Manor.[8] In 1316 the vills or manors from which, and their holders, from whom, feudal aids were demanded in the Hundred of Irchenfeld, showed that Richard de Baskervile, was Lord of Orcop.[9] This is the last documented mention of the Baskerville family in connection with Orcop, until 1528 when Sir James Baskerville settled the Manor upon his wife.[10]

The Mynde Collection at Aberystwyth provides much useful material to complete the gaps of the missing years, since so many of the leases of land in the Orcop manor are still in existence.[11] From these it can be ascertained that in 1364 Richard Baskeruill was Lord of Orcop, as detailed in the lease below.[12]

***1364.***

> *"Sunday next after the feast of St. Bartholomew.*
>
> *1. William Knap.*
> *2. William Heen.*
>
> *Grant of a messuage in Orcopp which William Wyrhale, formerly acquired of Dominus Richard Baskeruill, Lord of Orcopp, and Joan his wife. Witnesses, Rees ap David ap Yeuan, William ap Roppard, William ap Wilcock, Hugh Gough, Yeuhan ap Yeru. Dated at Orcopp".*

An Inquisition was held on the 28th April 1499[13] which showed that James Baskerville, knight, was seised the day he died of the manor of Orcop in fee. His eldest son Walter Baskirvile was to succeed him, and then Walter's eldest son, James. The document is worded as follows:-

*"He was seised in fee of the undermentioned castle and lordship and being so seised, by a certain charter indented, together with his last will thereto annexed, sealed with his seal of arms, the date of which charter is at Eardisle, 16 January, 8 Henry VII, enfeoffed Edmund Andeley, Bishop of Hereford, Thomas ap Morgan, knight, William Morgan, clerk, James Scudamore, Walter Vaughan of Hergest, William Morgan and Thomas ap Gwillym esquires, thereof with its appurtenances, English and Welsh, and of all other his lands within the March of Wales, and by the said charter declared that his will and intent upon the said feoffment was that the said feoffees should be seised thereof to his use for life, and after his decease, for the payment of his debts and legacies, and after their discharge for the use of Walter Baskervile esquire, his elder son for his life only, and after his decease, to the use of James Baskervile, elder son of the said Walter, intail, with remainder in default to John Baskervile, whole brother of the said James, the son, intail, with remainder in default to Philip Baskervile and Thomas Baskervile, third and fourth sons of the said Walter, successively intail, with remainder in default to his own right heirs. He was seised to him and the heirs of his body and of one Sibilla, daughter of Walter Deveraux, knight, late his wife, of the undermentioned manors of Staunton and Letton by the gift of Walter Deveraux, knight, and John Assheby, clerk, as by their charter 12th June, 33 Henry VI appears. He was seised the day he died of the under-mentioned manor of Orcop in fee".*

Sir James had succeeded his father John Baskerville in 1455, and had supported the House of York in the Wars of the Roses. The Inquisition further notes that the Manors of Staunton and Letton, also of Stretton next Sugwas were all worth 10 marks, and that Orcop, which was held of George, Earl of Shrewsbury, as of the Lordship and Hundred of Wormelow, was worth 100 shillings, and the services were unknown.

Another document in the Mynde collection confirms that Walter Baskerville was possessed of the manor prior to 1509.[14]

*"tempus Henry VII*

*1. Walter Baskervyle, knight.*
*2. Richard Jenkyn.*

*Grant of messuages and lands which Thomas Jenkyn, father of the said Richard held by copy of the Court Rolls of Orcoppe, one tenement called Burnettes and one tenement formerly of Hoel her . . . (torn). Rent 9/6d. annually. Suit of Court of Orcoppe. Heriot".*

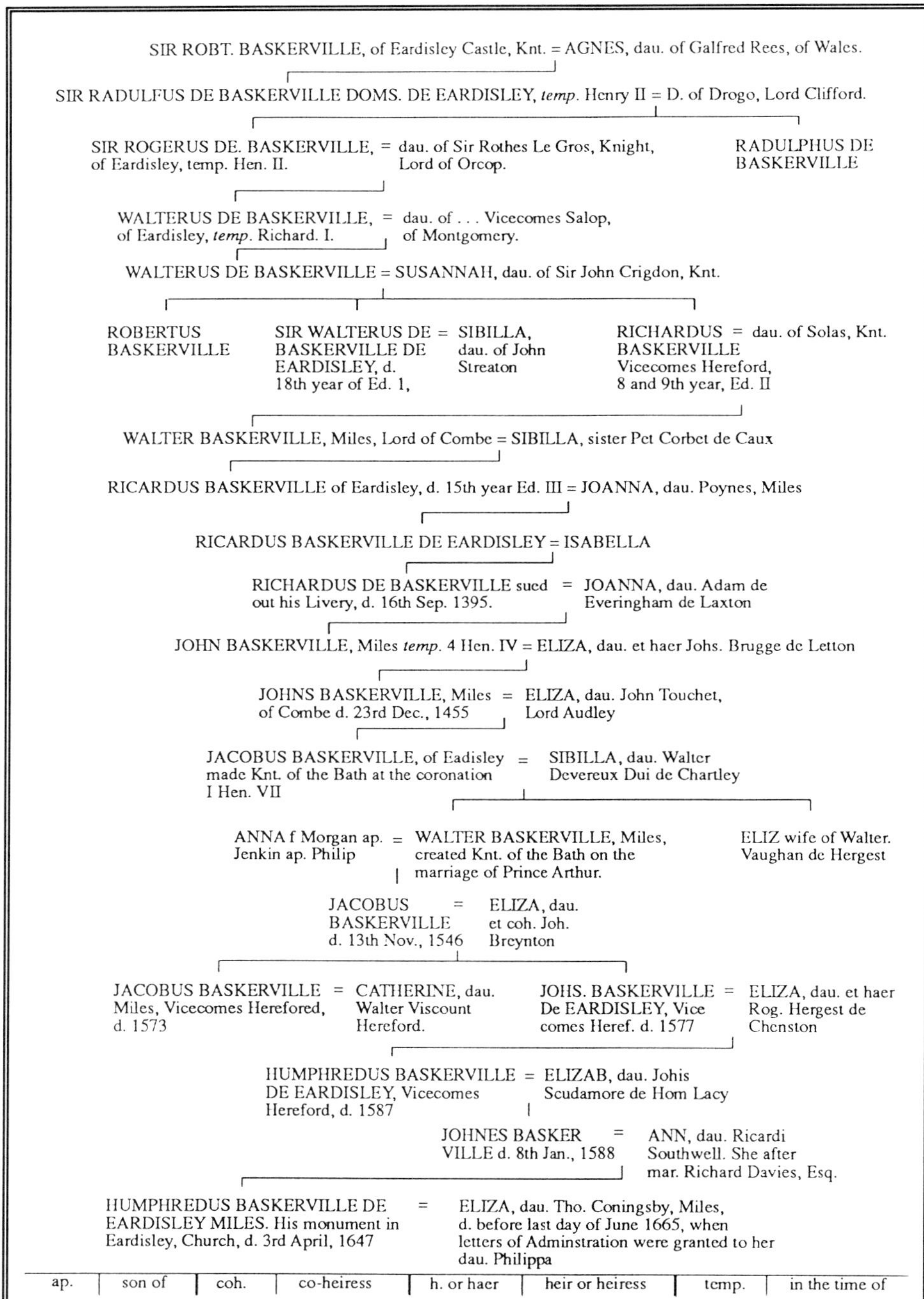


***Part of the Baskerville family tree***

The same Burnett remains today, a small, prosperous farm of 30 acres.

Leases dated 1509 and 1513 show James Baskirvile to be Lord of Orcop.[15]

***"1513/14. Jan 21.***

*1. James Baskirvile Esq., Lord of Orcop.*

*2. Ievan ap David.*

*Lease for 99 years of lands and tenements which formerly belonged to Wilcock Bayly in bondage there, and a messuage with a close adjoining in Orcop being customary land called Dreweslond. Rent 5/4d. annually with suit of court and heriot".*

No name resembling this is to be found now in Orcop.

***The Hoskyns family of Harewood.***
***For many years Lords of Wormelow.***

Nine other leases dated from 1540 to 1564 show Sir James Baskerville to be Lord, but from then until 1614 the Baskerville family do not appear on any of the intervening manuscripts. How-ever, the Calendar of Domestic State Papers shows that Sir James Baskerville was a Justice and Commissioner of Muster of troops to garrison Ireland in Hereford in 1570.[16] His son, Sir Humphrey Baskerville was Sheriff of Herefordshire in 1585.[17] The fortunes of the Baskerville family seem now to be on the decline, and there is a record in the Hereford City Library which shows that Sir Humphrey Baskerville, the last of the family to hold Orcop, had redeemed the manor of Orcopp with all messuages, gardens, orchards and farms belonging, from a mortgage to John Mansell of New Wyndsor, Berkshire.[18] This redemption was not permanent, and the following is a resumé of a document in the Mynde Collection.[19]

*"1614. May 20*

*1. Sir Humfrey Baskervile of Eardisley, knight.*
*2. Thomas Lello of the Inner Temple, London, gent.*

*Articles of Agreement in consideration of £310 for the conveyance of the manor of Orcopp, free of any incumbrances made by the said Sir Humfrey Baskervile . . ."*

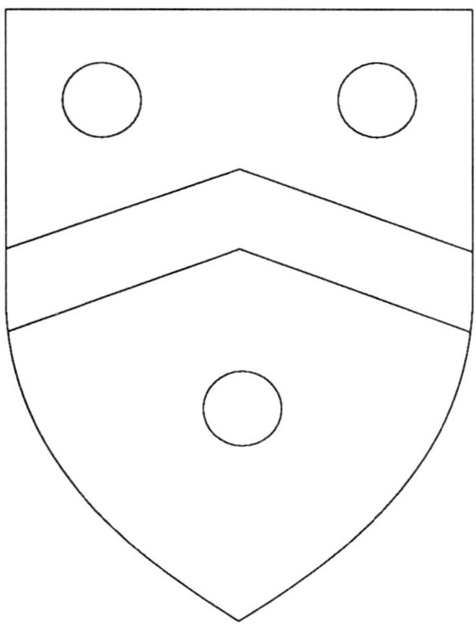

***The Baskerville family of Eardisley Castle. Lords of Orcop from the early 12th century until 1614.***

Sir Humphrey Baskerville declared for the King in the Civil War, but was not actively engaged in fighting. It is said that the income of the Baskerville estate had dwindled from £3,000 per annum to £300.[20] Sir Humphrey married Elizabeth, the third daughter of Sir Thomas Coningesby of Hampton Court, Hereford. He died on the 3rd April 1647, and was buried in Eardisley Church. What was probably the Baskerville Chapel is now used as the vestry, and overleaf will be found a photograph of the brass tablet on the floor which indicates his grave. Close by is the stone indicating the grave of his daughter, Phillipa, but the lettering and coat of arms are very worn, and did not photograph successfully.

This period, from the commencement of the 17th century, saw a steady rise in the fortunes of the Pye family who had lived on the Saddlebow Hill, (part of which is in Orcop parish) since 1443, and who had also acquired, through the marriage of John Pye of Saddlebow with Agnes, daughter of Roger Andrew, the Mynde, which at that time was a small township, later to become the Mynde estate of Much Dewchurch. A lease in the Mynde collection shows that this marriage had taken place by 1448, since 100 acres of arable land, 100 acres of pasture, 40 acres of wood and 20 acres of meadow in Mynde were granted to them, and to other children of Roger Andrew.[21] The Pye family, was, therefore, prominent in land ownership in Orcop for some time before the failure of the fortunes of the Baskervilles, and their own acquisition of the Mynde property. This John Pye's grandson, Walter, who died in

1575 married one of the co-heiresses of Philpot Price of Orcop, who was "of a great famulis" originating from Tre Wyne in the Black Mountains on the borders of Brecknockshire and Herefordshire.[22]

***Here lyeth the body of Sr Humphrey Baskervile of Eardisley Castle in the County of Hereford, Knight, who marrid Elizabeth the third daughter of Sr Thos Coningesby of Hampton Court, Hee had 2 sonnes Thomas and Henry & on daughter Philippa and deceased the third day of April Anno Dni 1647.***

From Thomas Lello the Manor descended to his son, Henry Lello of Hereford, who in 1633 sold it to Sir Walter Pye of the Mynde, and his son, Sir Walter Pye, the younger. The consideration money was £560.[23] From this date until 1723 the Pye family were Lords of Orcop. This period of 90 years is well documented due to the Mynde collection, and gives valuable information as to the life of the Pyes, and the customs of the Manor.

By the early 18th century, the Pye fortunes were also at a very low ebb, and the Mynde estate, together with its many lordships, was continually mortgaged, eventually being conveyed to James, Duke of Chandos, Marquis and Earl of Caernarvon.[24] The last of the Pyes to own the Mynde was Charles Pye, who, in 1714 mortgaged "the honour and castle of Kilpecke, with manors and Lordships including Orcop" to the Duke of Chandos for £13,000, as detailed in the Mortgage Deed at Aberystwyth. In 1720 there was a further Mortgage Deed involving £22,000, and finally in 1723 the estate became the property of James Brydges, Duke of Chandos. He was Herefordshire born, and a member of an old and distinguished family whose seat was Wilton Castle, at Ross-on-Wye. He was a great speculator in property, living in much splendour, although financially he was living a hand to mouth existence dependant on his success or otherwise in investments. He never resided in the mansion on the Mynde Estate, although he was responsible for the building of the very fine banqueting hall which is stated to be the finest in the county by N. Pevsner in his book on Herefordshire. It is five bays long, and two storeys high, with a coved ceiling and giant Corinthian pilasters. There are medallions over the doors with busts in profile of King Egbert, King Alfred, William the Conqueror, Edward III and Henry V. Above the fireplace can be seen the coat of arms of the Symons family who were to own the property after Brydges. The present owner of the Mynde, Mr W.A. Twiston-Davies, allowed me to wander at will over the empty mansion which has not been occupied for several years. There is still much mid 17th century panelling in some of the rooms, although the building has been altered and extended a great deal since it was built late in the 15th or early 16th century.[25]

*The Pyes of Much Dewchurch.* *Symons of Much Dewchurch.*

The Duke of Chandos was at this time Lord Lieutenant of Radnor and Herefordshire, and had intended to reside at the Mynde when attending Hereford, but there is no record of his having done so although he improved it, kept horses and cattle there, and stocked a cellar with cider and beer. The Mynde had a large deer park which also provided him with venison. By 1726 he had decided to sell the estate as he had pressing economic problems; he had already mortgaged part of it to Richard Symons, who is described as a citizen, merchant and fishmonger of London. The consideration money of £28,400 was finally paid, and the estate passed over to Richard Symons on 17th August 1726.[26] This transfer has been variously put at 1740 and 1750 in the Wormelow Manuscript, and Robinson's "Manors and Mansions of Herefordshire". The Deed in the Mynde collection is dated 1726, and manuscripts from then on bear the name of Symons.

The Symons family remained in possession of the Mynde until 1928 when the last descendant, Thomas Edward Raymond Symons, who had been a Major in the Grenadier Guards in the First World War, and was severely wounded, died at the early age of 39. He and his friend, Henry Ambrose Clive, a descendant of a distinguished Herefordshire family who came to the county about 1750, willed to each other their estates during the First World War, and on his death his estate became the property of Captain Clive. The mother of T.E.R. Symons continued to live at the Mynde until her death in 1949, when Captain H. A. Clive took up residence until his death in 1960, when it was sold to the present owner Mr W.A.Twiston-Davies.

The Symons family were connected in the early 18th century with agriculture and law, and a document in the Mynde collection mentions one, John Symons of Clowerwall, Gloucester (Clearwell), yeoman, as far back as 1620. Another John Symons of Clowerwall was in practice as an attorney with his brother, Thomas Symons, who resided in London, and there are many letters dating from 1692 to 1719 regarding their practice. The Richard Symons who purchased the Mynde was a brother to John and Thomas Symons. The family spent much of their time at the Mynde, and the Church at Much Dewchurch gives mute testimony to their prosperity, by their ornamented memorial tablets, to their charities which are listed on the Charities Board under the tower, and to the many tragedies in the domestic life of several generations of the family as evidenced by the inscriptions on the tombs of their children, few of whom lived to reach their majority.

The influence of the Lord of the Manor in more recent times as it affected Orcop is to be seen in the giving of land by Thomas George Symons in 1858, on which to build a school. The piece of land given, according to its Deed, "for the education of the children of the poorer classes for ever" was offered in such an altruistic manner that all reclaim to the property was waived to heirs and successors; when the school eventually closed in 1964, this had some awkward repercussions. The land for the Vicarage was given by Thomas Raymond Symons in 1911. All the lands in Orcop belonging to the Mynde Estate were sold in 1916, and although Captain Clive was considered to be still Lord of the Manor of Orcop, no one at the present time is very certain of the position.

*The Mynde, 1992. The mansion, built originally by the Pyes, added to over many generations, given its great banqueting hall by Lord Chandos, and finally abandoned a few years ago. Documents, kept by the families who lived here, and nowadays preserved at the National Library of Wales at Aberystwyth, have been of inestimable value in tracing the history of so many aspects of life in Orcop.*

# Chapter Six

## References


| | | |
|---|---|---|
| 1. | J. Williams. | Llyfr Baglan. London. 1910 Edition. City Library, Hereford. p. 259. |
| | Written between 1600 and 1607 this is a compilation of the pedigrees of the nobility and lesser gentry of Northern Gwent (Monmouthshire) and Ergyng, the south west portion of Hereford, including Archenfield. | |
| 2. | J.H. Matthews. | p. 108. |
| 3. | J.H. Matthews. | p. 108. Pipe Rolls 14 H.11. |
| 4. | V.H. Galbraith. | p. 80 |
| 5. | J.H. Matthews. | p. 108. Red Book of the Exchequer, Rolls Series, vol. II. p. 602. |
| 6. | J.H. Matthews. | p. 109. I.P.M. 28 H.111. No. 1. |
| 7. | J.H. Matthews. | p. 109. Charter Rolls. 37 H.111. |
| 8. | J.H. Matthews. | p. 109. Breviate of Pleas, 6. Edw.1. |
| 9. | J.H. Matthews. | p. 15. |
| 10. | J.H. Matthews. | p. 110. |
| 11. | On checking through the schedule of the Mynde collection I typed out details of papers which related to Orcop in some way or another amounting to 18 foolscap pages, and to approximately 180 manuscripts of which so far I have been able to peruse two thirds. There are other manuscripts which although not specifically mentioning Orcop, probably have some connection, e.g. estate accounts etc. | |
| 12. | – | Mynde Collection. 87. |
| 13 | – | Calendar of Inquisitions Post Mortem. Henry VII. Vol. II. p.71. No. 112. |
| 14. | – | Mynde Collection. 159. |
| 15. | – | Mynde Collection. 96. |
| 16. | – | Calendar of Domestic State Papers. 1581-1590. Hereford City Library. Entry 10th May 1570. |

| | | |
|---|---|---|
| 17. | – | Calendar of Domestic State Papers. 1581-1590. Entry February 6th 1585. |
| 18. | – | Local Collection Deed Box, Hereford City Library. Number 5783. Date 1613/14. |
| 19. | – | Mynde Collection. 25. |
| 20. | C.J. Robinson. | Herefordshire Castles and their Lords. Hereford. 1869. p. 47. |
| 21. | – | Mynde Collection. 288. |
| 22. | J. Williams. | Llyfr Baglan. p. 96. |
| 23. | – | Mynde Collection. 5252. |
| 24. | – | Mynde Collection. 5254. |
| 25. | – | R.C.H.M.E. Herefordshire South-west. p. 50 and 51. |
| 26. | – | Mynde Collection. 723. |

Orcop Castle Mound based on a drawing by E.A. Downman, 1904.

The ancient Lordships that attached to the Mynde were included when the estate was purchased by the late Mr. W.A. Twiston-Davies, and have now been handed down to his son, Mr. Audley Twiston-Davies, the present owner.

# Chapter Seven

## THE PYE FAMILY

The members of the Pye family most closely connected with Orcop were the Lords of the Manor from 1633, who were as follows:-

| | | |
|---|---|---|
| *Sir Walter Pye.* | *Baptized 1st October 1571.* | *Died 9th January 1635.* |
| *Sir Walter Pye, his son.* | *Born1610.* | *Died 1659.* |
| *Walter Pye, eldest son of Sir Walter Pye, the younger.* | *Born 1631.* | *Died 1690.* |
| *Robert Pye, son of Sir Walter Pye, the younger.* | | *Died 1680.* |

*Elizabeth,* Robert's daughter married to Henry Gorges of Eye, Herefordshire, who took over the administration of the Manor. Born 1677, died 1708.

Mention of the earlier members of the Pye family, and some of the customs of Archenfield are found in the following.[1]

> *"To the Bishop of Durham, Chancellor of England, c.1420.*
>
> *Complaint of Thomas Barre of co.Heref. John Aberhale of Irchinfeld lately sent John ap Pee, Walter ap Pee and others, his servants, with other Welsh malefactors to the number of sixty, all in warlike array, to Deweswall in the said county, and there did cut Complainant's corn and hay, to the value of 20 l. and carried the same to Irchinfeld, which is a free lordship, having in itself recovery at Hereford of all manner trespasses made or supposed in the said lordship; which said John is principal officer and hath all the governance there".*

In the Church of Saint David at Much Dewchurch can be seen several tombs and memorials to the Pyes. The earliest are those of John Pye, the son of John Pye who had acquired the Mynde through marriage (see page 54), and his son Walter Pye, who married Margaret, a co-heiress of Philpot Price of Orcop (see page 55). John Pye, who died in 1547, seems to have been much travelled, as well as much married![2]

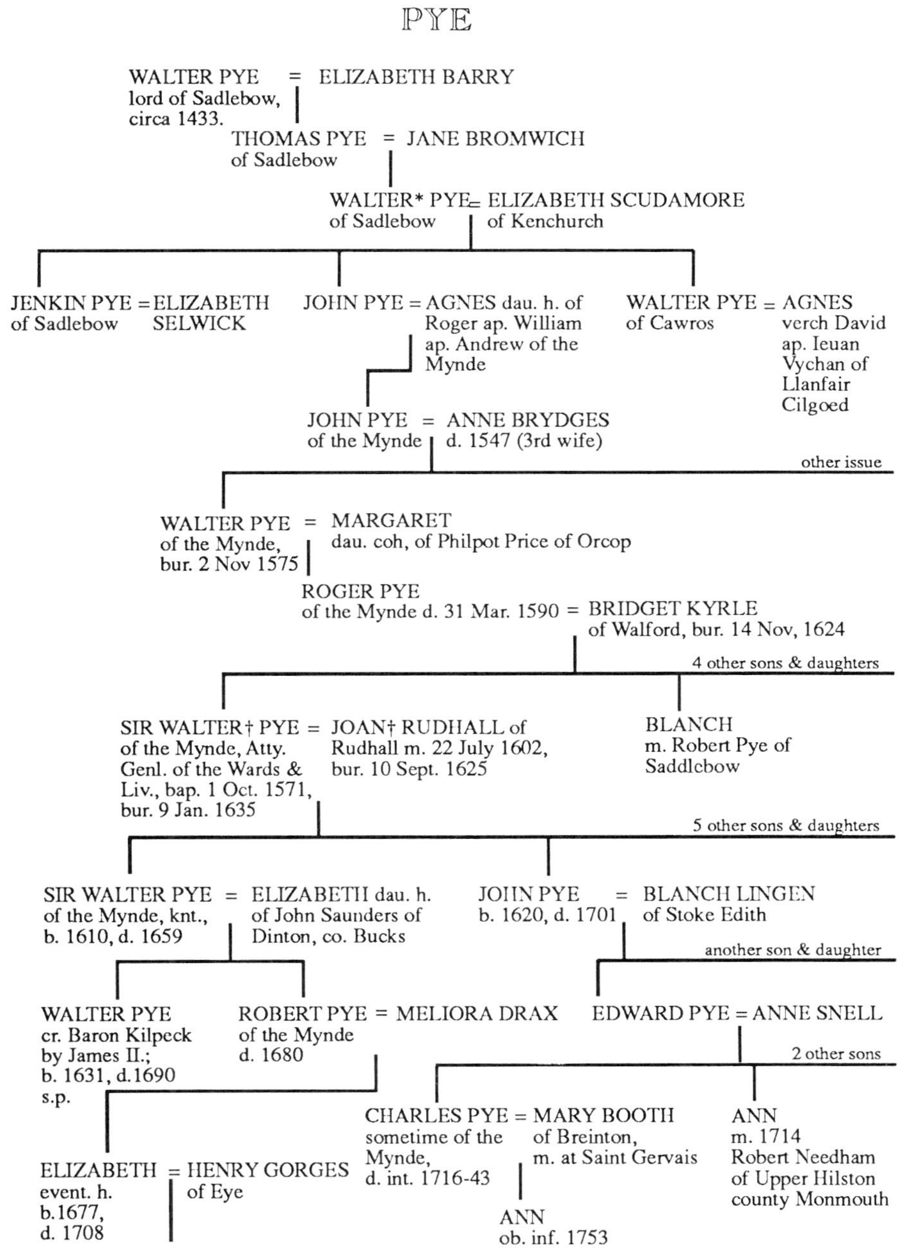


* The *Llyfr Baglan* calls him John thrice, Walter once.
† He was born in or before 1569, for he is named in the Heralds' Visitation of that year.
† The *Llyfr Baglan* calls her Elizabeth

ABBREVIATIONS

| | | | |
|---|---|---|---|
| S.P. | without children | dau. h. | heiress of |
| co. | county | dau. coh. | co-heiress of |
| inf. | infant | ap. | son of |

***Part of the Pye Family Tree.***

*"John Pye of the Mynde, sone of Jon Pye, seconde sone of Jon Pye of Sadlebowe, esq., maried 3 wiefes; his first wief was Anne, daughter to Sr. Richard Delabyre, knight; his seconde wief was Anne Brigees; and his third wief was Alrothes, daughter to Sr. Robert Whitney, Lord of Whitney. Hee had bye theme 42 children; and hee had bye concupines 22 childrene; Soe that in all hee had 64 children, as hitt appeareth upon his Towmbe in the Churche of Much Dewchurche. The said John Pye was ate Rome, at Jerusalem, and at the sepulcher of Christ. Hee did the 24 actes of Chilvalrye w'ch fewe men could do them all".*

The official family tree names Anne Brydges as his third wife.

The writing on John Pye's tomb is almost illegible; the monument to which the above refers is an altar-tomb which shows the effigies of John Pye depicted in costume with a pointed beard, and Walter, his son, in costume with a long cloak.

Although the family tree of the Pye family can be followed quite accurately with regard to the family at the Mynde, (see family tree, page no. 61), it is less clear when dealing with the family at Saddlebow. From leases in the Mynde collection it would seem that there were Pyes not only on Saddlebow, but also in Orcop itself. This is hardly surprising in view of the above inscription!

***"1541.***

*October 8.*
*1. Thomas Appy of Sadelbow, gent.*
*2. Walter Apy of Orcop, gent.*

*Grant of all the lands and tenements in Orcopp in the Lordship of Irchynfyld which grantor inherited after the death of his father".* [3]

From the family tree it can be ascertained that there is no Thomas Pye mentioned as around that date, the only Thomas being the second, mentioned in the 15th century. There are, however, instances of leases between the Pyes at the Mynde and others, being witnessed by their relatives at Saddlebow. The Church Registers show entries of baptisms and deaths up to 1698, but after that date the family appear to have moved from the district.

The Manor of Orcop first came into the Pye family in 1633 (see page 55) shortly before the death of the first Sir Walter in January 1635. His magnificent tomb at Much Dewchurch can be seen in the photograph overleaf. The actual helmet which he wore can be seen surmounting the tomb above his coat of arms. Part of the tomb of John and Walter Pye referred to above can be seen in the bottom right-hand corner of the photograph.

Sir Walter was born in 1571, going firstly to Oxford, and then on to a legal training at one of the smaller Chancery Inns, then finally into the Middle Temple.

He qualified in 1597, and by 1616, he, together with his brother Robert, later to become Sir Robert, were becoming prominent in public affairs as clients and servants of Buckingham.

> *"In view of Walter's qualifications and Robert's later career, it can be inferred that the former acted as a legal adviser, the latter as a financial manager in the Villiers entourage".*[4]

***Tomb of Sir Walter Pye in the parish church, Much Dewchurch. Two figures are misssing.***

Walter Pye then progressed to an appointment as Judge on circuit in South Wales, and in 1620 Buckingham's influence saw him installed as Attorney of the Court of Wards and Liveries. He was knighted in 1630, and the value of his office was, at a minimum estimate, some £1500 per annum. In his book concerning the Civil Service in the time of Charles I, Dr. G.E. Aylmer says.[5]

*"The surprising things about Walter Pye are firstly the amount he spent on land purchases, improvements, and building* before *he attained major office; secondly, the sheer rate at which he continued to buy and spend for his entire career of which record survives. His purchases began in 1602-3, his only incoming capital item in those early years was the £300 portion with his first wife, received in 1606. In addition, his father died some time before 1611, and he inherited a modest landed fortune of £100 or £126.13.4. per annum. By 1620 he had spent about £7,600 on land purchases, buildings and other improvements (including £120 to arrange the lease of the judicial seal in South Wales). This included the purchase of Kilpeck for over £1,000 in 1610, and £330 or more for renovations and a new water supply at his country seat, the Mynde".*

A document in the Mynde Collection dated March 15th 1629, acknowledges the receipt of £930 in full payment of £1520 from Sir Walter for the rectories of Glaseburie, Devynnog, Talgarth, Pipton and Wentworth in the counties of Brecon and Radnorshire.[6] There exists today in the small Elmhirst collection at Worsborough Bridge, near Barnsley, Sir Walter's private account book, and Dr. Aylmer says from this one can sense the great attachment he had to the Mynde, and to the countryside in general. He says he was born at the Mynde, it came to him by a long descent, he liked the situation, there was an easy water supply which cost him £90, and there was plenty of good fuel within the vicinity, together with hay and pasture.

As can be seen by the photograph of his tomb, he had 7 sons and 8 daughters, and the family circle at the Mynde was also increased by the bringing up of several of his god-children, the heir to the Walwyn family of Much Marcle, Fulke Walwyn, and the children of the Lingen family from Sutton Freen.[7] This may have been occasioned by Sir Walter's official responsibilities as Attorney of the Court of Wards and Liveries. In later years, his daughters Alice and Margaret, married Henry Lingen and Fulke Walwyn, and the families of Pye, Lingen and Walwyn were to be embroiled in the fierce combat between the Royalists and Roundheads. All three family homes were fortified against Cromwell's men, and in 1643 the Mynde was attacked and severely damaged. An entry in the Parish Register of Much Dewchurch reads –

***"February 1643.***

*Francis Lea, a poor, maymed soldier, was buried this third day of February".*

Another interesting sidelight on Sir Walter, is given by John Beale, a Herefordshire writer, who in 1665 was Chaplain to Charles II. He states that Sir Walter Pye was his uncle and writes of him:-[8]

*" . . . his memory was so clear and accurate that he could name every English gentleman (yeoman too, some would say), his ancestors' pedigree, coats of arms, their chief mansions, and other revenues, and being employed to make search into estates, he was well feed to remember names, families and estates and oft as I waited on him, he would diligently inquire whence, through what towns, by what houses I passed, and could better describe my way, than I, who had so lately viewed it".*

From the foregoing it would seem he was admirably suited to his position as Attorney General of the Court of Wards and Liveries, a Court which was instituted in the reign of Henry VII for the purpose of regulating inquiries upon the death of the King's tenants, ascertaining heirship, and the rights of the King to marriage wardship.

A portrait of Sir Walter appears on the following page 66. This was painted by Cornelis Janssens who was one of the most fashionable portrait painters in England during the years 1618-1628.[9] One of his early patrons was Lady Philadelphia Wharton, who was a grand-daughter of Lord Hundson, who resided at Arkstone Court, Kingstone, in Herefordshire. Since Sir Walter also had lands in Kingstone, no doubt he came into contact with the painter through a mutual acquaintanceship. His tomb at Much Dewchurch was sculpted by another Dutchman of the same name, but there was no relationship between the families. The portrait of Sir Walter now hangs in the picture gallery at Kentchurch Court having been purchased from the sale at Moccas Court, to the west of the county, some years ago. Since one of Sir Walter's daughters, Frances, married Henry Vaughan of Moccas, was widowed, and married a member of the Cornwall family of Berrington, who then became owners of the Moccas Estate, its presence there is explained. It is equally right that it should now hang in Kentchurch since several members of the Scudamore family of Kentchurch Court married into the Pye family.

On the death of Sir Walter in 1635, his son, also Walter, became the owner of the Mynde and Lord of Orcop. The Inquisition dated 1637 which follows shows the extent of his lands in Herefordshire.[10]

*"Inquisitiones Post Mortem. 12 Car.1. (1637) Pars.1., No. 123. Hereford.*

*Sir Walter Pye, knight, was seised in his demesne as of fee of and in the castle and manor of Kilpeck, with the appurtenances, in Kilpeck, Trevill, Kevernoll, the Meend, Lanhithock, Kainechurch and Much Dewchurch, in the county of Hereford; the capital messuage and tenement of lands called the Meende, in the parish of Much Dewchurch; the appurtenances, in the county aforesaid; lands in Welsh Newton, Pembridge, Garway, Llanrothall, Tretire, Orcopp and Kainechurch; lands called Longmeadowe, Oxeleasowe, and the Old Land, formerly Quarrell's and Greene Meadowe, in Didley and Grafton in the parish of Saint Devoreux; a messuage and lands in Wynnall in the county of Hereford, with a field called Sandpitt*

*Field there; Sidnall Field, Spitell Field, Rowmore Field, Hollowmore Field, Overfield, Allensmore; the manor of Bruttescourte; houses and lands in the parish of Kingston; the manor of Pitchers Ocle; lands and houses in Ocle Pitchard, Castleton, Momiton and Lugmeadow; the manor of Lyers Ocle.*

*Walter Pye, knight, is his son and next heir, and is of the age of 25 years and upwards.*

*Kilpeck and the Meend are holden of the King in chief, by knight service.*

*Welsh Newton, Pembridge Castle, Garway, Llanrothall and Tretire are holden of the King as of his Manor of East Greenwich, in free and common socage, by fealty only."*

***Walter Pye, knight, Attorney General of our Lord James, late king of England, and of our lord Charles, now King of England, of the Court of wards and Liveries, and Chief Justice of Great Session of the Counties of Glamorgan, Brecon and Radnor, son and heir of Roger Pye of the Mynde, esquire, son and heir of Walter Pye of the Mynde, esquire, son and heir of John Pye of the Mynde, esquire, son and heir of John Pye of the Mynde, esquire, and of Agnes his wife, daughter and heir of Roger Andrew of the Mynde, esquire. On the 22nd day of July in the year of Our Lord 1602, and in the 44th year of the reign of our Lady Elizabeth, formerly, Queen of England, he took to wife Joan Rudhale, daughter of William Rudhale of Rudhale in the County of Hereford esquire; by whom he had seven sons and eight daughters.***

***From the inscription on the tomb of Sir Walter Pye in Much Dewchurch Church. (See page 63)***

Sir Walter Pye, the younger, was a staunch Royalist, commissioned to travel to Rome on a secret mission to the Pope, on behalf of the King in 1642.[11] A letter in the Clarendon State papers written to Edward Hyde, later to become the Earl of Clarendon, states that Sir Walter had an audience with the Pope's nephew in March of that year. By July 1643 he was one of the nine noblemen who led the attack on Brampton Bryan in North Herefordshire. He was taken prisoner at the seige of Hereford, and imprisoned at Gloucester and Bristol, but "at the end of June new troops were raised in Herefordshire, and the county assessed at £1200 a month, free quarters being granted to the soldiers. Sir Walter Pye was again at liberty and returned to the county."[12]

The purchases made by the first Sir Walter, and those which were completed by his son between 1626 to 1637, amounted to approximately £25,400, some £19,000 being on land, buildings and improvements. The income that the second Sir Walter enjoyed was probably something between £2000 and £2,500 per annum. Dr. Aylmer states that his father's funeral cost £2000, and he also had to arrange dowries for his sisters, so that he was soon in financial difficulties. He sold lands and timber for £2,350 in 1637, and more land for £2,410 in 1639. He lent the King £2000 in 1640, and managed to raise troops for him in 1642-43, and in 1646 he compounded for an annual income of £1,350. The following document dated 1658 shows that, one year before he died, he was still selling portions of the estate.[13]

***"1658.***

*Sir Walter Pye of the Mynd and Katherine Pye, the only daughter of the said Sir Walter Pye, acknowledge payment from Brandon Hillyard, a citizen and goldsmith of London and Henry Lawley of London, merchant, the full sum of £3,400 this 20th day of July, being the purchase of the Manor and Lordship of Lennthall Earls".*

This original Deed is placed in a file of miscellaneous papers from a private collection in the Hereford City Library, and I came upon it by chance.

Although he was active in the Royalist cause, Sir Walter the younger, was also, like his father, deeply attached to his country home, and from the document below, it would appear he was not unappreciative of loyalty from his servants.[14]

***"1638/9.***

*March 22. Sir Walter Pye of the Meende, knight. George Whiting, late servant of Sir Walter Pye, knight, deceased, late father of the said Sir Walter, and Mary, wife of the said George Whiting.*

*"Grant of an annuity of £6.13.4. issuing out of the lands in the tenure of Walter Webb, parcel of the manor of Orcopp, in consideration of the good service that George Whiting had done to the said Sir Walter Pye, the father, and Sir Walter Pye the son".*

He appears to have interested himself in the agricultural side of the Mynde as evidenced by the following account in his own hand, and bearing his signature.[15]

***"1640.***

*Corn in the House to be accounted for.*

| | |
|---|---|
| *Mungcorn* | *243 bushels* |
| *Wheat* | *70 bushels* |
| *Rye* | *42 bushels* |
| *Mault* | *264 bushels* |
| *Peas in the Barne unwinnowed* | *30 bushels* |
| *Corn in the ground. Wheat, Rye and Barley* | *20 acres.* |
| *Lent grain, Peas and Oats –* | *12 acres.* |

(Mungcorn is a mixture of different seeds sown together in order to come up in one crop, wheat ground with rye or barley. Lent grain was that sown about Lent time).

*Cattle of all sorts.*
*Eight draught Oxen*
*3 breeding mares with coltes*
*1 other breeding mare with a colte*
*4 two-year old mare coltes*
*4 cart horses*
*1 stoned horse*
*1 stallion vocat' (called) Spratt.*

*Wood to be fallen upon Saddlebowe's ground and to be sold and accompted for.*
*Wains, cartes and wheels to be sold and accompted for.*
*Rent due and behind from Orcop for the last quarter, £4.13.9."*

Sir Walter died in 1659, one year before the Restoration for which he had sacrificed so much, and was buried at St. Clement Dane, in London. His Will named his eldest son Walter as his heir, then his second son Robert, and in the last resort, his own brother John, and their heirs. This was to cause many problems in the years ahead.

Walter inherited an estate which had become much impoverished from the prosperous days of his grandfather, the first Sir Walter. His name is to be seen on leases from 1660 to 1668, but thereafter his younger brother, Robert, had taken over the estate and the Lordship of Orcop. The documents in the Mynde collection indicate that Walter was unmarried and intended to remain so. Accordingly, he passed over more and more of the estate to Robert before 1668, and certainly by 1674 as shown by leases and receipts in the Mynde collection.[16] Walter is last noted as Lord of the Manor of Orcop in a Court Roll dated 1663. [17]

The Restoration of 1660 swept away the dour face of Cromwell's Puritanism, and saw the return to the Established Anglican Church. There was, however, much persecution of non-conformists, particularly Puritans, Roman Catholics, and dissenting clergy. The year 1673 saw Parliament demanding that all those of any official standing should take the sacrament according to the rites of the Church of England, those who refused to do so were listed as recusants and liable to severe penalties.

While I have not found any firm evidence as to the religious convictions of Sir Walter Senior, and Sir Walter the younger, there is no doubt that the latter's eldest son Walter, was an adherent to the Church of Rome. In 1688 he followed James II to France and into exile. James created him Baron Kilpeck (the name of a village close to the Mynde), and he died at Whitbourne in his native Herefordshire in March 1690. His title was not recognised in England since it was conferred after James II's abdication.

Robert Pye, however, appeared to be a staunch Protestant; he was also Royalist and a Justice of the Peace of Hereford. He married twice; first in 1667 to Mary, the daughter of Sir Edmond Bray of Northampton,[18] and again in 1674, his second wife, Meliora, being the daughter of Sir James Drax of London.[19] It would appear that the estate was far less likely to be subject to fines or seizure if under Robert's control, apart from the fact that since Robert was likely to have an heir, there would be direct descent from Sir Walter Pye the second. One cannot help thinking that it was rather a clever manoeuvre on Walter's part to protect the Pye inheritance which had certainly done its part in bringing back the monarchy. It is a matter of conjecture just how strong Robert's religious convictions were.

Robert Pye is named Lord of the Manor on a Rent Roll of 1674 so presumably the ownership of the Mynde estate had been successfully passed on by that time.[20] His tomb in Much Dewchurch consists of a black marble slab placed in the nave of the Church with his coat of arms, together with those of Bray and Drax, drawn thereon. The inscription in Latin states simply –

> *"The remains of Robert Pye, esquire, son of Walter Pye of the Mynd in this parish, knight; who died 30th January in the year of grace 1680, aged 42."*

There is nothing to indicate the tragic circumstances in which he died; neither J.H. Matthews nor the writer of the Wormelow manuscript were apparently aware of the nature of his death, when preparing the history of Much Dewchurch.

At this time there were two large property owners in Much Dewchurch, Robert Pye and John Bodenham, a descendant of the ancient family from Rotherwas, who resided at Bryngwyn. Bryngwyn has had many mansions built on its land, the last of which was built in 1868 by the Rankin family who endowed Hereford City Museum and Library. Sir James Rankin MP who died in 1915 was Chairman of the Managers of Orcop School. The family mansion has now become a light engineering works, and part has been divided into flats for its employees.

John Bodenham was a fervent Roman Catholic, while Robert Pye was, as has been mentioned, a staunch Protestant. Religious disputes were as common in Herefordshire as elsewhere at this period, and the accusation made by Titus Oates of an alleged plot against the Protestant religion in England in 1678 had caused much anti-Catholic feeling. Father Kemble had been executed at Hereford in 1679, and in 1680 a proclamation was issued commanding all Catholics to take the Oaths of Abjuration and Allegiance before the Justices of the Peace in Quarter Sessions in Hereford. John Bodenham had refused to attend, and a warrant was issued which Robert Pye, in his position as a Justice of the Peace, was determined to enforce. Bodenham had shut himself up with his servants in the house, and had fired upon constables, who accompanied by Pye's servants, had come to arrest him. Accordingly, in the next Quarter Sessions, a fresh warrant was issued, and Robert Pye decided to serve this in person. The following is copied from a Fly Sheet, published in London in April 1681, which is now in the British Museum Library. A further record of the trial is in the State Paper Office in London.

*"A True Relation of a late barbarous assault committed upon Robert Pye, Esq., one of his Majesty's Justices of the Peace for the County of Hereford, who died thereof 30th January 1680 by John Bodnam Esq., a notorious Papist whom he went to apprehend for refusing to obey the orders of the Quarter Sessions whereby he was summoned to take the Oath of Allegiance.*

*Prior to this incident there had been attacks on Protestant Justices, and several warrants were granted at the Quarter Sessions against John Bodnam as being known as an obstinate and violent Papist, and still refused to take the oaths which the law requires. He kept close in his house making it as a garrison, defending himself, against the constables and their assistants, some of whom he shot and wounded.*

*Some time after this, that is to say on the 12th January last, it was Mr Pye's misfortune to spy his unruly neighbour, Bodnam working in his own grounds, whereupon having at the same time an Order of Assizes for the said Mr Bodnam's apprehension about him, and thinking that himself, that his oath and the duty of his place, in honour obliged him to apprehend an offender who had so often offended, he went to him and commanded him to surrender himself as a prisoner to the law. Mr Bodnam having a hedge bill in his hand replied, according to the usual language of his Papist Litany, "Damme, stand off, or I will cleave you down". The Justice made answer, "Mr Bodnam, you know I am too much a man to fear you". It seems he had formerly hand to hand taken him prisoner, and let him go upon his parole, which he afterwards perfidiously and dishonourably broke, and for his justification sent him word that no faith was to be kept with hereticks. Mr Pye, having therefore given him to understand as before, that he did not fear him, told him further in these words, "I come, not now as a single person, but as a magistrate according to law to apprehend you, and therefore I require you to surrender yourself peaceably". This Mr Bodnam refused to do, Mr Pye bravely and vigorously pressed in upon him, which this same Papistical butcher perceiving stepped back, and in good earnest let fly at his head with his hedge bill, and having stunned the valiant magistrate with the first, with the second blow fell'd him to the ground; presently company coming in prevented the immediate murder of the gentleman and seized upon the criminal Bodnam.*

*The wounded Mr Pye recovered his senses some time later, but it was only to increase his pain. For after he had continued ill for about 18 days in a lingering condition, upon 30th January last he departed this life, the sacrifice of Papistical disobedience and rebellion, not only to the unspeakable grief of his family and relations, but to all who had the honour of being acquainted with him. Nor is he less lamented by all true Protestants as well in the same, as in the adjacent counties. It is true the murderer will be doubtless hanged, but here is the severity of the case, we have lost an industrious and valiant magistrate, the Papists only a loose, base, butcherly villian.*

*Now it is a hundred to one but that as soon as this same caitiff (despicable knave) shall be hanged, the papists will deny that there ever were such persons as Mr Pye or Mr Bodnam, and perhaps that there is no such county as Hereford, but such blots in their Scutcheons as these will not be so easily wiped away . . ."*[21]

The wish of the writer, however, was not to be granted since Bodenham was tried for the murder at the March Assizes at Hereford, before Baron Atkins and Mr Justice Levins, but appears to have been discharged on pleading his Benefit of Clergy, as he was paying his fines as a Popish Recusant on the Recusant Rolls from 1676-84. His will dated 21st September 1705 names his eldest son, Charles, as his heir, and the Register of Papist Estates lists Charles Bodenham of Dinedor in 1717 as owning the Manor of Bryngwin.[23]

A footnote to this sad affair is provided by the following deposition which again gives no hint of the dramatic events which preceded it.[24]

*"Exchequer Depositions by Commissions. 2 Jac. 11. (1686). Michaelmas. No. 39. Hereford.*

*Meliora Pye, widow, versus Edward, Peter and Elizabeth Pye, infants.*

*As to the debts of Robert Pye of Kilpeck, esq., of Kilpeck late husband of the said Meliora, daughter of Sir James Drax. The said Robert was son of Sir Walter Pye, of Kilpeck, knt. by whom some of the debts were incurred.*

*The debts were very numerous and heavy. One was to William Pye. Money was owing to Sir Edmond Bray for the maintenance and education of Frances Pye, daughter of Robert Pye by a former wife. Frances had died unmarried. The plaintiff had a daughter, Elizabeth Pye. Property at the*

*Mynde, Kilpeck, Much Dewchurch, Saint Devereux "and the partes thereabouts" were settled on the plaintiff as her jointure. Robert Pye held the manor of Kilpeck.*

*Depositions taken at the Royal Oak in the city of Hereford. Mention is made of Edward Pye, merchant, and of lands of Robert Pye called Linton Park. At his decease, the chattels of Robert Pye were appraised at £478.14.1 There were "severall old trees and stoggall trees growing upon the several lands of Mr Robert Pye dec'd . . . which said woods were converted into cordwood and sold to Ironworks."*

*The following is a list of the debts. Most of them were paid by the widow.*

### *Debts*

| | £ | s | d |
|---|---|---|---|
| Mr Abraham Seward of Hereford | 35 | 0 | 0 |
| Ann Ballard of Langrove | 40 | 0 | 0 |
| James Collins of ffoye, gent. | 51 | 10 | 0 |
| " " " | 60 | 0 | 0 |
| Elizabeth Davys, servant. | 1 | 10 | 0 |
| Anne Williams. " | 3 | 3 | 0 |
| Elizabeth Hill. " | 2 | 10 | 0 |
| Thomas Caunt | 7 | 14 | 0 |
| William Jones. " | 1 | 10 | 0 |
| John Brackley, Royal Exchange, London. | 3 | 0 | 0 |
| Christopher Hill of the Savoy, London. | 2 | 7 | 0 |
| Iris Whitwell, servant. | 4 | 18 | 0 |
| Margery Bryan, Hereford, for meat etc., | 10 | 0 | 0 |
| Rowland Andrewes, Hereford, joiner, for Robert Pye's funeral. | 22 | 4 | 0 |
| Henry Waldron, the Temple, London. | 30 | 0 | 0 |
| John Lambert, joiner (see end notes) | 10 | 0 | 0 |
| John Rogers of Llandinabo, gent. | 29 | 10 | 0 |
| Rowland Andrews | 30 | 0 | 0 |
| Alice Clifford, widow. | 40 | 0 | 0 |
| Hester Stratford, spinster. | 80 | 0 | 0 |
| James Heath | 20 | 0 | 0 |
| Edward Powell, Much Dewchurch. | 1 | 15 | 0 |
| Walter Baker, Much Dewchurch. | 5 | 0 | 0 |
| Thomas Miles, of Lanwarne, butcher. | 2 | 0 | 0 |
| Rowland Andrews | 50 | 0 | 0 |
| William Pye of Thruxton (See end notes) | 30 | 0 | 0 |
| Joan Lambert (See end notes) | 30 | 0 | 0 |
| Thomas Price, Much Dewchurch. | 1 | 15 | 0 |
| Much Dewchurch Poor Rate. | 10 | 0 | 0 |

| | | | |
|---|---|---|---|
| John Williams of Lanwarne. | 3 | 10 | 0 |
| Edward Biddolph, gardner, wages. | 14 | 0 | 0 |
| Robert Symonds, mercer, Hereford. | 30 | 0 | 0 |
| | 662 | 16 | 0 |

Robert's widow, Meliora, continued to live at the Mynde with her daughter, Elizabeth, the only living child from Robert's two marriages.

It was not until Walter's death in 1690, as mentioned above, that her right to be there was really questioned, when John Pye, the third relative mentioned in her father-in-law's will, endeavoured to prove through the Chancery Court that the estate should come to him and his heirs.

Meliora died in 1699, John in 1701, and in the meanwhile, Elizabeth had married Henry Gorges of Eye, in Herefordshire. Henry Gorges entered public life being elected knight of the shire for the county of Hereford in 1698.

On the death of Elizabeth in 1708, the Estate was claimed by Charles Pye, grandson of John Pye, and so the battle was joined once more. It had commenced in 1691, continued on and off until 1718, and must have been a hollow victory since he eventually let, mortgaged, and finally sold to the Duke of Chandos.

The documents relating to this action, together with abstracts of deeds from 1567 to 1702 are in the Mynde Collection, and are prolific to an extreme. The papers give no indication of how long the Gorges family continued to reside at the Mynde. Henry Gorges and Elizabeth had 9 children, of whom Meliora lived the longest, dying at the age of 43 years. There is a tablet to her memory in the tower of the Parish church at Much Dewchurch which runs –

> *"Here lyeth the body of Meliora, daughter of Henry Gorges of Eye, of whom may with truth be offered that few women had an equal, and not many men, a superior understanding. Nobody had more exalted notions or friendship, but alas how rarely could she have expected to find honour and sincerity equal to her own. She lived in the esteem of all persons of merit, and died greatly lamented, especially by the poor.*
>
> *11th February, 1744."*

With the selling of the Mynde estate to James, Duke of Chandos, the connection of the Pyes with Orcop ceases, and no trace of the family or even the name remains in the immediate neighbourhood. One of the first Sir Walter's sons, William, of Thruxton, however, ensured that the family name lives on in his Charity which embraces 26 parishes. (See page 153.)

# Chapter Seven

## REFERENCES


| | | |
|---|---|---|
| 1. | J.H.Matthews. | p. 117. |
| 2. | J. Williams. | p. 57. |
| 3. | – | Mynde Collection 44. |

The Welsh 'ap' meaning 'son of' appears in such names as ap Rees, becoming Preece; ap Robert – Probert etc., This compares with the Scottish 'Mc', Irish 'Mac' and the English suffix 'son' at the end of a name e.g. Johnson, Davidson etc.

| | | |
|---|---|---|
| 4. | G.E. Aylmer. | The King's Servants. Pub. London. Routledge and Kegan Paul. p.308 ff. |
| 5. | G.E. Aylmer. | p. 308 ff. |
| 6. | – | Mynde Collection 186. |
| 7. | M. Munthe. | Hellens. London. 1957. p. 85. |
| 8. | J. Hutchinson. | Herefordshire Biographies. Hereford. 1890. p. 13. |
| 9. | H. Reade. | Woolhope Club Transactions. Hereford. 1927-8-9. Paper read 28.8.1928. |
| 10. | J.H. Matthews. | p. 106. |
| 11. | M. Munthe. | Detail from Clarenden State Papers. Vol. 11. p. 142. Bodleian Library. Oxford. |
| 12. | – | Archaeologia Cambrensis. 1864. |
| 13. | – | Hopton Collection,Hereford City Library. |
| 14. | – | Mynde Collection. 56. |
| 15. | – | Mynde Collection 5097 |
| 16. | – | Mynde Collection 3513, 851-3, 252, 855. |
| 17. | – | Mynde Collection. 5172. |
| 18. | – | Mynde Collection. 851-3 |
| 19. | – | Mynde Collection. 855. |
| 20. | – | Mynde Collection. 5153. |

| | | |
|---|---|---|
| 21. | – | Hopton Collection. Hereford City Library. |
| 22. | J.H. Matthews | p. 102. |
| 23. | – | Register of Papist Estates. Hereford County Record Office. |
| 24. | J.H. Matthews | p. 107. |

Lambert was the name which carried on longest at Orcop in the Church registers. The John and Joan Lambert referred to in the list of debts could have been John Lambert who was buried on 14th August 1686, and Joan Lambert who was buried on 1st September 1686. The Lambert family were tenants on the Mynde Estate for many years.

The William Pye referred to is likely to be the donor of the Charity mentioned at the end of the chapter.

| | | |
|---|---|---|
| 25. | R. Gorges. | The Story of a Family through 11 Centuries. Boston, U.S.A. 1944. |
| 26. | – | Mynde Collection 2962-2976. |

The small Elmhirst collection referred to on page 64, may now be in a local library or record office since Mr. Elmhirst is now deceased. I have been unable to trace its whereabouts.

Regarding the religious convictions of Sir Walter Pye senior, and his son, Sir Walter Pye the younger, see page 69, family tradition and information researched by the late Colonel Kellow Pye of Hampshire, indicated that they were Roman Catholic. John Pye, 1620-1701, who instituted Chancery proceedings to regain the Mynde, was a known recusant, Sir Walter and his son, were never listed a such.

# Chapter Eight

## Aspects of Life in the Manor of Orcop in the 17th, 18th and 19th Centuries

The Historical Manuscripts Commission in London have no record of any Court Rolls belonging to Orcop Manor, but there are six in the Mynde Collection at Aberystwyth which date from 1622 to 1683. In addition, I have traced copies of a further twenty five court Rolls dated from 1737 to 1808. These latter rolls are in a private collection to which I have kindly been given access, and it has been possible to include many extracts which give a broader and more detailed picture of life in the Manor. One of the most interesting of the earlier Rolls is quoted below:-[1]

***"12th June 1663.***

> *The presentment of the homage at the Court Baron of Walter Pye, Esq., holden for the Lordship of Orcop.*
>
> *We present that our tenure is socage of ancient demesne, and that we do not know or acknowledge any heriot, custom or relief to be found from any of the free tenants within the Lordship.*
>
> *We present it convenient and advantageous for our said Lord and his tenants of the said Lordship or Manor that the common within the same be depastured with their own cattle, and that no tenants put a greater number of cattle thereupon than shall be proportionable and answerable to their estates respectively. To the end that as well foreigners' cattle as the supernumeraries of the tenants may be impounded for a restriction of surcharge accomplished, we desire that a pound be erected by the Lord at the Green within the said Lordship for the use of himself and his tenants for the purpose aforesaid, and for other occasional distresses wherein the tenants will voluntarily assist, and we desire that the Bailiff be required carefully to take notice of and impound such foreigners and supernumary cattle as aforesaid.*
>
> *We refer ourselves to the presentments made at former courts touching encroachment upon the Lord's waste, and do now present Henry Hughes for encroaching 1½ acres, William Meredith of Orcop Hill encroaching ½ acre, Lawrence Willin for ½ acre.*

*Whereas William Smith, he hath part of John Gethings land, of the yearly value of 50 shillings, the whole being £24 per annum, and the chief rent 19/6d. We do, by consent of both parties, apportion the said rent, namely 17/- to be paid by Gething, and 2/6d. by Smith. We do also by consent of both parties apportion the chief rents of Thomas Price's estate being in whole 2/6d, Mr Thomas Philpotts 1/10d. and Thomas Price to pay 8d.".*

***The Pound. On the hill known as Stars' Pitch, (at one time, Penmaine Lane).***

The word 'socage' is Anglo Saxon, meaning tenure of lands by certain determinable service, while 'ancient demesne' was the name given to manors held by the Crown in 1066. "Whether they were still in the King's hands or were held by a subject, those dwelling on them, the 'tenants in ancient demesne' enjoyed certain customary privileges of their own, some of which were unknown elsewhere."[2] The free tenants are stating here that they do not pay any type of fine or heriot to their Lord, on the decease of any one of them, to enable their heir to succeed to the tenure of the property and lands they occupy. The reference to Chief Rent also precludes the freeholder of the property from any other service to his lord except for the payment of this rent, and attendance at the manor court. Another term for Chief Rent is 'quit rent'. The following definition of 'socage' is also helpful:-[3]

*"Socage had an exceedingly important part to play in the development of the land law, for with the passing of feudalism all free tenures became*

*progressively assimilated with it. Significantly the word socage is a Saxon word, and neither the word nor the tenure existed in Normandy before the Conquest. Indeed, it is one more evidence of the Conqueror's conservatism, that socage not only survived, but increased in importance. Bracton was of opinion that the term is derived from soc, the French word for a ploughshare. Again, Domesday Book has a good deal to say about the sokemen, who are found tilling the land of the manor. Socage, it is suggested, is the tenure on which they hold at this time. It is certainly an agricultural tenancy, and although after the Conquest it is possible to find examples of kings granting land in socage, in origin it is the tenure upon which those freemen who actually cultivated the land of the manor hold that land. It is immune from burdensome feudal incidents. There is no scutage, no wardship, and no marriage. It is distinctly English in origin, although the Normans not only retained it, but gradually came to prefer it to other tenancies."*

***The bridge over the Garron, near the Green Farm. Here was the dam which held back water for the Lower Mill. In the big flood of 1957 water flowed a foot higher than the top of the parapet. Referred to in Court Rolls as "the greate bridge over the Garron near Orcop's Church."***

The Court Roll above written helps to date the period during which Walter Pye, (the elder son of the second Sir Walter Pye, later to become Baron Kilpeck), held the lordship of Orcop. The manuscript refers to "Walter Pye Esq.," when the free tenants are asking their Lord to erect a pound. That he did not do so is seen in statements by tenants in cases regarding the rival rights of the Manor of Wormelow who testify that the pound was built by Robert Pye, his younger brother, who died in 1680.

With regard to the Court itself, the term 'Court Baron' was believed to be a court which exercised jurisdiction and administered the custom of the manor to freeholders only, presided over by the lord, but a court in which the tenants themselves gave judgment. There was also a 'customary court' for the copyhold tenants, presided over by the lord's steward only. I quote again as follows:-[4]

> *"Undoubtedly, this is what some legal writers at a later date thought the manorial system of courts was, but Maitland (F.W. Maitland), doubted whether there was so clear a distinction between court baron and court customary as has been suggested, and in addition, since the number of freeholders in many manors was small, he thought judgment was normally given in the lord's court by the suitors, whether the case concerned freehold or copyhold land. Such suitors, were, in his opinion, the freeholders, the unfree tenants acting merely as presenters."*

Although the Orcop Manor Rolls refer to a Court Baron, this was always held in the presence of the Steward or Deputy Steward, and the 'homage' or jury was composed of both free tenants and copyholders so I am inclined to support the suggestions quoted above. Since Orcop Manor was sizeable, 2403 acres, it probably had 'leet' jurisdiction which allowed its suitors to correct roads and fences in decay, overflowing of ditches, and encroachments on the highway.[5] The later Court Rolls contain many instances of such presentments. The Court Leet was held at Wormelow and Harewood, and each inferior manor paid suit and service to the Lord of Wormelow Manor and Hundred.

The Leases in the Mynde Collection also help to differentiate between the various types of land occupiers in Orcop in the 17th century.

***"November 10th 1648.***[6]

> *Sir Walter Pye and Walter Houthy of Orcop, Labourer.*
>
> *Lease for life of 6 acres in Saddlebow Hill in the parish of Much Dewchurch, joining to the lands of John Cicill on the east part, the highway leading from Baggalidyeard to Rosse on the south, and the common called Saddlebow Hill on the west.*
>
> *Rent 6/8d. and 6 fat chickens and a dozen eggs annually. Heriot 6/8d."*

Leases at this time often stipulated "a heriot of the best beast" and "suit of court" which meant attendance by the tenant at his Lord's Court.

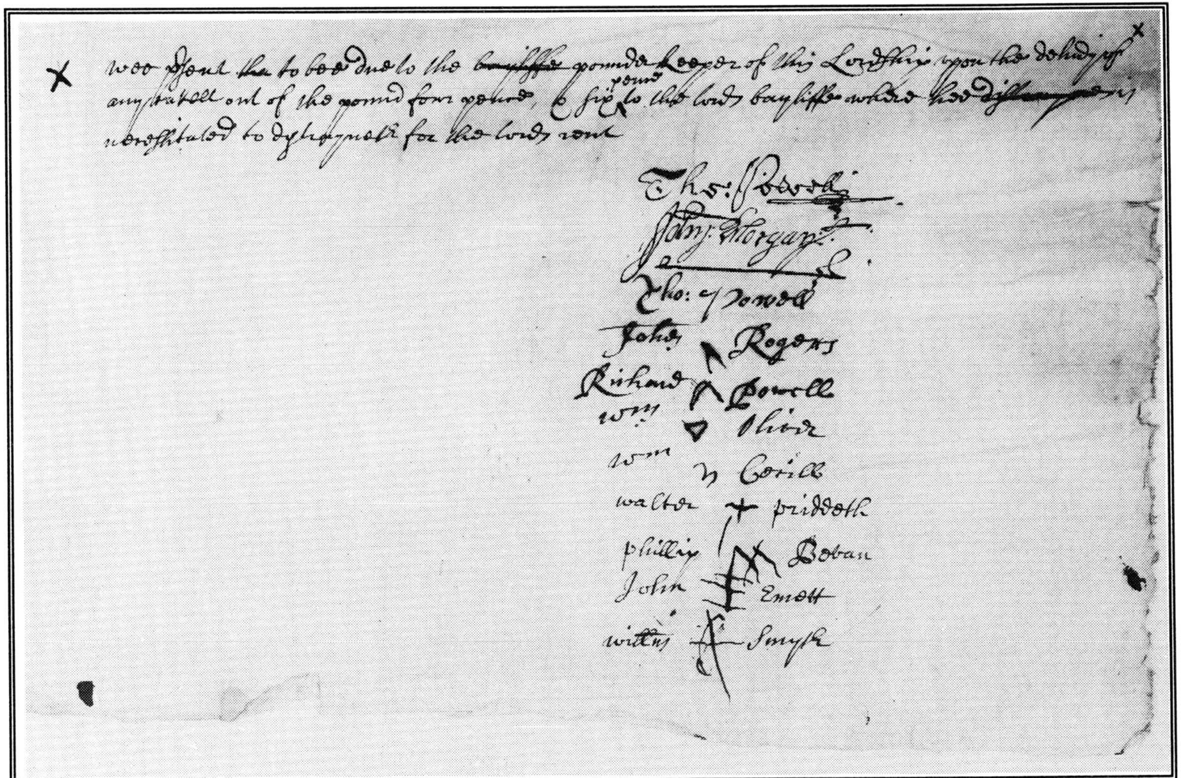

Tho: Powell
John Morgan
Tho: Powell
John Rogers
Richard Powell
Wm Olivr
Wm Corill
walter priddoth
phillip Boban
John Emott
willm Smyth

*Mynde 5174. Part of a Court Roll dated 19th November 1674 which sets the amount due to the pound keeper of 4d. a pounding as sworn in an affidavit, see page 84. Of the 11 freeholders signing the Roll, only three could write their names, note the various marks of the other eight.*

*"1577/8. February 17.*[7]

> *1. Gruffith a Pye of Moche Dewchurche, gent., and Katherine, his wife, Robert a Pye and Joan, his wife.*
>
> *2. Olyver Thomas, Gwenllyon his wife, and James Olyver, their son.*
>
> *Lease for 3 lives of a tenement and lands in the parish of Orcoppe in the tenure of Thomas Meredythe. Rent 3/4d. and a couple of capons annually. Heriot 5/-."*

This meant that the lease was to be for an indeterminate period, but that, on the death of one of the three tenants, a heriot of 5/- would have to be paid, if it was the wish of the other two, to add another life to the deed.

The following details from another document in the collection show the continuance of the tradition of partition of lands by the old law of gavelkind.

*"1599/1600. Feb 20.*[8]

> *1.Robert Newton of Slymebridge, co. Gloucester, Brodeweaver, and Thomas Newton of Longehope, co. Gloucester, yeoman, two of the sons and co-heirs of Robert Newton, late of Westburye, deceased, their father, and brother and co-heirs of Henry Newton, their brother, of certain gavelkind lands in Irchingfield, co. Hereford, yeoman.*
>
> *2. John Wyllym of Newton in the parish of St. Wanerdes, weaver.*
>
> *Grant in consideration of £4 of their parts in the messuage and lands called Newton and Grenewaye as of their right in gavelkins lands in Irchingefild as two of the brothers and co-heirs of Henry Newton, one of the five brothers and co-heirs of Robert Newton, being their parts of his part of the said messuages and lands into four parts lying in the parish of St. Wanerdes and Orcopp now in the tenure of John Wyllym and Bartholomew Jowldinge."*

These properties still exist and carry the same names today, Newton farm and Greenways. It is suggested that the partition of lands by gavelkind accounts for the number of small fields existing in Orcop.[9]

Many leases were for 21 years as follows:-

***"1637/8. Jan. 10.[10]***

> *Walter Pye of the Mynde. John Gunter of the parish of Orcopp, yeoman. Lease for 21 years of a messuage and lands in the parish of Orcopp called Hondies Farme. Rent £5 annually".*

This farm too exists today, and is still known as the Hondys.

The Lord of the Manor surely kept a good table for he was well supplied with chickens, eggs and grain throughout the year as a result of rents paid in kind as well as in coin. The terms of one lease dated September 29th 1651 for land outside, but adjacent to Orcop parish run:-[11]

> *"Lease between Sir Walter Pye and Anne Verywer, widow and her son of Much Dewchurch for lands in Much Dewchurch. Rent £16, ten bushels each of wheat, muncorne and peas, 2 fat geese, six fat chickens and a couple of fat capons annually. Lessees shall also render service in lessor's husbandry with the wain or plough and 6 oxen with 2 labourers on two days annually and eight thraves of rye straw annually."*

A thrave is the equivalent of 24 sheaves of grain forming two stooks. The above is one of the few documents in the whole collection which stipulate the giving of aid on the estate, in addition to the money rent and goods in kind.

Some idea of the poverty of the parish at this time can be gained from the information given in the Herefordshire Hearth Tax List of 1671 which shows that of the 42 parishes in the Wormelow Hundred only 4, (of which Orcop was one), had just one inhabitant paying tax. It is interesting to note that Robert Pye at the Mynde was paying tax for twenty hearths, and Sir William Powell, who held the patronage of Orcop Church, was paying for 12. The Rev. Jeremy Jackson of Garway who at times served Orcop Church was paying tax on 3 hearths.[12]

Orcop was also assessed for Ship Money in 1631 to the sum of £8.9.9.[13] and although so remotely situated, did not escape the attentions of the marauding Scots who pillaged it to the amount of £37.11.2. in 1645 during their siege of the City of Hereford.[14] It is recounted by Miles Hill who was employed by Parliament to get in provisions for the Scots in 1650, that the total of all the plunder gained in Herefordshire was £31,743.5.2. His account entitled "A true and Impartial Account of the Plunderings, Losses and Sufferings of the County of Hereford by the Scottish Army during their siege before the City of Hereford Anno. Dom; 1645" says:-[15]

> *"This is an abstract taken of the losses, damages and plunderings of one hundred and six small parishes within the county of Hereford by the Scottish Army commanded by General Leven, in the prosecution of which were divers boxes, doors, chests and trunks broken open and rifled,*

*severall families undone, most of all their cattle, horses and goods taken from them, much money, plate, jewels and all kinds of rich household stuff, rings and other rich commodities as wearing apparrel, linnen, books, the plate and linnen of divers churches, all the horses, mares and colts that ever they set their eyes upon as well from friends as others as the reader may see if he pleases in an inventory".*

***The vault of Thomas Abrahall died 16th November 1735 aged 77, and his wife, Sarah, died 1st February 1708, aged 44. See page 84 and 104***

***Vault 1992.***

Orcop is, as has been shown, situated in a valley between hills. Along the edge of some of these hills, namely, Saddlebow hill, Old Hall Wood, Little Hill and Garway Hill were many quarries, valuable sources of material for the building of homes, for roofing of houses and outbuildings, and paving of roads. The tenants of the manor were given permission by the Pyes to haul stone from these quarries for their own use. Stone was used as well for repairs to estate property, and for use at the Mynde itself. It was obviously necessary to ask permission from the Lord of the Manor at the Mynde to haul stone, but it would appear never to have been refused. There is one instance, however, of the system presumably being abused for we are told that when Henry Gorges was Lord of the Manor, and was riding, one day, over the common waste of Orcop, he noticed that stone had been taken from one of the quarries and a house built with it. Upon enquiry, and being told who had done this, he stated that the offender, one Thomas Abrahall, should be made to bring the stones back "in his teeth".[16] Turf was also cut and hauled by tenants from Orcop Hill to make a bowling green at the Mynde.[17]

Orcop appears to have been a very insular village in those days, due, no doubt, to the remoteness of its position, and so it remained until well after the turn of the 20th century, and the age of the popular motor car. There is the instance of a woman who asked leave of the Lady of the Manor, Mrs. Meliora Pye, (Robert Pye's widow), to enclose a piece of ground on Orcop Hill in order to build a house. Permission was granted, but, some years later, the woman, being widowed and wishing to marry a second husband, who was not of the parish, was threatened by some parishioners who wanted to take possession of the land for the use of the parish. Mrs Pye supported the woman who remained in possession of the land until her death, when her son inherited it.[18]

Those who received permission to enclose land on the commons of Orcop, and who built cottages there, did not, by so doing, have the rights to pasture their animals on the common. After the Pound was built, probably about 1670, in Robert Pye's time, there are instances in the Mynde documents of animals being impounded, and an affidavit sworn by one man, John Jones, stated that he kept the pound and was paid 4d for every pounding, and kept it in repair. There was still a pound in 1809 since a dispute had arisen between the cottagers and the Lord of the Manor which led Thomas Symons to seek Counsel's Opinion. I do not know the events that preceded this, but the Counsel's Opinion was as follows:-[19]

> *"In answering this question, I must take it for granted that Freeholders have an undoubted right of Common of Pasture, and that the Cottagers have none. In such case the Freeholders have a right to distrain the cattle or pigs of the cottagers, damage feosant, but if they, or the Poundkeeper detain them after a tender of sufficient amends for the damage done, and the charges of the distress, such detention is illegal, and will subject those who detain them to an action. In the present case the cottagers have yielded to the demands, which seem exorbitant and have paid the money, which as it seems to me, is an admission of the amount of the damage done, and they cannot now have any remedy for the exaction. The Poundkeeper should return the charges, and pay the money in each case to the person who impounded the cattle and who set the damage.*
>
> *Signed. H. Dampier.*
>
> *April 15th 1809."*

Presumably the freeholders were taking unfair advantage of the cottagers by demanding excessive dues for the damage done by the animals belonging to the cottagers. Today there are the remains of the pound on the land belonging to the Lower Mill Farm, which borders onto the Green Farm, (see photograph on page 77). It is known as the "pound" by many villagers, and is situated within half a mile of the old village although at the end of the parish. Another Court Roll of Orcop Manor is dated 20th January 1651, and concerns a man's attempt to establish the existence of a pathway.[20]

> *"To this Court cometh Thomas Price and prayeth a view to find out the ancient bridle way out of the King's Highway leading from Orcop's Green towards Bagalyard to the Cockshoot and so far to Saddlebow's Butts and to him it is granted."*

This was witnessed by five tenants, together with the names of six villagers who were to be the Jury in the View.

> *"Ordered that the Jury do meet and view the place in question before the eve of Christmas, and return the verdict to the Steward before the 1st April under the penalty of each of twenty shillings."*

This ancient bridle path can be identified with the photograph on page 86. In a later chapter regarding the mills of Orcop, it will be seen that there was once a mill near the Old Shop or the Brooklands, its present name, and Thomas Price, who wished to find the bridle path, lived near the mill in 1640, and in a rent roll of 1674, was described as the tenant of the mill. Almost directly opposite the site of the mill an old footpath is marked on the Ordnance Survey Map; today the path is marked by a hedge which follows the path right up to the Cockshoot Wood and to Saddlebow's Butts. Possibly Thomas Price had recently taken over the lease of the mill (which remained in the name of Price up to 1735), and wished to establish the ancient bridle way for the convenience of his customers.

The eighteenth century was a time of great change in Orcop Manor since the Lordship passed from the Pye family to the Duke of Chandos, and then to the Chandos family. The last member to administer the estate and the manor for the Pyes was Robert Pye's son-in-law, Henry Gorges, and when his wife died, there was a long legal struggle for possession.

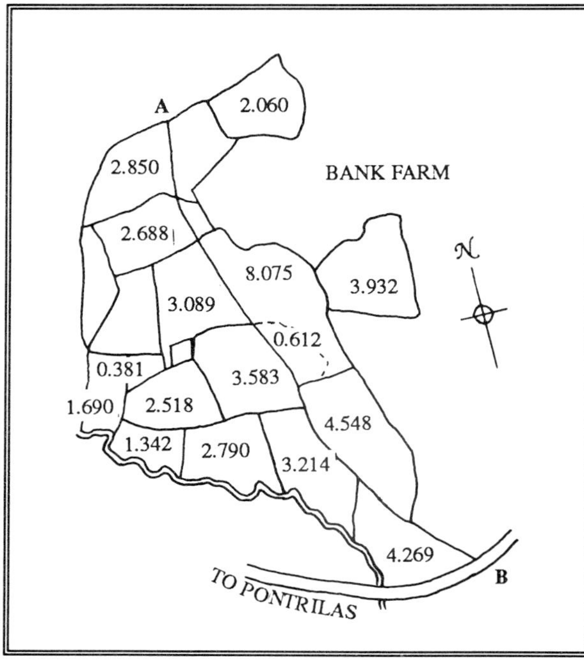

***The Bank Farm 1966. This farm has now been incorporated with Brooklands Farm. The line of hedges "A-B" marks a large part of "the ancient bridle way" referred to on page 85. The photograph is taken from near "A" looking south.***

A schedule of rents of the Orcop Manor dated 1717 which was prepared for Charles Pye when he recovered the Manor, only to immediately mortgage it, provides fascinating reading with regard to current livestock prices.[21]

| | £ | s | d |
|---|---|---|---|
| Widow Lambert for the Hendros (now called Hendre) | 11 | 8 | 4 |
| Also 2 bushels oats, 2 capons, 6 chickens | | 5 | 6 |
| Moores and Meakes Farm | 11 | 3 | 4 |
| 6 bushels Oats, 2 capons, 6 chickens, 4 hens. | | 11 | 6 |
| Thomas Jones, now Jonathan Beavan. | | | |
| Moiety (part) of a tenement. | 1 | 10 | 0 |
| plus 2 geese, 2 capons, 6 chickens and 2 days work in harvest. | | 7 | 4 |
| John Stringer | 1 | 14 | 0 |
| 6 chickens | | 1 | 6 |
| Thomas Price, late Joseph Price (Mill) | 7 | 10 | 0 |
| 2 bushels oats, 6 chickens | | 3 | 6 |
| Yearly salary for collecting Orcop Chief Rents. | 1 | 0 | 0 |

The Orcop Chief Rents amounted to £8.15.0. per year out of which £3.6.8. had to be remitted to the Lord of Wormelow Manor since it was a superior Manor, and Orcop paid Suit and Doome to the Lord of Wormelow. This question of chief rents was to raise many legal problems in the time of the Lordship under the Symons family. Where an inferior manor was held under the jurisdiction of a larger manor, the chief rents that were collected from the freeholders were remitted complete to the superior lord. In the case of Orcop, this was not done, and it would appear that the Manor of Orcop was a law unto itself, but whether by some ancient tradition or by deliberate falsification cannot now be determined.

Richard Symons of London purchased the estate from the Duke of Chandos in 1726, and by 1735, his son, John Symons, who was then 27 years old, had married Anne Colebrooke, (a farm in St. Weonards bears the name of Colebrooke), and was Lord of Orcop. John Symons, who went to University at Oxford, had a sum of £1600 advanced by his father for his education and travel abroad from 1727-1732.[22] The long legal struggle by Charles Pye to regain the Mynde from the Gorges after the death of Elizabeth Gorges (nee Pye, daughter of the murdered Robert), and the subsequent mortgaging and remortgaging of the Estate, had led to a certain neglect of the administration of the Manor of which the new Lord of the superior Manor of Wormelow, Stephen Ashby, was probably well aware. As stated before, the Common of Orcop was particularly valuable, being possessed of many quarries, and in 1735/6 Ashby presumably decided, in view of the fact that

Orcop Manor owed Suit and Doome to Wormelow, that he would claim the common of Orcop to be within the bounds of the Manor of Wormelow. The account of the perambulation of Wormelow Manor (see page 42) shows that Orcop certainly did come within the Manor of Wormelow, but since it had long been established as a separate Lordship, it would appear that it was only necessary to provide Doomesmen to sit in judgement at the Hundred Court and to pay certain Chief Rents. The test case was a plea of trespass on Orcop Hill, (otherwise called Orcop Common, on the boundary of the manor), where William Abrahall, son of Thomas Abrahall, had dug stone and taken it away. There are 17 documents in the Mynde Collection,[23]2 briefs, notices and bills of costs regarding this case which took place at Herefordshire Assizes in the summer of 1736, and although since commencing proceedings, Stephen Ashby had died, his heirs carried on with their efforts to eject Abrahall from two parcels of land on the Common. The case on this occasion went in favour of John Symons, but 9 years later in 1744/5, the new Lord of Wormelow Manor, who obviously doubted the verdict, one Richard Clark, decided to raise the question again. This time, Thomas Rudge, an erring tenant of Symons, who had taken over the tenancy of a cottage on the waste following the death of his father, William Rudge, was chosen to be the main witness. He had formerly applied to be admitted as a tenant for that part of his father's house in which he lived, but since his father was very impoverished, the parishioners feared that he (the father) might become chargeable on the parish, and so, the son's claim was dismissed, the father remaining the tenant.[24] The son, Thomas Rudge, promised to pay his father a rental for the room he lived in and for part of the land. The evidence was collected for this case at the Swan and Falcon in Hereford, on the 15th July 1746. The background to the case provides much food for thought. The brief states:-[25]

*"The action has been brought by Rudge at the instigation of Mr Clark, Lord of the Manor of Wormelow, not only to assert his right to the cottage in question, but likewise, to the whole waste or common in Orcop which he insists is within the manor of Wormelow, whereas Mr Symons claims it is belonging to and within his manor of Orcop which was formerly part of the estate of the Pyes of the Meend. Solemn tryal Summer 1736, Hereford Assizes. Stephen Ashby was Lord of the Manor at this time, and in order to try this right brought an ejection against William Abrahall, a tenant of Mr Symons on the said waste, but by neglect of the persons concerned, the papers of such trial are lost, which we comprehend the new Plaintiff is not ignorant of, and therefore, as many of our old witnesses at the last trial are dead, he has a mind to make this second attempt.*

*After the last verdict all the tenants on the waste attorned to Mr Symons, and amongst them, William Rudge, the plaintiff's father, who by writing under his hand, agreed to become Mr Symons' tenant for the cottage in question at 6d. per annum, a rent continued until his death which happened at Christmas 1743. Upon his death Mr Symons' agent called on the new tenant, Thomas Rudge, for the rent in arrear, but he refused to pay and declared he was advised by the steward of the Court of Wormelow not to pay arrears, or to attorn or pay Mr Symons any further rent for the said cottage. Upon which Mr Symons on the 11th February 1744 caused a distress to be made for 6 years rent due Michaelmas 1744. Gave him notice to quit or pay 2/6d. This has occasioned the present suit, for Plaintiff immediately repleveyed the goods and declared in the Hundred Court of Wormelow, but Mr Symons has since removed it into the Common Please and obliged them to declare as above."*

'Repleveyed' means the taking back of what has been distrained upon giving security to try that right at law.

The defendants, William Gwatkin and David Pritchard, who were bailiffs acting for Symons, acknowledged seizing goods from Thomas Rudge as follows:-

*"1 pewter dish, 2 small pottage pots, 1 brass pan, 1 axe, 1 spade, 1 frying pan, 1 warming pan, 1 bed, 1 bedestead, 3 blankets, 1 rug and 1 small kettle."*

They further stated that the cottage, which was erected on waste called Coneygar Hill, was the cottage and freehold of Mr Symons, and because the goods were in the cottage encumbering the same and doing damage there, they had the right to distrain upon them. On reading through the Court Rolls I noticed that William Rudge and his son had been presented at a Court Baron in 1738 for erecting a cottage and enclosing a garden on Coneygar Hill, and together with others, had been told to throw open the enclosure and pull down the building before the next Court Baron in a few months time. This erection of cottages and enclosing of waste ground was a familiar cause of presentment; the offenders were usually fined 3/4d and since these fines were carried on from one Court Baron to the next, the cottages and enclosures do not appear to have been demolished. I had an interesting conversation on this point with a gentleman in the National Library of Wales at Aberystwyth who had been working among old Estate records for many years, and he told me that when these encroachments were made, it was formal procedure to bring them to the Court Baron, and the fines were purely nominal. Having brought the encroachments into the jurisdiction of the Manor Court, it enabled the Lord to establish his ownership of the buildings since they were on common land and he was "Lord of the Soil". The rents charged were often very low, but the buildings provided additional revenue, and were an added asset to the estate. He also mentioned that valuable work had been done recently by a gentleman in Shropshire, since deceased, who had also come across the rival claims of two Lords of the Manor to cottages on the boundaries of their manors. Unfortunately, time prevented further discussion on this fascinating topic since we both had long journeys to get home, but it was interesting to know that this was the procedure usually adopted as it appeared to me that many of the cottages had survived the orders of the jury.

The name Coneygar Hill is mentioned several times in old deeds, together with the name Abrahall's Yat (or gate), and during the case of 1745/6, its position was a vital factor in the fight to establish where the bounds of Orcop manor ended, and those of Wormelow began. These names have never been known to anyone still living in Orcop today, and I have spent a great deal of time endeavouring to trace where they could be. Piecing together acreages and directions given in old leases provided a general direction of the whereabouts of Abrahall's Yat. By checking the Tithe Map of Much Dewchurch, together with cottage agreements, it would seem that Abrahall's Yat was the land at the extreme eastern end of Orcop Hill, and that part of it bordered on to Much Dewchurch.

The date of the lease below indicates that the Abrahall family were well known in the parish by the early 16th century. For the entrance to their property to be a local landmark makes one think that they had a sizeable holding. The document that mentions Gorge's threat to Abrahall for quarrying on Orcop Hill indicates that he lived at the "Burnettes" or in that vicinity. The name is a very ancient one, and it is likely that the tenement in those days stretched further than it does now.

***"1551/2. March 3.*** [26]

> *1. James Baskervyle of Erdesley, knight.*
>
> *2. John Lewes and Katerine, his wife.*
>
> *Grant of a messuage called Conyngars with 24 acres of arable land in Orcoppe extending in length near the way leading from Orcoppes Grene to Aberhales Lydatt and in breadth between the highway aforesaid and the hill called Conyngar Hyll . . ."*

The farm at the bottom of Orcop Hill called "the way" is the Green Farm, and one of the fields bordering the road up to Orcop Hill is called in the Tithe Apportionment Book, "Conygree" while in a Rental Book of the Mynde Estate, an entry reads "cottage and land called Coneygree, 15/-." Today the cottage, is named "Coney Cottage." Perhaps the most satisfactory discovery regarding these old names came from an affidavit sworn by the Steward for Wormelow which shows the animosity which the case had caused.[27]

> *"George Roberts, of Llanwarne, gentleman, maketh oath that having been appointed by the court in Trinity time last to show the place in question, he attended on Thursday the 7th day of August last at the place appointed for the stewards and jury, together with William Gwatkin the younger, the other shower, and there proceeded from the place appointed for their meeting towards the place in question, and before the said showers and jurors came to the said place in question, Thomas William Gwatkin riding*

*before the jurors stopped at a crossway a considerable distance from the place in question, and pointing down one lane and up another lane said "there are the boundaries of the Coneygar Hill" to which this deponant objected saying that we had nothing to do with the Coneygar Hill, being decided by the rule of court to show only the place in question. This deponant further said that from the said crossway, they, the showers and jury, proceeded to the place in question, being a cottage let in the possession of one, Thomas Rudge, and this deponant having desired the gentlemen of the jury to take notice of the said cottage and view the same, being the place in question, this deponant rode off. When the lessor (John Symons)of the plaintiff (Rudge) asked this deponant if he would show Abrahalls Yatt being a place at a considerable distance from the cottage, and being a gate leading into Costain Woodlands called Scudamore's Hill belonging to the Lady Scudamore, and no part of the place in question, this deponant replied "no", adding that he had shown the said cottage, and comprehended he had nothing more to do in pursuance of the rule, whereupon the said Mr Symons and William Gwatkin rode with the jury from the said cottage towards the place called Abrahalls Yatt, and the said William Gwatkin said the edge of the upper side thereof adjoining to the said Lady Scudamore's lands was the bounds of Mr Symon's manor of Orcop, and riding further on to the common called Orcop Hill, the said William Gwatkin, said "here or hereabouts is the end of Coneygar Hill" or words to that effect."*

The lease of Conyngars and the affidavit places Abrahall's Yat somewhere between the end of Conyegar Hill which is known today as Little Hill, and Orcop Hill, the latter at that time being common and waste. The "Burnettes" is in this area. It was much later when gathering information regarding Orcop Baptist Chapel that this was confirmed.

The Costain Woodlands were probably what is shown on Ordnance Survey Maps as Scudamore Hill Wood; the former name is unknown in Orcop, and I have found no other mention of it in documents. An affidavit sworn by William Gwatkin, the Steward of Orcop, confirms the statement made by Roberts, but comments that Roberts travelled over the disputed ground in the reverse direction.

The affidavits sworn by many Orcop villagers show that they never doubted that the common of Orcop belonged to the Lord of Orcop. There are many instances similar to the following:-[28]

*"Affidavit sworn by John Baker, aged 74 years.*

*To prove that he raised wallstone and paving on waste called Orcop Hill by Mr Gorges's order about 40 years ago for his use at the Meend, that he was bred and born in the parish of Orcop, always understood that ye Conygar Hill and all the parish was in the Manor of Orcop, never knew or heard that anybody ever halled stone or tyle on the waste of Orcop without leave from ye family at the Meend, Lords of Orcop. Remembers to have heard a Court was kept in Mr Robert Pye's time about 60 years ago, but was not at it being then out at service in a neighbouring parish.*

*Thomas Abrahall, aged 53 years.*

*About 22 years ago remembers he applied to Mr Woodhouse, agent to the Duke of Chandos, for leave to raise stone on Orcop Common to repair his house, and had leave to raise the stone. Never heard tell until lately that anybody had any claim to the waste of Orcop except the family at the Meend."*

The following affidavit of Walter Gwatkin, who was at one time, Mr Symon's bailiff, concerns the impounding of stray animals.[29]

*"Walter Gwatkin, 64 years.*

*To prove ye payment of one year's rent by William Rudge and frequent promises by him to pay arrears.*

*To prove a distress made on Thomas Powell, Bailiff of the Manor of Wormelow for arrears of rent for a tenement and about an acre of land on ye waste of Orcop, and ye rent paid in consequent of that distress of two shillings and six pence for ye charges of it.*

*To prove ye Conygar Hill was also reputed and esteemed to be within the Manor of Orcop.*

*To prove that no tenants of the Manor of Wormelow were ever thought to have any right to pasture on the waste of Orcop, or any others except ye freehold tenants of ye Manor of Orcop; that about 4 years ago he impounded the sheep of one, Giles Walter, of the Manor of Wormelow for trespass on ye waste of Orcop, and received a promissory note for 1/6d. on his delivering them, and that sometime ago he impounded ye cattle of one, John Gilbert, of ye Manor of Kilpeck, and received one shilling satisfaction."*

Another unusual affidavit is short and lacking explanation, but runs as under:-[30]

*"John Russell.*

*To prove of £3.0.0. in lieu of a Deodand on account of an accidental death of a person on Orcop Hill."*

A deodand is any personal chattel which is the immediate cause of the death of a human being. The deodand was supposed to be forfeited to charitable or pious purposes. On another occasion an entry in the Court Roll states –[31]

> *"We present that since the last Court there happened to the Lord of the Manor a Deodand which moved to the death of Thomas Evans on Orcop Hill within this Manor, and that three shillings the value thereof was paid into the Steward's hands in open court for the use of the Lord of this Manor."*

Since payment was made to the Lord of the Manor, I interpret the word 'deodand' as being another word for 'heriot' although this is not the standard definition which is the one already given. (See end note).

Maps were used to prove the old grant of lands near to Conygar Hill extending in length from Orcop Green to Abrahall's Yat, but unfortunately there is no trace of them in the collection, and one can only assume that they have now perished.

It is interesting to note that several bailiffs of Wormelow Manor asked permission of the Mynde to have houses built on the waste of Orcop where they lived although serving the Lord of Wormelow. Amongst these were Thomas Powell, Lewis Powell and William Rodd, whose widow still remained in Orcop, (see inventory attached to her will, page 99).

Together with the sworn affidavits of many villagers comes the official documentary evidence of the past. The case for the Lord of Wormelow stated –

> *"Walter Pye and Baskervilles paid suit for the Manor of Orcop. At the former trial the purchase deed was produced from the Duke of Kent, (former owner of Wormelow Hundred and Manor), and an extract from Court Rolls to prove it was ancient demesne, and produced other court rolls from Henry VIII from which it appears that Orcop was presented as a vill within the jurisdiction of Wormelow, and that the tenant had suffered recovery and paid fines in the Court of Wormelow for lands in Orcop. Also produced were Writs of Right to the steward to make partitions of lands in the reign of Mary. Also produced the Bailiff's account from 1641 for 3 years in which they charged the customary heriot after the death of Sir Walter Pye, doomesman £1.2.0. and also several court rolls whereby it appears that the tenant of Orcop had served his Jury at Wormelow Court Barons. Also produced some presentments of offences in Orcop, and encroachments and fines estreated (levied). Also proved that Orcop men have served and been served in Wormelow Manor Court, also one incident of an estray horse taken in Orcop in 1735, the year before last trial and that the doomesmen pay different rents and Orcop pays £3.6.8."*

The case for the Lord of Orcop stated –

*"The manor was bought from the Duke of Chandos. Orcop is a manor held in Capite (a tenant in capite, or in chief – one who holds lands immediately of the King), and pays £3.6.8. (which by some means Wormelow has permission from the Crown), and yet it is an independent Manor.*

*We have a copy of an old record called Testa de Neville out of the Exchequer which was pleaded and allowed in the Abbot of Craylands case in Parliament, 7 Edward III, which shows that the freemen and Welchmen in Urchinfield hold their lands in Capite of the King rendering £30.7.6. and ought to find 49 men in the King's Service for 15 days in Wales at their own costs which tallies with the subsequent record.*

*Also a copy of a Grant from the Tower 24 February 37 Henry III, to Walter Baskerville and his heirs of free warren in all his demesne lands in the Manor of Horcop in Hirchinfield so that the lands be not in the bounds of the King's forest.*

*Also copies of the Inquisition Post Mortem of Walter de Baskerville 24th May 28 Henry 3 whereby it is found that Sir Walter holds of the King in Capite the Manor of Orcop with the appurtenances in Urchinfield in free socage paying therefore 60 shillings and to find two men for the said manor, two men for its appurtenances in the King's service against Wales at his own costs and one day and one night towards England and that the Manor was then £7 per annum.*

*We have also many Leases and Counterparts of Leases from the Baskervilles as Lords of the Manor, divers undertenants of severall parts of the demesne lands in the times of Edward IV, Henry VII, Henry VIII, Edward VI and Queen Elizabeth.*

*We have also the rolls of three Courts kept for our Manor to wit, one 20 James I, and two more in the reign of Charles II where encroachments on the Common were presented.*

*To show that great disputes arose and were carried on and continued in the Pye family for about 40 years whereby the rights of the Manor were neglected.*

*N.B. As the Plaintiffs allow several ancient mesne Lordships under them of which they reckon this one, and they call Suits and Dooms, and that they have each their Courts Baron, and that they collect of their severall undertenants in small sums just as much Chief rent as they pay in Gross to the Lord of Wormelow, how in that (as well as in other respects) we apprehend we vary much from the rest, for Orcop pays only a rent of £3.6.8. and receives Chief rents from its tenants amounting to £8.15.7. per annum."*

The case was discharged in favour of Orcop and the Mynde, and costs of £52.5.6. were awarded to John Symons, the decision being given on 5th December 1746. There is an account which runs:-

| | £ | s | d |
|---|---|---|---|
| Paid £5 for witnesses' meals. | | | |
| Dinner for 12 gentlemen (the jury on view perhaps?) | 1 | 15 | 0 |
| Wine | | 2 | 0 |
| Punch | | 2 | 6 |
| Ale | | 15 | 0 |
| Hay and corn for horses | | 2 | 8 |
| | 2 | 17 | 2 |

After the case had been settled the tenants who had cottages on the common attorned to John Symons, two typical examples are quoted below:-[32]

*"I, William Philpotts, do hereby attorn tenant to John Symons for 1 barn and sheep's cot with a stable, wain house, work house and 2 parcels of land containing 1 acre by ye same, more or less, situated on Coneygar Hill on the waste of the manor aforesaid, and now in the occupation of John Weare, at ye yearly rent of 2/6d, and I have this day paid unto ye said John Symons 1d. for part of rent on account of my attorning tenant aforesaid. Dated 29th January 1747."*

*"I, Thomas Tutrell, attorn to John Symons for 1 cottage and half an acre of land situated on Coneygar Hill at ye yearly rent of 6d. payable at Michaelmas, and I have this day paid to John Symons 1d. in part of rent and on account of my attorning.*

*Dated 12th December 1746."*

The rentals of other cottages with up to 1 acre of land varied from 3d. per year to 1/- per year.

John Symons instituted regular courts and from 1737 to 1747 these were held twice a year. After this there is a gap in the rolls until 1779 when they continue less frequently until 1808. The homage usually comprised ten to twelve men, both freeholders and tenants, together with a further two men who were sworn in as assessors. All those who defaulted by their non-attendance were fined 2d. and below are a few examples of the varied presentments which were made in these rolls.

For not repairing bridle ways, fines of 3/4d. 5/- and 10/- [33]
For not erecting stiles in a footway, 3/4d[34]
For not repairing the bridge over Orcop Mill stream 5/-[35]
John Watkins for not scouring and cleansing his ditch 5/-[36]
For a bridleway out of repair and very dangerous to passengers 3/4d[37]
For stopping up a footway leading from Coneygar Hill to the Burnett being an ancient footway (Abrahall's Yat perhaps?). 20/- [38]

Milbourne Pritchard for digging a ditch before a stile from the Pennant to Orcops Church.

Ordered to fill same up or put a bridge over it. 5/-[39]

Certain husbandry way from Orcops Green to Orcops Hill to be repaired. 5/-[40]

Thomas Medmore and Thomas Wood for not putting up a gate at Strodwen (Stradway) land in a way leading from Strodwen to Orcop Hill. 3/4d[41]

We present that Thomas Maddox, late a tenant of this manor died since the last Court by an accident in a Quarry within the said manor, but what accrued to the Lord thereupon the Jurors cannot set forth.[42]

William Waters for keeping goats without keeping them under the direction of the Lord.[43]

We present 1 strayed sheep.[44]

William Rogers and James Treherne for quarrying on team roads. 39/-[45]

Thomas Parry for falling and converting ash timber on Garway Hill. 10/-[46]
(Hard, straight grained wood useful for handles of tools, plough fittings etc.)For erecting a pig sty on the waste. 10/-[47]

Thomas Evans for erecting a barn upon Garway Hill. 10/-[48]
We present the pound being out of repair.[49]

By 1786 the fines for non-attendance had been increased to 6d. each for labourers and 1/- each for team holders.[50] The villagers were so jealous of their traditional rights that they were even prepared to indict the Lord of the Manor himself. The following entry appears –[51]

*"We present Sir Richard Symons, Baronet, Lord of the Manor, for two bridges on the Church Path."*

The fine was limited to 20/- should the repairs not be done by the next Court. A Court Roll dated 24th November 1779 provides interesting facts regarding the occupations of some of the inhabitants of Orcop at that time. There were twenty seven presentments for encroachments and building on the Lord's waste, and among the occupations were the following:-

Sawyers, Masons, Labourers, a Publican, Carpenters, a Tyler, a Weaver and a Thatcher.[52] The fine for encroachments was usually 3/4d. but in later years, fines were not stipulated, they were merely limited to 20/-. These rolls provide much information regarding the existence of footpaths, bridle ways, team roads and husbandry ways, and since the names of those who had to carry out the repairs are given, it helps to give an idea of where the inhabitants lived. It also helps to account for the fact that Orcop only had one Enclosure Act for 275 acres since the number of presentments for earlier encroachments show that much of the common and waste had already been possessed before 1814, the date of the first meeting regarding the Enclosure Award.

John Symons died in 1763 leaving no heir, and since his father, Richard Symons, had stipulated that each person who inherited should adopt the surname and arms of Symons, the son of his daughter, Anna, Richard Peers, inherited the Mynde and assumed the name of Symons. He was created a baronet on the 23rd May 1774, [53] and died, unmarried, in 1796 when the title became extinct. An extract from a local paper in 1774 states that £35 was distributed among the poor of the City of Hereford, a donation from Richard Symons of the Meend.[54] The following week a fat ox was to be provided for his poor parishioners.

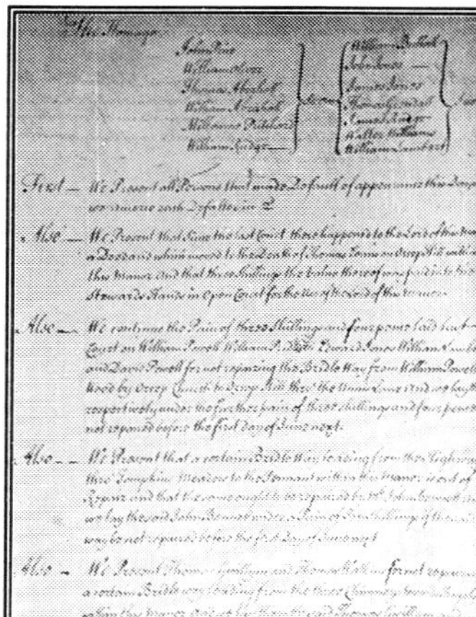

***Photograph of copy of a Court Baron of John Symons held on 28th October, 1737.***

Another item in the same journal dated 6th November 1777 shows the harsh treatment meted out by some of the magistrates at that time for what would appear to us to be trivial offences.[55]

*"Committed to County Jail by John Scudamore, James Meredith of Orcop, labourer, charged with killing a hare in the night and having same in his possession. To remain in gaol for three months unless the sum of £20, the penalty inflicted by Act of Parliament, shall be sooner paid."*

The Quarter Session Rolls for Herefordshire are not catalogued, and although I checked through those for 1740, 1744, 1746, 1754, 1751, 1778, 1800, 1805 and 1875 to 1888, I found little reference to Orcop. Many cases in the later years referred to drunkenness and assault, while those of the earlier years often comprised cases which were reported and not proved, or cases which, although reported, were held over to later sessions and then were missing. Cases would be brought for such things as stealing a quantity of hay worth 2/-, for stealing 4 cheeses valued at 8d, and 1 lb. of woollen yarn valued 2d, for stealing tile hammers worth 6d, and tile-peckers worth 5d, for stealing money, shirts and silk handkerchiefs, cotton stockings and gowns, but when one attempted to follow these up, nothing could be traced with regard to verdict and sentence.

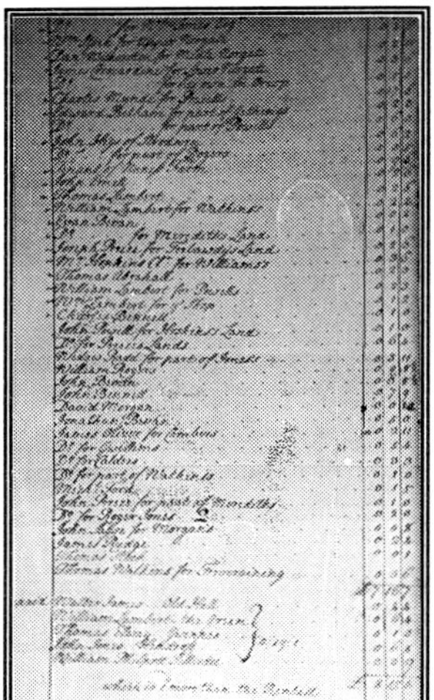

***Photograph of a list of Orcop Chief Rent, date approximately 1700-1720.***

The remoteness of Orcop attracted a "notorious horse stealer" to Garway Hill in 1774. The local paper had some fascinating entries regarding David Williams, alias Deo Deliro, who was late of Builth Wells and a clockmaker by trade. He is described as –[56]

> *"A middle sized man about 60, wearing a light brown wig with a single curl, and a cap under his wig, and a light brown coat and waistcoat and dirty leather breeches."*

He made his headquarters at Cold Nose, a farm on Garway Hill, now called White House. This farm was not part of the Mynde Estate, being variously owned by wealthy landowners and magistrates and let to tenant farmers. He stole horses in Denbighshire and Somerset, and brought them to Orcop. The newspaper tells us that –[57]

> *"David Williams is an old and notorious offender having been imprisoned in Denbighshire for coining, and last year in our gaol for horse stealing from which he was discharged by proclamation. A singular discovery was made, it is said, last week in the parish of Orcop, where in the middle of a thick wood a stable was found almost underground, which undoubtedly was formed for the purpose of stabling such horses as this fellow and his family might steal. For Williams regularly brought up his sons to this felonious practice. This is part of a numerous gang dispersed over the kingdom, and by exchanging horses stolen in one part of the country for those stolen in the opposite, they have for long escaped the pursuit of justice."*

Some while afterwards, David Williams escaped from a constable, together with his son and a servant who aided him in his assault on the constable. The last entry I found ran –[58]

***"29th September 1774.***

> *Felons under sentence of transportation set off under guard in order to be shipped to his Majesty's plantations in America included David Williams, the notorious horse thief."*

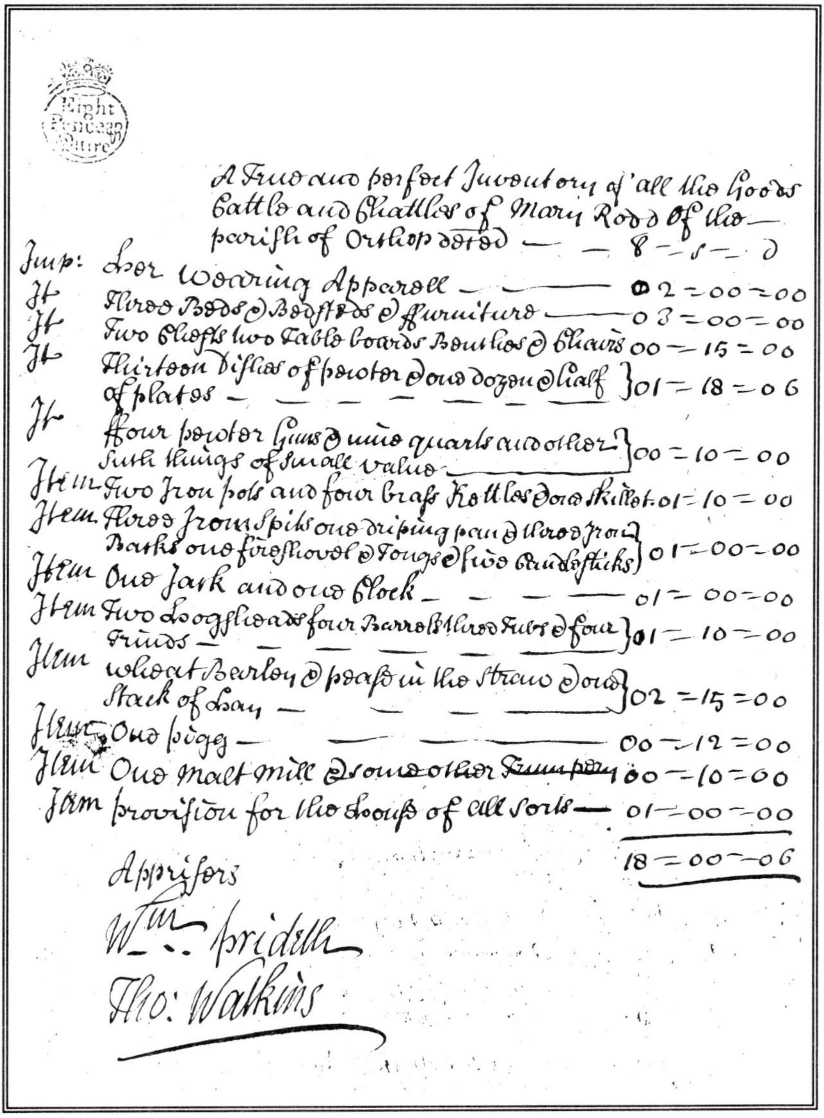

A True and perfect Inventory of all the Goods Cattle and Chattles of Mary Rodd of the parish of Orcop dated — 8 — 5 — 0

| | | |
|---|---|---|
| Imp: | Her Wearing Apparell | 02 = 00 = 00 |
| It | Three Beds & Bedsteds & furniture | 03 = 00 = 00 |
| It | Two Chests two Table boards Benches & Chairs | 00 = 15 = 00 |
| It | Thirteen dishes of pewter & one dozen & half of plates | 01 = 18 = 06 |
| It | ffour pewter guns & nine quarts and other such things of small value | 00 = 10 = 00 |
| Item | Two Iron pots and four brass Kettles & one Skillet | 01 = 10 = 00 |
| Item | Three Iron Spits one driping pan & three Iron Racks one fireshovel & Tongs & two Candlesticks | 01 = 00 = 00 |
| Item | One Jack and one Clock | 01 = 00 = 00 |
| Item | Two Hogsheads four Barrels three Tubs & four Trunds | 01 = 10 = 00 |
| Item | wheat Barley & peas in the Straw & one Stack of Hay | 02 = 15 = 00 |
| Item | One pigg | 00 = 12 = 00 |
| Item | One malt mill & some other Trumpery | 00 = 10 = 00 |
| Item | provision for the House of all sorts | 01 = 00 = 00 |
| | | 18 = 00 = 06 |

Apprisors

Wm Pridell

Tho: Watkins

***Inventory of Mary Rodd, Widow.***

***Her husband was Bailiff of Wormelow Manor, see pages 93 and 104. Goods included Pewter guns, Jack for rotating a spit, and a goodly number of cooking utensils.***

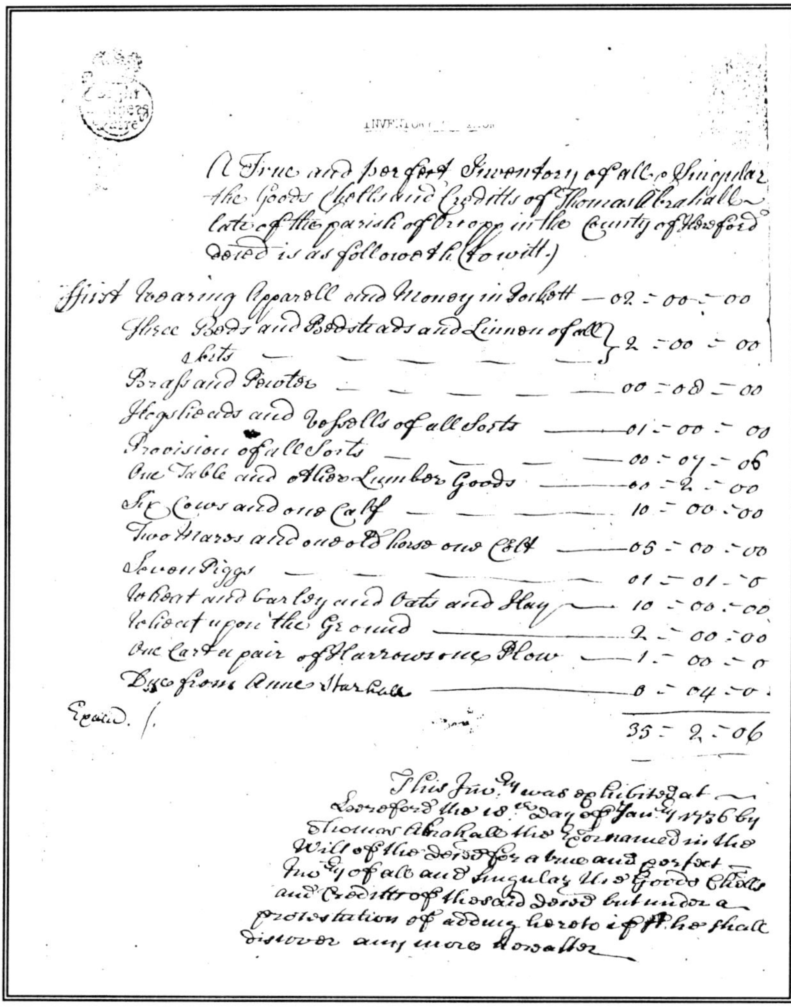

A True and perfect Inventory of all & Singular the Goods Chatells and Creditts of Thomas Abrahall late of the parish of Orcop in the County of Hereford deced is as followeth (to witt)

| | |
|---|---|
| First Wearing Apparell and Money in Pockett | 02 = 00 = 00 |
| Three Beds and Bedsteads and Linnen of all Sorts | 2 = 00 = 00 |
| Brass and Pewter | 00 = 08 = 00 |
| Hogsheads and Vessells of all Sorts | 01 = 00 = 00 |
| Provision of all Sorts | 00 = 07 = 06 |
| One Table and other Lumber Goods | 00 = 2 = 00 |
| Six Cows and one Calf | 10 = 00 = 00 |
| Two Mares and one old horse one Colt | 05 = 00 = 00 |
| Seven Piggs | 01 = 01 = 0 |
| Wheat and barley and Oats and Hay | 10 = 00 = 00 |
| Wheat upon the Ground | 2 = 00 = 00 |
| One Cart a pair of Harrows one Plow | 1 = 00 = 0 |
| Due from Anne Abrahall | 0 = 04 = 0 |
| | 35 = 2 = 06 |

Exaid. /

This Inv.ry was exhibited at Hereford the 18.th Day of Jan.ry 1736 by Thomas Abrahall the Executor named in the Will of the deced for a true and perfect Inv.ry of all and singular the Goods Chatts and Creditts of the said deced but under a protestation of adding hereto if he shall discover any more hereafter

***Inventory of Thomas Abrahall, 1736.***

***Extracts from his will are on page 104. His tomb in Orcop churchyard is shown on page 83.***

The power of the Manor and Hundred Courts was steadily diminishing by the end of the 18th century, and a Suit Roll dated 1st May 1778 which lists 62 names of those Orcop residents owing suit and service to the Court of Orcop, shows that only 14 attended.[59] Likewise at an earlier Hundred Court held at Harewood End for Sir Hungerford Hoskyns in October 1758, there was only one representative from Orcop, and the absentees were fined ten shillings. Comment is made that from the paucity of attendants and the absence of all excuses it would seem that the rights of the Lord were disputed.[60]

As already mentioned cottage rents were in the region of 3d to 2/6d per year for those erected on the common in the mid 18th century, but by 1830 the rentals for cottages with an acre or more of land were in the region of £1.10.0. to £3.0.0. per year. There were, however, many cases of rents for a cottage with 4 plocks of land being 10/- a year, of a cottage with 3 roods of land being 7/- a year, and occasions where an entry in the Estate Rent Books states "Old Ralph, cottage 5d a year" and where one woman who rented a cottage for 6d a year on Saddlebow Common wanted to add a small corner of common to her holding, the land was rented to her at 2d per year. One would like to think that the rents were related to the tenant's circumstances, and to the size and condition of the buildings and land. Presumably these token rents were agreed in order that the Lord of the Manor did not forfeit the right of ownership of the common and waste lands of the village. There are instances in the book of various cottage agreements where it is stated that a tenant took over a cottage in very poor condition, and that he was charged a reduced rent for 3 years, and given materials with which to repair it. There is one interesting agreement for a cottage called Birch Cottage in Much Dewchurch parish; the rent in 1825 was £4 per year, and £3 of this was allowed as payment for the tenant bringing the post to the Mynde. This carried on for many years, although by 1850 the allowance appears to have been reduced to 1 guinea per year. Another entry which catches the eye is the one where the tenant who paid £1 a year for a cottage on Orcop Hill was given notice to quit for having wire in his possession, presumably for the purpose of poaching.

The probate inventories provide one with some indication of the wealth and poverty of some of the freeholders and tenants of the Manor. Examples are given below:-

*"Edward Betham, died 8th November 1732.*[61]

*Inventory of goods, chattels, of Edward Betham apprized by Charles Greenaway and James Lambert, Apprizors.*

| | £ | s | d |
|---|---|---|---|
| A pair of gears prized at (harness, tools) | | 4 | 0 |
| A yoke and a hammer | | 1 | 6 |
| Three hundred of lath | | 1 | 0 |
| Three beams | | 2 | 0 |
| Four drosks and five bittails (not known) | | 1 | 0 |

| | | | |
|---|---|---|---|
| Spokes prized at | | 2 | 0 |
| The cyder and the hogshead | | 3 | 0 |
| Hay prized at | 1 | 0 | 0 |
| Two prafstows (cannot trace meaning) | | 3 | 0 |
| Three vessels and two drams | | 5 | 0 |
| A bedstead prized at | | 1 | 0 |
| Overplus money | 1 | 5 | 5 |
| A pot prized at | | 2 | 0 |
| A chest drawers, bed and bedstead | | 10 | 0 |
| Six bushels of barley | | 8 | 0 |
| Four bushels of beans | | 10 | 0 |
| A cheese press prized at | | | 6 |
| A pair of cart limbers | | | 6 |
| | 4 | 19 | 11 |

There is a Lease dated 3rd September 1659 between Sir Walter Pye and an Edward Betham for a tenement named "ye Butts" at a rent of 1/- annually.[62] The building was in the Butts quarry, and this Edward Betham was most likely a descendant living in the same property since his widow was called for the defence at the trial of 1735. She stated that her husband had quarried at two quarries which he assumed were on his land.

*"Elizabeth Walter. Will proved 20th June 1755.*[63]

A true and proper inventory of all and singular goods, chattels and credits of Elizabeth Walter, late of the parish of Orcop, widow, deceased.

| | £ | s | d |
|---|---|---|---|
| A brass pot | | 2 | 6 |
| Her wearing apparel | | 5 | 0 |
| Two pewter dishes | | 2 | 0 |
| A brass kettle | | 7 | 0 |
| A feather bed and bolster | | 15 | 0 |
| Debts due to deceased | 2 | 15 | 0 |
| | 4 | 6 | 6 |

*Signed by Hannah Medmore, Executrix.*

Hannah Medmore was Licensed by the Bishop of Hereford as a Midwife in Orcop parish on 9th February 1766.[64]

*"Thomas Lambert.*[65]

A true and perfect inventory of the goods and chattles of Thomas Lambert late of the parish of Orcop and County of Hereford, deceased, apprized this 9th day of November 1726 by us, William Pridith and Thomas Watkins as followeth:-

| | £ | s | d |
|---|---|---|---|
| His wearing apparell | | 5 | 0 |
| One bed and bolster | | 10 | 0 |
| Three pairs of old ragged sheets and one old blanket | | 5 | 0 |
| Two small yearling heifers | 2 | 10 | 0 |
| Oats and pease in the barn | 1 | 10 | 0 |
| One small stack of hay | | 10 | 0 |
| One small tub and one old kinderkin (type of barrell) | | 4 | 0 |
| Two old coffers | | 3 | 0 |
| Old pair of tongs, one frying pan, two dishes and two spoons | | 1 | 0 |
| A chattle lease for about 81 years, unexpired value. | 8 | 0 | 0 |
| | 13 | 18 | 0 |

The Lambert family were well known in Orcop, and there are over 70 entries in the Church registers relating to them, but they have quite died out now. This Thomas Lambert was Churchwarden for several years. A "chattle lease" was another name for leasehold or an interest in land so this was probably a 99 year lease.

The will of William Priddith who apprized the goods of Thomas Lambert shows that he was one of the wealthier freehold farmers. He lived at Caerwendy Farm which is not now considered to be in the parish of Orcop although it owed suit and service to the Manor of Orcop. It is situated about 1 mile south west of the Church.

*"William Priddith, Caerwendy. Dated 9th April 1736. (Extracts).*[66]

*To my wife Lucy, two beds with their appurtenances and furniture of the best room, one chest of drawers, one hanging cross, four tablecloths, one dozen diaper napkins, 4 pewter dishes, one dozen pewter plates, and all my plate except my silver tankard, after her decease to be divided amongst my three daughters, Elizabeth, Mary and Margaret.*

*To my son William Priddith, my largest silver tankard, and all the residue and remainder of my household goods, all my corn implements and husbandry goods, cattle, chattles, and personal estate and all deeds, indentures, bonds, bills, notes of hand etc., and property in St. Weonards, Orcop and Garway."*

His three daughters were to have £300 payable one, two and three years after his decease, together with one bed with appurtenances, three pewter dishes and one dozen pewter plates. He also had one married daughter Ann Donne, and it is interesting to note that the Tithe Schedule shows 74 acres on Garway Hill owned by Benjamin Priddith Donne so the family connection with the parish still existed 100 years later. Such items as pewter porringers and dishes, beds, bolsters, sheets, wains, tubs, all types of barrels, oxen and cattle were all tabulated in many of the inventories and wills, sometimes a small sum would be bequeathed to the poor of the parish. The inventory of the goods of Mary Rodd, widow, shows that her home was well furnished when compared with other widows. Her husband, William Rodd, was one time Bailiff of Wormelow, and built a house on Conygar Hill.[67] A copy of the actual inventory can be seen on page 99.

I was fortunate to be able to trace the Will and Probate Inventory of Thomas Abrahall who had taken stone from the quarry without the leave of Mr Gorges; this family remained in Orcop until about 1750 and from then on seem to have left the district. The one vault tomb still remaining in the churchyard is Thomas Abrahall's tomb, and a photo can be seen on page 83. His first wife died in 1708, and he married again in 1710. Extracts from his Will are as follows:-[68]

*"To my son, Thomas Abrahall, my new bedstead and all furniture thereto, all my stock in trade and all implements belonging thereto, and all implements of husbandry, except two pair of old wheels which I had given and bequeathed to my sons Walter and William. To my wife Ann, the best bed and bedstead and all the furniture thereto belonging, and also all the brass and pewter that was her own before our inter-marriage, and one brewing tub, one barell, 1 vessel, 1 hogshead and the best chest.*

*I give to my daughter-in-law, one pair of flaxen sheets now in her mother's possession. I give to William Abrahall 2 hogshead, 1 good one and 1 indifferent one. I give to my son Walter, 2 hogshead, 1 good one and 1 indifferent one. I give to my son John, one new hogshead and one he hath in his possession.*

*I give all the rest, residue and remainder of my goods and furniture and household stuff under-before mentioned to be equally divided between and amongst my said 4 sons, Thomas, William, Walter and John. Share and share alike, except 5 hogsheads which I do hereby give to my said son, Thomas Abrahall only.*

*I give to 30 poor housekeepers the sum of £3 to be distributed at my funeral by my executor herein. Also the £3.1.0. now in my box is to be used for my funeral."*

The copy of the Probate Inventory can be found on page 100. The Will stated that Thomas Abrahall was a cordwainer (shoe maker) in addition to his farming activities. His sons are noted as tenanting lands on Orcop Hill and Coneygar Hill, (Little Hill) for about 20 yeas after his death.

Sir Richard Symons died in 1796 and the estate then devolved on his sister's grandson, Thomas Raymond, who received Royal Licence to use the surname of Symons and bear the arms of Symons.[69] Thomas Raymond Symons was Lord of Orcop until his death at the age of 74 in 1818. He divided his time between London, Lyme Regis and the Mynde, but his agent, Thomas Harvey of Ross-on-Wye, kept in constant touch with him regarding the affairs of the estate. One letter from Harvey concerning the Orcop part of the estate ends with this sentence –[70]

> *"Your donation of 1/6d. to the poor families was thankfully received to the number of 64."*

His son, Thomas Hampton Symons, succeeded him, but died in 1831. It was during his lordship that the Orcop Enclosure Award received parliamentary assent, and many cottages were built on portions of land which he let previous tenants rent in addition to their original holdings. Unfortunately, the only record which would give the exact locations of many of these was the book of plans in which each plot was numbered, but this does not appear to have survived. The Rent Books only stipulate "a cottage on Orcop Hill", and since most of these buildings were built on the waste land which was allotted to T.H.Symons at the time of official enclosure, there is no check on them in the Tithe Schedule. I have traced the sites of several cottages which have been demolished, and thanks to the help of many Orcopians who have long memories, or who can remember names given to barns and buildings after their respective tenants, I have been able to trace where some of these buildings were, and who lived in them which has been most rewarding. When one considers the population of Orcop was 631 in 1851 after making allowance for the larger families of those days, there were obviously many more dwellings in the parish then than remain today.

The rentals of the Mynde Estate were collected twice a year, usually for two days at the end of March, and two days at the end of October, and in 1855, the rental of the whole Estate was in the region of £3,100.0.0. per annum. This did not include the rent arrears which were considerable in many cases, and appear to have been allowed to mount up for several years. The Orcop rents in 1903 were between £700 to £800.[71]

Thomas George Symons inherited the estate on the death of his father in 1831, and died on the 15th November 1868. He was responsible for the establishment of Orcop School. A Valuation of the goods at the Mynde assessed after his death amounted to £910.3.0. (see page following).[72]

After his death, although the family continued to live on the estate, the mansion was variously let to aid the income, and outlying parts of the estate were gradually sold. The sale held on 28th August 1916 virtually severed the connection of the Mynde with Orcop since all property there was relinquished to new owners. The traditional heriot was paid as recently as 23rd May 1905 at the Court Leet held at Harewood End, when £1.2.0. was paid to the Lord of Wormelow by the Lord of Orcop, Thomas Raymond Symons, being £1.0.0. heriot due on the death of his father, and 2/- for one suit called Orcop Green.[73]

This, the last recorded payment, brings to a close a manorial tradition, the seeds of which were sown by the 12th century, and which survived, however tenuously at times, right through to the 20th.

*Valuation of goods at the Mynde on the death of T.G. Symons, signed by George Pye, of Hereford, Auctioneer, amounting to £910.3.0.*

***Coach House***

*Mail Phaeton. Brougham. 4 Wheel Dog-cart. Coburgh. 2 Wheel Dog-cart.*

***Nag Horses.***

*Brown Harness Horse. Bay Harness Horse.Pony. Bay Nag Horse. Donkey.*

***Saddle Room.***

*Side Saddle. Pair Game Bags. 2 Men's Saddles. Set Double Hardness, brass mounted. Single Harness, plated. Set Double Harness, plated. 3 Riding Bridles. 3 Hunting Plates. Bits Dumb Jockey and Longing Rein. 3 Buckets. Plated harness.*

***Pigs.***

*40 Fat Pigs. 2 Breeding Sows. 2 Ditto. 12 Stores.*

***Wainhouse.***

*Burgen and Keys Mower. Spring Cart. Spring Waggon. Pony Cart. Donkey Cart.*

***Implements.***

*3 Wagons. 2 Carts. 6 Pikes. 6 Rakes. Cattle Crib. Pair Wood Harrows. Water Carriage. 3 Ladders. Ground Car. Chaff Engine and Belt. 2 Haul Rakes. Turnip Cutter. American Hay Rake. Corn Bin. Chaff Kipe. Wood Plough. 2 Sheep Troughs. 3 Dozen Hurdles. 2 Rick Clothes, Lines and Poles. Horse Power and Thrashing Machine. Winnowing Machine. Wheelbarrow.*

***Hay, Straw, Crops etc.***

*2 Ricks of Hay. Part Rick of Hay. Clover. Hay in Barn. Wheat in Granary. Straw in Barn. Growing Wheat. Growing Clover.*

***Cattle.***

*Barren Cow.. Shorthorn Bull. 2 Aged Cows and Calves. Barren Cow. 8 In Calf Cows and Heifers. 5 Three-Year-Old Heifers. 4 Yearling Heifers. 1 yearling Bull. 3 Weaned Steer Calves. 2 Weaned Heifer Calves.*

***Sheep.***

*54 Ewes. 56 Lambs. Two-year-Old Rams. 35 Feeding Sheep.*

***Horses.***

*Two-Year-Old Cart Colt. Two-Year-Old Nag Colt. Aged Pony. Aged Black Cart Mare. Aged Bay Cart Mare.*

***Poultry.***

*20 Ducks. 40 Fowls.*

***Gearing.***

*3 Links Long Gear. 3 Links Cant Gears. 1 Links G.O. Gears.*

***Casks and Cider.***

*23 Hogsheads. 800 Gallons Cider.*

***Total £910.3.0.***

# Chapter Eight

## REFERENCES


| | | |
|---|---|---|
| 1. | – | Mynde Collection. 5172. |
| 2. | H. Cam. | The Hundred and Hundred Rolls. Merlin Press, London. p. 163. |
| 3. | G.W. Keeton. | The Norman Conquest and the Common Law. London. 1966. p. 152. |
| 4. | G.W. Keeton. | p. 142. |
| 5. | C.W. Chalklin. | Seventeenth Century Kent. London. 1965. p. 42. |
| 6, | – | Mynde Collection. 68. |
| 7. | – | Mynde Collection. 227. |
| 8. | – | Mynde Collection. 223. |
| 9. | Rev. Preb. Seaton. | History of the Deanery of Archenfield. Preface. |
| 10. | – | Mynde Collection 300. |
| 11. | – | Mynde Collection 193. |
| 12. | J.H. Matthews. | pages 25 to 29. |
| 13. | J. Duncumb. | History of Herefordshire. Volume 1. p. 104. |
| 14. | Rev. J. Bird. | Herefordshire Antiquities. Visitation to Churches 1845. Pilley Collection. Hereford City Library. |
| 15. | H.L.V. Fletcher. | Herefordshire. |
| 16. | – | Mynde Collection. 2899-2918. |
| 17. | – | Mynde Collection. 3113. |
| 18. | – | Mynde Collection. 2813. |
| 19. | – | Mynde Collection. 3100. |
| 20. | – | Mynde Collection. 5171-6. |
| 21. | – | Mynde Collection 2972. |
| 22. | – | Mynde Collection 3373. |
| 23. | – | Mynde Collection 2996-3012. |
| 24. | – | Mynde Collection 3111-6. |

25. – Mynde Collection 2813.

26. – Mynde Collection 155.

27. – Mynde Collection 2911.

28. – Mynde Collection 2813.

29. – Mynde Collection 3111-6.

30. – Mynde Collection 2977-94.

31. – Private Collection. Court Roll 28th October, 1737.

32. – Mynde Collection 1970-1974.

33. – Private Collection. Court Roll 28th October 1737.

34. – Private Collection. Court Roll 28th October 1737.

35. – Private Collection. Court Roll 28th October 1737.

36. – Private Collection. Court Roll 5th May 1738.

37. – Private Collection. Court Roll 2nd May 1737.

38. – Private Collection. Court Roll 2nd May 1737.

39. – Private Collection. Court Roll 5th December 1739.

40. – Private Collection. Court Roll 28th April 1741.

41. – Private Collection. Court Roll 18th October 1742.

42. – Private Collection. Court Roll 22nd October 1747.

43. – Private Collection. Court Roll 15th November 1780.

44. – Private Collection. Court Roll 22nd July 1788.

45. – Private Collection. Court Roll 24th October 1808.

46. – Private Collection. Court Roll 23rd October 1801.

47. – Private Collection. Court Roll 23rd October 1805.

48. – Private Collection. Court Roll 23rd October 1805.

49. – Private Collection. Court Roll 24th October 1808.

50. – Private Collection. Court Roll 22nd July 1788.

51. – Private Collection. Court Roll 15th November 1780.

52. – Private Collection. Court Roll 24th November 1779.

53. – Mynde Collection. 1251.

54. – Pugh's Hereford Journal. 10th February 1774. Hereford County Record Office.

55. – Pugh's Hereford Journal. 6th November 1777.

56. – Pugh's Hereford Journal 16th April 1774

57. – Pugh's Hereford Journal. 21st October 1773.

58. – Pugh's Hereford Journal. 29th September 1774.

59. – Mynde Collection 5177.

60. – Wormelow M.S.S. Hereford City Library.

61. – Hereford Probate Records. Hereford County Record Office. Index, Book 8. p.190.

62. – Mynde Collection 93.

63. – Hereford Probate Records. H.C.R.O. Index Book 10, p.95.

64. – Pamphlet issued by the Woolhope Club, Hereford.

65. – Hereford Probate Records. H.C.R.O. Index Book 8.

66. – Will in Hereford City Library.

Local Collection of Hereford Wills.

67. – Hereford Probate Records. H.C.R.O. Index Book 9. p.12.

68. – Hereford Probate Records. H.C.R.O. Index Book 9. p.54.

69. – Mynde Collection 5251.

70. – Mynde Collection 2484.

71. – Private Collection. Account Book.

72. – Mynde Collection 510.

73. – Rolls of Courts Baron and Courts Leet, 1806-1905 for Manor and Hundred of Wormelow. Hereford County Record Office.

*Deodand*

The word used in English law for the weapon with which a man committed homicide, to be surrendered first to church, later to the King. In the case of an animal killing a human being this was forfeit, case in 1842 of fining an engine which killed a man. Since the Manor was ancient demesne the Lord had the right to receive the fine that was assessed.

(First Book of English Law). O. Hood. Phillips, London. 1953.

# Chapter Nine

## THE OLD MILLS

Orcop has the ruins of an old grist mill adjoining the farm known as the Lower Mill, but so far as I can ascertain from older parishioners this has never been in working order in their lifetime, but they can remember their parents talking of carrying corn to be ground there.

The mill itself was probably working in 1851, since the 1851 Census lists the following:-

| | | | | |
|---|---|---|---|---|
| *Mill* | *William Banton* | *21 years* | *Miller* | *Head* |
| | *Peter Gwatkin* | *23 years* | *Grinder* | *Servant* |
| | *Luke Preece* | *24 years* | *Labourer* | *Servant* |

while at the nearby Lower Mill Farm the following are listed –

| | | | |
|---|---|---|---|
| *Lower Mill.* | *Ann Banton* | *47 years* | *Farmer of 64 acres 3 labourers, Head of household.* |
| | *James Banton* | *24 years* | *Farmer's son.* |
| | *Thomas Banton* | *14 years* | *" "* |
| | *Ann Banton* | *19 years* | *" daughter.* |
| | *Eliza Banton* | *11 years* | *Scholar.* |
| | *Elizabeth Banton* | *9 years* | *Scholar.* |
| | *Emily Banton* | *5 years* | *Scholar.* |

Ann Banton's husband, William Banton, a miller was buried in 1850,[1] and in 1856 she had moved to the Tything Barn Farm in Orcop whilst her son, William, occupied Lower Mill.[2] The drawing of the mechanism is on page 114. The building itself is now in a very dangerous state; the roof has fallen in, and, although most of the machinery is still there, it has collapsed, but a photograph of the mill stones can be seen on page 118. The Rev. Dredge's notes (see page 129) stated that, at the beginning of this century, the mill-race and weir were out of order. "The disappearance of the latter has been a boon to the parish as now the water is able to pass more freely away, and floods which used to be very frequent have almost ceased". The Lower Mill Farm and the Mill at no time belonged to the Mynde estate so it is difficult to trace any further documented facts about it.

*Lower Mill Farm. Tudor doorway leading from the kitchen.*

*One of the oldest buildings in Orcop. This is the granary built on the west end of the building.*

***This is the view of the Lower Mill showing the mechanism. The water-control gate was controlled by a rope leading into the mill. The leat was clearly defined until 1956, but as a result of regular ploughing it can no longer be seen.***

The name Lower Mill had always made me wonder, long before embarking on this story, why it was so named. If there was a Lower Mill, surely there must have been an Upper Mill? No one in the village had any observations to make on the subject, and on checking through the notes of the Rev. Dredge, I noted that he commented that he had heard there had once been another mill higher up the Garron. I then checked the names of fields in the Tithe Schedule which bordered onto the Garron, and found that field number 345 was named Wear Meadow, (The Oxford Dictionary give "weir" and "wear" as having the same meaning), while another a little further on, numbered 307, was called Millwood pasture. I then explored the Garron around this area, and found distinct traces of the mill leat in a small meadow close to the Brooklands Farm. On discussion with the owner, Mr George Sayce, I learned that his father, who had owned the farm for many years before he had taken it over, had suffered losses to his sheep on several occasions because the leat was much deeper then, and when there was a heavy rainfall, the leat filled with water and the sheep would fall into it and drown. Over the years they had endeavoured to fill it up.

*The Brooklands. The house from the south 1992. Both millstones can be seen in the centre of the lawn.*

*The mill leat along which water was carried to the mill looking east*

The next step was to check which of the fields nearby had any traces of a building on the Tithe Map. Field number 391 had a building shown, but in the schedule it was listed only by number with no details except measurement which was just over ¼ of an acre. Mr Sayce told me that for years, when they ploughed the field in the corner nearest to the Garron, they had uncovered a great deal of stone. Another link in the chain was the discovery of something, which, I am almost ashamed to say, I had seen for many years without realising its import. On the lawn at the back of the farm is part of a cider press containing flowers. This stone is raised up by another larger circular stone – a mill stone of the Derby peak variety! This stone was less expensive than the French burr stones which were cemented together with plaster of Paris and iron binding hoops, as shown in the photograph of the stones still in the Lower Mill. Whereas the French stones were more expensive and used for grinding wheat to a fine flour, the Derby peak stones were cheaper, easier to dress and generally used for grinding barley, oats, beans and peas, in fact, for grist. I was told that this stone had been found some years ago in one of the barns where it had been used for a step, and that another similar one was to be found in the bed of the stream which runs under the road, and alongside the field in question to feed ultimately into the Garron. All had begun with conjecture, although admittedly, backed by some reasonable facts.

*Reclaimed stones from The Old Mill. 1992.*

Documentary evidence was now called for, and here the Mynde Schedule showed the existence of several documents, which helped to prove without doubt that the Upper Mill was a reality, and that it was situated in just the spot located. The Court Roll quoted on page 85 showed that Thomas Price who was the miller, had asked for a Jury to view the ancient bridle way to the Cockshoot, and the photograph on page 86 shows that way, which is almost opposite the Brooklands farm. A rent roll of 1717[3] showed that the mill was still in the possession of a Price. The first Lease in the Mynde collection relating to a mill is detailed as follows:-[4]

*Lower Stone from Mill.*

***"1584. August 18th.***

*1. James ap Powell of Llangarren, gent. Robert ap Powell and Thomas ap Powell.*

*2. Roger Pye of Meende in the Parish of Dewchurch Magna, gent.*

*Grant in consideration of £5 of a parcel of land over which a water-course leads to the mill of the said Roger in Orcopp with the said water-course which land and watercourse extend in length between the two meadows of Roger Pye in Orcopp, of which one lies on the west part called terra Henthrustlandes, and the other lies on the east part and called terra Wyrralles, and in breadth extending from the old course of the river Garran on the south part to the land of the said Thomas ap Powell on the north part. Witnesses. John Kyrle, William Pye, Hughe Jones, John Moris, John Wyllym, John a Pye." Latin.*

***Lower Mill. The dovecot over the door of the house. Most of the older farms had these.***

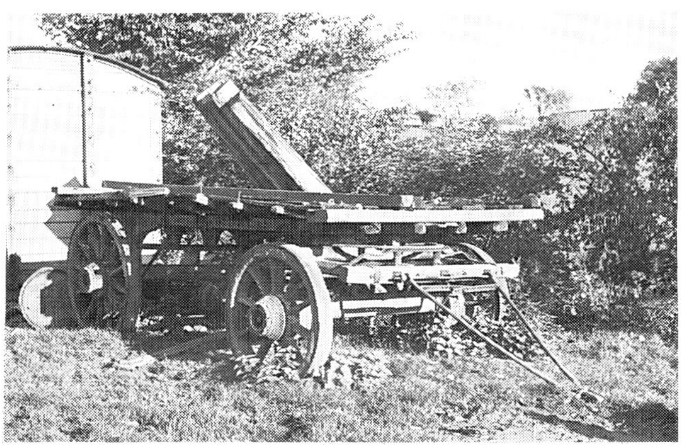

***An old farm wagon at Lower Mill farm. This was once the property of the Green Farm and was obtained when the Green changed hands in 1961, being used to carry away other purchases.***

Wyrrales land was so called after a certain William Wyrhale who leased land in Orcop from Richard Baskerville in 1364.[5] The name is not known at all in the village nowadays, and so I have not been able to check exactly where the land is, but the land to the west, called Henthrustlandes, would be the old name given to the Hendre farm of today, while the old course of the river is on the south side of the watercourse to the mill. Wyrrales land today would be somewhere between, and part of, both the Brooklands and Moat farms. When showing these details to Mr and Mrs Sayce, I was delighted to hear the remark, "we've always called that field, Pye's meadow". Why, they did not know; but it demonstrates how a place retains its name and title down the centuries.

***The millstones in the ruins of Lower Mill.***

The next lease is dated 1640.[6]

***"1640, April 6.***

*Sir Walter Pye of the Meend, knight.*
*Thomas Williams of the parish of Orcop, yeoman.*

*Lease (counterpart) for 21 years of a water grist mill in Orcop and a parcel of pasture lying beneath the water course (½ acre), one meadow (3 acres) adjoining the mill lying between the brook called*

*Garran and the way leading from Bagerlidiat towards Rosse, and a parcel of pasture (2 acres) lying on the upper side of the said way between the lands heretofore of Thomas Gylbert, gent, and Richard ap Probert. Rent £7.10.0. and 6 chickens and two bushels of oats annually."*

The measurements given here are approximately the same as those of the lands adjoining the mill. This is all the documentary evidence that was available until 1805, when the following Lease occurs.[7]

***"1805, March 1.***

*John Symons, Thomas Williams of Orcop, miller.*

*Lease of a ruinated cottage, decayed mill and lands in the parish of Orcop. Rent £5.2.0. per annum."*

This Lease states that Thomas Williams "shall repair and keep in tenantable and substantial repair the said dwelling house and water corn mill, and the tackle or inside work thereof, buildings, gates, stiles over gates, hedges, ditches and drains belonging". There is also a note with it to say that Thomas Moore would give £5 a year for it as it is, and would pay an added rent, if repaired, should Williams not retake the mill. On checking through the Church Registers I came across the following entry:-[8]

***"Burial Register, 1813-1889.***

*Thomas Williams. Upper Mill. Buried 24th March 1814. aged 50 years."*

Still later in the Register was the following entry:-[9]

*"John Watts, Upper Mill. Buried 24th September 1822, aged 14 years."*

The next discovery came only recently through a book of Leases of property on the Mynde Estate, some of which date from 1831.[10] I found a lease which runs as follows:-

*"Evans, Thomas.*

*I, the undersigned Thomas Evans, of the parish of Orcop in the county of Hereford, Labourer, do hereby agree to rent of Mr John Cooke, of the Chase, Ross, the Receiver of the Rents and Profits of the Mynde Park Estate, from the second day of February last, seven several pieces or parcels of Arable land, meadow and pasture land called the* Old Mill lands *containing by admeasurement Twelve acres Two roods and Two perches situate in the parish of Orcop in the County of Hereford, late in the occupation of William Banton as Tenant thereof, for the term of one whole year so on from year to year until six calendar months notice in writing shall be given by either party to quit at the end of the first or any subsequent at and under the yearly rent of Ten pounds payable half yearly in equal portions . . . And I further agree to plough, sow, manure and cultivate the arable lands in a due and regular course of husbandry, and spend, use and consume all the hay, clover, straw, dung, muck, soil and compost which shall yearly grow, arise or be made on the said premises. And I further agree to keep and leave the fences of and belonging to the said premises in proper order and repair. As witness my hand this 20th day of July, 1838.*

*The mark X of Thomas Evans."*

The land had previously been in the occupation of William Banton, who was the husband of Ann Banton, mentioned at the commencement of this chapter, and whose son was at the Lower Mill in the 1850's. Since this date was near to the Tithe Map Schedule date (1842), I then checked to see if Thomas Evans still occupied lands under the Estate. His name was in the schedule, and he occupied lands which were arable, pasture and meadow, measuring 12 acres and 21 perches, and the numbers of the fields were adjacent to and included the field 391 where the Upper Mill had been. Photographs of the old leat, and mill stones at the Brooklands Farm are on pages 115 and 116.

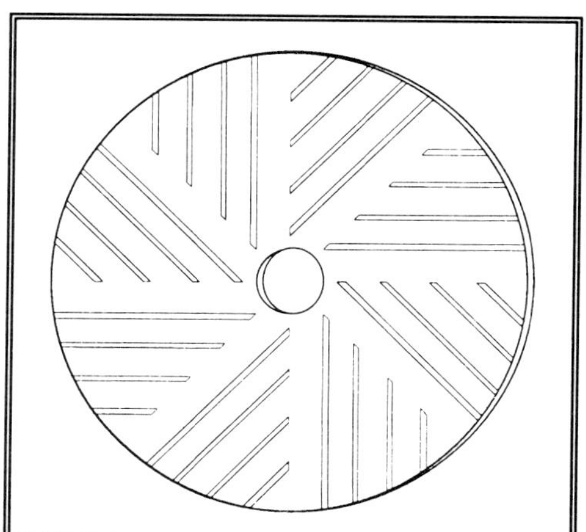

***Common Dressing for a 4ft dia. millstone as found in the Lower Mill.***

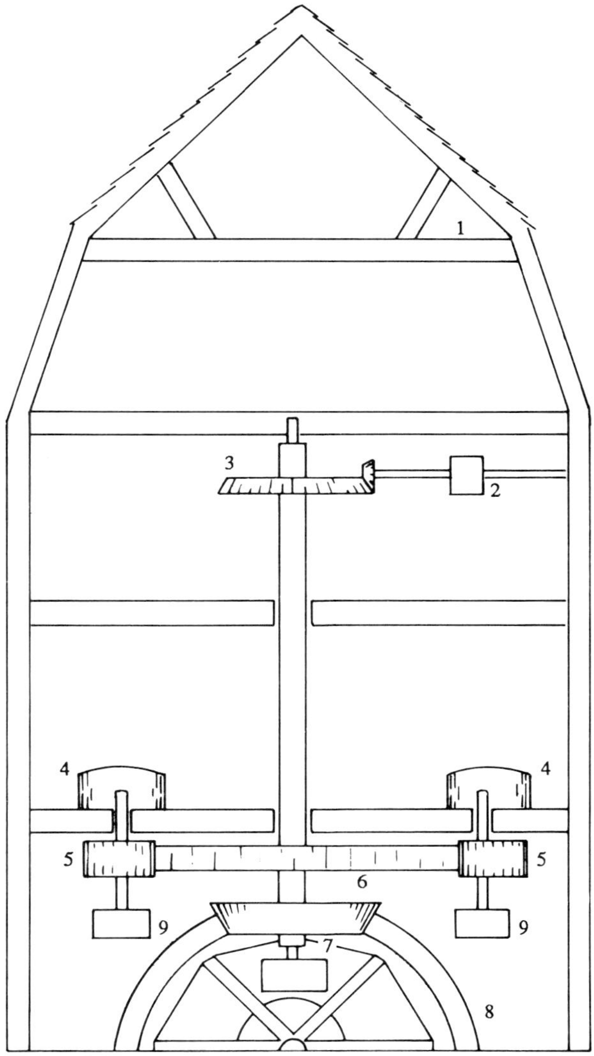


1. Mansard roof
2. Pulley to drive accessories
3. Crown wheel
4. Tun, encasing stones
5. Stone nuts
6. Spur wheel
7. Wallower
8. Pit wheel (water wheel behind)
9. Parts of hursting

***Based on a drawing from 'British Water Mills' Leslie Syson.***

***Drawing of a 2 Pair Mill***

# Chapter Nine

## References


1. – Orcop Church Registers. Burial Register 1813-1889 p. 46. Entry 361.
2. – Post Office Directory of Hereford, Worcester, Bath and Bristol 1856. Hereford City Library.
3. – Mynde Collection. 2972
4. – Mynde Collection. 201.
5. – Mynde Collection. 87.
6. – Mynde Collection 128.
7. – Mynde Collection. 671.
8. – Orcop Church Registers. Burial Register 1813-1889. p. 5. Entry 40.
9. – Orcop Church Registers.Burial Register 1813-1889. p. 11. Entry 88.
10. – Book of Leases. Mynde Estate Private Collection. p. 155.


Ann Banton's son, William, also farmed the Tything Barn farm, but his wife died at the early age of 28 years, and he died at Pengethley in 1888.

He was buried in Orcop Churchyard on the 9th March 1888. (Burial Register 1813-1889. p. 99. Entry No. 787).

# Chapter Ten

## THE PARISH CHURCH

The Parish Church is situated in the south east corner of the parish. It is dedicated to St. John the Baptist, although the Royal Commission's Book of Historical Monuments refers to the Parish Church of St. Mary.[1] So far as I can ascertain the former dedication is correct, but there have been occasions when documents have arrived for the Church with the title St. Mary's. There is no evidence to show that if the Church was dedicated to St. Mary, when and why the dedication was altered.

> *"The building is of roughly coursed local sandstone rubble with ashlar dressings, and the upper part of the tower is of timber, the roofs covered with modern slate. The 12th century piscina suggests a pre-existing church of that date, but the present nave and north aisle were erected in the first half of the 13th century. The chancel was rebuilt c.1300. At some uncertain period the nave-arcade was partly reconstructed and the north aisle was lengthened westward. The West tower was added probably early in the 16th century. The building was drastically restored in 1860 and again in 1907; the north vestry is modern, as is the stone casing of the tower, the west end of the north aisle and the south porch".*[2]

The Church has three windows dating to 1300 in the chancel, and another of the same date in the north aisle, although a Visitation of Churches made in 1845 states that the east window in the chancel had fragments of old stained glass.[3]

> *"The tower which is early 16th century is in two stages, the lower with a modern stone casing, the upper of timber and surmounted by a pyramidal timber spire set on a louvred base. Within the ground stage of the tower, partly carrying the upper storey, is a timber framing consisting of four angle posts, resting on sleepers against braces against the north and south walls, two braced ties against the west wall, and diagonal braces against the east wall arched over the tower arch. The second stage is of plain timber panels grooves into vertical posts. The louvred base to the spire is set back behind the general wall face with the intervening space covered by a sloping roof; it has been partly rebuilt but retains some old timbers. The spire is modern."*

*"The roof of the nave is of early 16th century date and of braced collar-beam type, in two bays, with moulded and cambered tie-beams. The north aisle has a lean-to roof, probably of 16th century date, but with modern wall plates".*[4]

***Photograph of a water colour of Orcop Church, 1820. Hereford City Library***

It appears from the foregoing that the restoration of 1860 of which, incidentally, no record can be found in the Faculty Registers of the Diocesan Office, or the Cathedral records of Articles of Enquiry, was carried out with such ardour that much of the character of the church was lost for ever. One plan of a series still exists in the Church records, which show the work that was undertaken. The Visitation of 1845 already referred to speaks of two windows into a rood loft over the chancel arch, the arch itself being a flat arch with a square headed orifice on each side. The pulpit was of plain oak and in the south east of the nave, whereas now it is of sculptured stone and situated in the north west of the nave. In the north aisle there was a small piscina in the south wall, and steps leading up to the rood loft. The tower and bells were divided from the nave by an arch, screen and square headed door of wood. There was a door into the chancel on the south wall, over which was a shallow space for a tympanum. The door can be seen in the photograph of a water colour painted in 1820 (see above). The porch, in 1845, was of stone with a window in each side, and had eight steps leading into the church of which three were decorated with "handsome crosses," whereas today there are only three stone steps. The Visitation also states that there was a large chest on the south side of the chancel; this was, no doubt, the original parish chest. Today the only chest is in the vestry, and is a very good example of a Jacobean Bible Box. (see illustration on page 126).

*Orcop Church Early 1963.*

There are several stone tablets attached to the walls of the church which were floor memorial stones before the restoration, and were removed at that time and re-mounted.[5] The church floor, now relaid with modern tiles, has a marked and continuous slope from the west wall of the tower downward through the nave to the chancel. In the Wormelow Manuscript it is stated that there was an inscription in the church which ran thus –

*"This Church was adorned in the year 1726.*

*William Priddith.*

*William Lambert."*

There is no trace of this inscription today. William Priddith and William Lambert were both Churchwardens of Orcop, although not at this particular date. The manuscript also states that "there is a font of plain stone standing in the great aisle dated 1664". Today the font is of sculptured stone, and is definitely of Victorian origin.

The Church plate is Elizabethan, the Cover Paten bearing the date 1576. It consists of a beautifully engraved chalice with an elaborate scroll, a cover paten and a silver alms dish. The silver alms dish has no hall or date mark, but is presumed to be early 17th century.[6]

*Interior of Orcop Church, taken from the tower looking east to the Chancel.*

The restoration of 1860 cost approximately £749,[7] and was carried out under the supervision of T. Nicholson, the Diocesan Architect at that time. The notes made by the Rev. Norris Dredge, Vicar from 1893 to 1909, state that a list of donations towards this figure was in the parish chest, but unfortunately, like many of the documents he mentions, these have disappeared. The church was kept in repair by the parishioners, a church rate being made and collected. It was not until Easter 1889 that a system of offertories was commenced. From the Parish Minute Book it states –

> *"The Vicar asked how the current Church expenses were to be maintained as there was a deficiency during the past year of 12/- which had been paid by the late Vicar. Mr Burleigh said (rightly) that the people had not been educated to give to God. It was agreed that the expenses were to be met by the Scriptural system of weekly offertories".*

Another £400 was spent on repairs in 1961. The woodwork in the tower was renewed and wired to keep out jackdaws who were causing havoc to the structure and sprayed against the death watch beetle. Pointing of walls, installation of a lightning conductor and many other maintenance items were carried out at the same time.

***The Bible Box.***

The Church has a fine peal of bells, numbering five, of which four dated 1663 to 1731, served the church until 1907 when the remaining treble bell was added. The bells are inscribed as follows:-

| | |
|---|---|
| ***1663.*** | *Fear God, Honour the King. John Morgan, Thomas Powell.* |
| ***1663.*** | *John Morgan, Thomas Powell, Churchwardens.* |
| ***1679.*** | *Fear God, Honour the King. John Lambert, C.W. Den.* |
| ***1731.*** | *Peace and Good neighbourhood.* |
| ***1907.*** | *God Bless Orcop. Robert Davies, Thomas Porter, Norris Dredge.* |

The bells have been examined by Mr Frederick Sharpe, who has recently had his first book on the church bells of Herefordshire published, and he told me that they are a fine peal of bells in very good condition. The notes left by the Rev. Norris

Dredge, together with some accounts in the Church records from the firm who supplied the fifth bell, Greenleaf and Tristram of Hereford, show that in 1907 the four bells were re-hung, a new frame being made since the original was unsafe, and the fifth bell hung at a cost of £139.12.6. Donations to the fund were made from all manner of subscribers from the Bishop of Hereford, Sir James Rankin, a local brewery and parishioners, from £2.2.0. down to shillings and sixpences. Church collections, concerts and dances, sales of work and teas were all organised to this end. *The Hereford Times* on 6th April 1907 wrote –

> *"The Church bells at Orcop which are among the oldest in this country have for some time past been silent, but at Easter they rang out joyous peals with all their old melody."*

***The Preaching Cross in the Churchyard. According to the Rev N Dredge's notes this was removed from beside the church porch at the time of the restoration and placed further away from the church, when new paths were cut. The socket stone is 2 ft 4 inches square by 1 ft 9 inches deep. The niche has a projecting hood all round. The shaft 10 inches square to octagon, is 4 foot high. Preb. Seaton states "The shaft was used some time as the base of a sun dial, and on the base are clearly the remains of a Holy Water Stoup".***

***Detail from "Standing Crosses of Herefordshire". A Watkins.***

After a service in church at which Prebendary Seaton was the preacher, there was a tea and concert in the schoolroom.

The oak cross on the altar was carved and given, together with an alms box by Mr Thomas Grice, who was active in Church and School affairs, probably at the beginning of this century. His descendants are still resident in Orcop. The brass vases were given by the Rev. Norris Dredge, and a beautifully embroidered book mark was worked by Miss G. Banks, a mistress in the School, in the early 1900's. The latter, after many year's use, was replaced in 1960. The oak lectern and hymn board were bought by parishioners in memory of the first Vicar, the Rev. Arthur Gray, M.A. who was Vicar from 1859 to 1889, and died on the 26th August 1903. He is buried with his wife, Isabella, and infant daughter behind the church. A brass plate is in the tower with the following inscription –

*"To the Glory of God and in memory of*
*Arthur Gray, M.A.*
*Vicar 1859 – 1889*
*entered into Rest 26th August, 1903.*
*the oak lectern was presented by his*
*former parishioners and friends.*

*N.J. Dredge.*

*W. Meadmore.*
*R.H. Davies.* *Churchwardens.*

The Lectern was dedicated by the Rural Dean and Vicar of Goodrich, the Rev. Prebendary Seaton at a service on the 24th May, 1904.

### *VICARS OF ORCOP*

*The living was a donative until 1859 and was served by the incumbents of neighbouring parishes.*

| | |
|---|---|
| *Rev. Arthur Gray* | *1859, resigned 2nd January 1889.* |
| | |
| *Rev. Joseph Bartholomew* | |
| *Davey Hopgood.* | *Instituted 29th March 1889.* |
| | *Resigned 1st April 1893.* |
| | |
| *Rev. Norris Dredge.* | *Instituted 26th April 1893.* |
| | |
| *Rev. William Slater Isherwood.* | *Instituted 11th November 1909. Died 1932.* |
| | |
| *Rev. Herbert Ball.* | *Instituted 1932, Resigned* |
| | *21st December 1941* |
| | |
| ***Orcop united with Garway 30th May 1939.*** | |
| | |
| *Rev. Stanley Elliott Skinner.* | *Vicar of Garway, served Orcop until his death 31st January 1942.* |
| | |
| *Rev. Frank Ridley Whittaker.* | *Instituted 2nd October 1942.* |
| | *Resigned 31st March 1951.* |
| | |
| *Rev. Herbert Douglas Dickin.* | *1951 until 29th February 1956.* |
| | |
| *Benefice of Orcop and Garway dissolved 19th September 1956.* | |
| *Benefice of St. Weonards and Orcop held in plurality by the Rev. Brinley Handel Hawkins.* | |
| | |
| *Rev. Brinley Handel Hawkins.* | *Collated to the Church of Orcop 28th December 1956. Resigned 17th April 1958.* |
| | |
| *Rev. Wilfrid Evans.* | *Instituted 21st August 1959.* |

*The Rev Norris Dredge.*

*St John's College, Cambridge. B.A. 1875., M.A. 1887. Curate of Christchurch, Preston, 1876-77. Colne, Lancs, 1877; Ainsworth, Lancs (sole charge) 1877-1880. Chesterfield 1880-1888 (with charge of Calow 1880-1884), Clay Cross, Derbyshire 1888-1893. Vicar of Orcop 1893-1909. Rector of Pettaugh, Suffolk, from 1909 until his death in 1919. One of his daughters, Genevieve, lives at Ufford, Nr. Woodbridge, Suffolk.*

*His rough notes regarding the village have been most valuable, particularly, with regard to his endeavouring to name most of the cottages in the parish, many of which have now disappeared. These notes were given to me by Mrs Florence Gatfield who found them some years ago among old books bought when the Vicarage was sold. Mrs Gatfield also loaned the photograph from which I was able to have a negative made for further prints.*

# Chapter Ten

## REFERENCES


| | | |
|---|---|---|
| 1. | – | R.C.H.M.E. South-west Herefordshire. p. 207. |
| 2. | – | As above. p. 208. |
| 3. | C.J. Bird. | Visitation of Parish Churches, 845. Pilley Collection. Hereford City Library. |
| 4. | – | R.C.H.M.E. p. 208. |
| 5. | Rev. N. Dredge. | M.S.S. notes. Deposited in Hereford C.R.O. |
| 6. | – | R.C.H.M.E. p 208. Also History of Archenfield. p.74. |
| 7. | – | Jakeman and Carver, Local Hereford Directory 1871. |

# Chapter Eleven

## THE PARISH CHURCH – ITS DEVELOPMENT

The first mention of clergy serving Orcop comes from the Registers of the Cantilupe Society from which the following details emerge:-

| | |
|---|---|
| ***September 18th 1277.*** | *Ordination at Leominster Subdiacone.*[1] *Johannes de Orcop ad titulum patrimonii.* |
| ***September 23rd 1335.*** | *Sub deacon, Hugh Orcope de Lyngeyn.*[2] |
| ***September 20th 1343.*** | *Ordination Rees Orcop in Chapel of Hyneham by Gloucester*[3] |
| ***1345.*** | *Presbiteri. Johannes, filius Willelmi Roberdes de Orcope*[4] |
| ***September 19th 1377.*** | *Sub deacon. William Orcope.* [5] |
| ***April 5th 1382.*** | *Ordination in Whitbourne Chapel* [6]*on the Vigil of Easter.William Orcop, his own benefice Priest.* |

These are the only clergy listed, there being a gap of five centuries until the 19th century. The register of Vicars of nearby Llandinabo shows, that one, Richard Orcop was priest there in 1391.

The Taxation of Pope Nicholas c.1291, shows that Orcoppe Church belonged to the Prior of Llantony Prima, near Abergavenny, that its annual value was £4, and that in 1317 the parishioners complained to the Bishop of Hereford that the Prior and Convent of Llantony Prima neglected the cure of souls in Orcop.[7]

The Valor Ecclesiasticus of 1535 shows that Arcoppe chapel was annexed by the Prior of Saint John of Jerusalem in England, that Thomas ap Ieuan was the curate, and that there was a pension of 13/4d. a year payable to the Prior of Llantony. [8] The annual value of the cure at this time was £5.11.10. The Bishop's Registers of 1536 state that the Chapel of Orcoppe was attached to the Priory of Llantony by Gloucester. There appears to be some discrepancy here, and from a copy of Thesaurus Rerum Ecclesiasticum the entry reads –[9]

*"Being an account of the values of all the ecclesiastical benefices extracted from records in the reign of Henry VIII by John Ecton, later Receiver General of the Tenths of the Clergy.*

*Arcop, alias Orcop Chapel. Prior Llantony XIIIs. 1111d.*
*Sir William Compton. Patron. Not in Charge".*

*Feb. 16.—The Bishop instructs the Official to inquire into the alleged neglect of the Parish of Orcop by the Priory of Llanthony Prima.*

Fol. 17b. LITTERA EXCITATIVA MISSA OFFICIALI CONTRA PRIOREM ET CONVENTUM LANTHONIE PRIME PRO CURA ANIMARUM ECCLESIE DE ORECOP.—Officiali suo salutem. Querelam gravem parochialis ecclesie de Orcop nostre diocesis recepimus continentem quod religiosi viri Prior et Conventus Lanthonie Prime, Menevensis diocesis, tanquam sibi appropriatam optinere dicuntur, curam animarum que in ea iminet dampnabiliter negligentes, eidem ecclesie per vicarium idoneum seu alium presbyterum sufficientem nullatenus faciunt deserviri nec sacramenta ecclesiastica ipsius parochie temporibus debitis ministrari; ita quod propter pastoris negligenciam aliqui infirmi de parochia predicta morientes sacramentis ecclesiasticis, proh dolor, caruerunt. Quocirca vobis committimus et mandamus quatinus, si certa est, dictorum religiosorum excessum tam periculosum, dampnabilem, et enormem per omnem censuram ecclesiasticam tam salubriter quam celeriter corrigere studeatis. Datum Gloucestrie, xvj° die Februarii, anno Domini M°CCC°xvij°.

***From the Registrum of Adam de Orleton, Bishop of Hereford, 1317-1327.***

***Translation***

***A letter provoked and sent to the Official against the Prior and Convent of Llanthony Prima for the care of souls in the Parish of Orcop.***

***Greeting to the Official. We have received a serious complaint from the parish of Orcop in our diocese containing information that those prior's men, the Prior and Convent of Llanthony Prima in the Diocese of Menevensis, just as they are holding on to what they have appropriated for themselves, so they are culpably neglecting the cure of souls which is involved in those things. In no wise do they cause this same parish to be served zealously by a suitable vicar or other sufficient priest, nor do they provide the church sacraments of the parish itself at the appointed times, so much so that on account of the negligence of the pastor, some infirm people from the aforesaid parish who are dying are deprived of the church's sacraments, to their grief.***

***Wherefore we commit to you and command you so that you may study to what extent is the deviation of the said prior's men so dangerous, culpable and irregular, if it is true, and may attempt to correct it as beneficially, as speedily by means of all ecclesiastical severity.***

***Given at Gloucester on the 16th February 1317.***

*The official Seal of the Prior of Llanthony Prima, near Abergavenny. This Seal was photographed by Mr F.C. Morgan, and is one of the collection of Seals in the Cathedral Library. Used for sealing documents at Llanthony 1317.*

One of the earliest of the Baskervilles, who were to become Lords of Orcop, soon after the foundation of Llanthony Abbey in 1136 gave the Church of Herdesley (Eardisley) with its tithes, and the Churches of Yazor, Cusop and Stretton, together with other gifts, to that foundation, so it is possible that when the Manor of Orcop came into the Baskerville family, through the marriage of a Baskerville to the daughter of a knight of Orcop, (see page 52), the church of Orcop was likewise given in charge to Llanthony Priory. Sir William Compton who was its patron, as previously mentioned, during the reign of Henry VIII, rapidly rose in favour being appointed in turn, Chief Gentleman of the Bedchamber, Constable of Sudeley and Gloucester castles, and to many other offices. He attended Henry VIII at the Field of the Cloth of Gold and at Gravelines in 1520. He died immensely wealthy with property in 18 counties, was Sheriff of Hampshire, Somerset and Dorset, and Sheriff of Worcester for life, by Royal Grant in 1516.[10] I have been in touch with the Archivists of both Llandaff Cathedral and Lambeth Palace Library with reference to the records of Llantony Prima and Seconda, but there do not appear to be any documents which would help to trace the earlier history of Orcop Church. Another interesting fact that emerges from the earliest documented mention of Orcop is that in the charter of 1138 (see page 44) it is mentioned that Orcop, along with other places in Herefordshire, was confirmed to Roger, son of Miles of Gloucester. Roger's wife, Cecily, was the daughter of Payn FitzJohn, who had been an itinerant justice for Henry I. Payn FitzJohn had been granted by the King all the possessions in Herefordshire of Hugh de Lacy, who was the founder of the Augustinian priory of Llanthony, when he died in 1121.[11] It was Miles of Gloucester who gave the land at Gloucester for the founding of Llanthony Secunda. So there is the other possibility that Orcop Church, possibly the pre-existing church suggested by the survey of the Historic Monuments Commission, could have been attached to Llanthony through the inheritance of Roger, son of Miles of Gloucester, and Cecily, his wife, daughter of Payn FitzJohn.

The next mention of a patron is in 1553 when Thomas Browne and William Breton paid £1596.7.8. to the King's representative for the manor of Llanwarne, and the advowson and rectory of Llanwarne, together with the tithes and oblations of the Church of Orcopp in tenure of Thomas ap Evene, and grant of all kinds of lands in Hereford, London, Bangor, Devon, Warwickshire, Oxfordshire, Worcestershire and Rutland.[12] The dissolution of Llanthony Secunda had taken place in 1538,[13] and the Thomas Browne mentioned lived at Much Dewchurch at Browne's Place which was afterwards to be known as the Mynde.[14] J.H. Matthews states that the Mynde had been known as Browne's Place and as Tregroes (the house at the crossroads). Mynde in those early days was a small township within the parish of Much Dewchurch. The Pyes were living in Orcop and on Saddlebow Hill, and in Much Dewchurch as noted on various leases in the Mynde collection.

They are referred to as "of Mynde" (1511), "of Dewchurch" (1566), but in 1578 and 1584 the leases refer to "Roger Pye of the Mynde" so possibly Browne's place was re-named at this time when presumably the Pye's took possession. Thomas Browne died in 1581, and at an Inquisition held at the Booth Hall, Hereford, in 1584, his estate was partitioned under the law of gavelkind, which still existed in Archenfield, after evidence had been given by many witnesses, some of them from Orcop, that such a law was the law of Archenfield, between his two sons, Edward and George.[15] Edward Brown was in possession of Harewood in 1604,[16] and it remained with the family until 1654 when it was sold to the Hoskyns family by John Brown. The Chapel of Harwodde in the Valor Ecclesiasticus of 1535 was also annexed to the Prior of St. John of Jerusalem with a yearly value of 35s.3d. a figure far below that of Orcop. Prebendary Seaton states that the dedication of Harewood chapel was, on its transference to the Knights of St. John of Jerusalem changed from St. Denis to St. John of Jerusalem, and that it was entirely despoiled at the destruction of the Religious Orders during Henry VIII's reign. One cannot help conjecturing whether Orcop was originally the Church of St. Mary, and at this time had its dedication changed to St. John the Baptist. As already stated, I have found no evidence to suggest any reason for the Church being referred to as St. Mary. The survey of the Church by the Historic Monuments Commission mentions that the nave is early 16th century, and that the tower was added and the nave also reconstructed at the same period.

*The Church of Orcop*

In the Parliamentary Survey of 1650 Orcop is stated to be an impropriate rectory worth £40 a year, William Powell, Esq., being the owner, with Edward Beatham, clerk, serving the cure, and receiving the small tithes.[17] It also states that the parishes of Orcop and Llanwarne are fit to be united. I have endeavoured to check whether the two parishes were ever joined but without success. Thomas Browne did hold the advowson of Llanwarne, in addition to the tithes and oblations of Orcop, but apart from that, I cannot trace any other documents. William Powell, later Sir William Powell, was born in 1622, and was buried in Sellack Church, near Ross-on-Wye, in 1680. His second wife, Mary, was the widow of John Bridges, baronet, and mother of James, Lord

Chandos, Baron of Sudley (see page 55). Edmund Browne of Harewood granted a lease of the impropriate tithes of Orcop for 100 years to John Powell of Pengethley and Fulham,[18] who was probably the father of William Powell, the original donor of the Orcop Charity (see page 155).

The next reference to a patron comes in the draft of the Act for Inclosing lands in the parish of Orcop.[19] The original meeting for this was held at the Mitre, Hereford, on the 23rd July 1814, and the document states –

*". . . and whereas James Woodward Esq., Joseph Terrett gentleman as Devisees in Trust under the will of Walter Roberts Esq., deceased are Rectors impropriate of the said Parish of Orcop and as such are entitled to all rectorial and vicarial tithes yearly arising within the parish".*

By the time this Act was officially implemented on the 24th July 1824, James Woodward had also died, and the only surviving devisee was Joseph Terrett who in the Inclosure Award was allotted 40 acres of the 275 acres enclosed (see plot 102 on enclosure map, page 199), in lieu of tithes. In the Mynde Collection there is a lease which states –[20]

***"June 1 1825.***

*Jane Palmer of the parish of Pencoyd, widow.*
*Thomas Hampton Symons.*

*Lease for the life of the said Jane of the tithes of the Lands of the said Thomas Hampton Symons in Orcop".*

This would indicate that for a short period Thomas Hampton Symons as Lord of Orcop had held the patronage of the Church. I cannot trace any relationship between the Palmers and Symons's. The Hopkins family of Pencoyd married into the Palmer family of Bolitree, Weston-under-Penyard,[21] and possibly Jane Palmer was the mother of William Palmer who in the Tithe Schedule of 1843 is named as owning the tithes, and is also mentioned in the Visitation of Churches[22] as being the Patron in 1835. There are several Palmer graves at Pencoyd and Weston-under-Penyard, but Jane Palmer's is not amongst them. An old book in the Diocesan Office, which has neither date nor title, gives the following information about Orcop.

*"Parish No. 264. Orcop. Donative (nothing charged). No tithes to Incumbent. Patron* Walter *Palmer £220.*

*2100 acres 1 rood 35 perches. Population 570".*

The population figure indicates this information to be round about 1841.

William Palmer had a son Walter, who was resident at Pencoyd Court, whom William Cobbett visited in 1821 (see page 18). In 1855 the Rev. M.H. Miller bought the tithes intending to settle at Orcop, but the district did not agree with him, and by 1860 he had sold the tithes to the Rev. Arthur Gray, who, in 1869, gave half of them as an endowment.[23] This was met by the Ecclesiastical Commissioners who on the 15th July 1869 granted a sum of £1500 towards defraying the cost of purchasing the Tithe Rents.[24] The Rev. A. Gray was the first Vicar of Orcop, and was patron of the living for some years, until his death in 1903, when the advowson went first to his wife, Isabella, who died soon afterwards, and then to the Rev. F.W. Bussell of Northolt, Middlesex,[25] then to George Crookes of Orcop Grange,[26] who transferred to Mrs Ada Cuthbert, who next transferred the right to Harrogate College Ltd., Walsall.[27] In 1939 the parish was united with Garway,[28] and a new Trustee was appointed, the Martyr's Memorial and Church of England Trust, on the 10th January 1940.[29] In 1956 the benefice of Orcop and Garway was dissolved, and on the 13th November 1958, Orcop was joined with St. Weonards and remains so today.[30]

The Rev. Arthur Gray built his own residence, the Grange, on the site of the old Tithing Barn, which property William Palmer owned in 1842, and exchanged several fields so that the land was more compact. His successors lived in various houses in the village until 1911 when Thomas Raymond Symons of the Mynde family, gave land in Orcop for a vicarage.[31] I have been in correspondence with the daughter of the Vicar of Orcop at that time, the Rev. W.S. Isherwood, (Vicar from 1909 until his death in 1932), who states that they were living then at Great Camdore over 2 miles from the church, (see page 218), and who remembers how overjoyed the family were when they moved into the new vicarage and had only one mile to walk to church. The vicarage (see photograph 2, page 137), was a pleasant building, not too large as in the case of so many. When the parish was united with Garway which had its own vicarage, the Ecclesiastical Commissioners decided to sell the building at Orcop. The vicarage was subscribed for by all denominations in the parish, although I can find no record of the amount subscribed. Many people have told me how resentful they were that the vicarage was sold by the Ecclesiastical Commissioners leaving the parish without a Vicar of its own. Orcop Church never gained any monetary or social benefit from the sale, (the amount realised went into Diocesan Funds), since it lost direct contact with its Vicar, who was seldom seen in the village except on Sundays. The method of disposal of the vicarage has done much to decrease interest in the church, and whenever money has been needed for maintenance, there are many who refuse help on the grounds that the money was given towards the vicarage and no one had the right to sell it. One sympathises with the people who feel that they were badly treated by those who should have known better.

*An aerial view of Orcop Church with School adjacent. Donovan C. Wilson, Hereford.*

*The Vicarage.*

# Chapter Eleven

## References


| | | |
|---|---|---|
| 1. | – | Registers of the Cantilupe Society. Hereford City Library. Registrum Thomas de Cantilupe, 1275-1283. |
| 2. | – | As above. Registrum Thomas de Charleton. 1327-1344. |
| 3. | – | As above. Registrum Thomas de Charleton. 1327-1344. |
| 4. | – | As above. Registrum John de Trillek. 1344 1361. |
| 5. | – | As above. Registrum Johanus Gilbert. 1375 1389. |
| 6. | – | As above. Registrum Johanus Gilbert. 1375 1389. |
| 7. | – | As above. Registrum Adam de Orleton. 1317 1327. |
| 8. | J.H. Matthews. | p. 110. |
| 9. | John Ecton. | Thesaurus Rerum Ecclesiasticum. Published 1742. Cathedral Library, Hereford. |
| 10. | W.E.A. Cooke. | M.S.S Hereford Patrons and Incumbents. Hereford City Library. |
| 11. | – | Official Guide Book, Llanthony Priory H.M.S.O. 1963. p. 4. |
| 12. | – | Calendar of Patent Rolls. 7 Edward VI. Westminster. Ref.11. p. 962. |
| 13. | – | Official Guide Book, Llanthony Priory. p. 8. |
| 14. | J.H. Matthews. | p. 152. |
| 15. | – | M.S.S. City Library, Local Collection. Interrogations and Depositions taken at Booth Hall, Hereford, 1584. |
| 15. | J.H. Matthews. | p. 102. |

| | | |
|---|---|---|
| 16. | J.H. Matthews. | p. 152. |
| 17. | Rev. Preb. Seaton. | History of Archenfield. Hereford. 1903. p. 74. |
| 18. | C.J. Robinson. | Manors and Mansions of Herefordshire. |
| 19. | – | Draft Act for Parliamentary Inclosure. Local Collection. Hereford City Library. |
| 20. | – | Mynde Collection. 475. |
| 21. | J.H. Matthews. | p. 118. |
| 22. | C.J. Bird. | Visitation of Parish Churches 1845. Pilley Collection. Hereford City Library. |
| 23. | Rev. N. Dredge. | M.S.S. notes. |
| 24. | – | Registers in Hereford Diocesan Office. Bishop's Register 1857-1869. p. 676. |
| 25. | – | Hereford Diocesan Office. Register 1919-1926. p. 19. |
| 26. | – | Hereford Diocesan Office. Register 1919-1926. p. 27. |
| 27. | – | Register 1919-1926. p. 410. |
| 28. | – | Bishop's Register 1938-1953. p. 40. |
| 29. | – | Bishop's Register 1938-1953. p. 66. |
| 30. | – | Bishop's Register 1958- 13th November 1958. |
| 31. | – | Bishop's Register 1902-1919. p. 487. |

# Chapter Twelve

## Parish Life

As the foregoing has shown, Orcop Church had no Vicar until 1859, and the Registers, which date from 1672, give little indication of life in the parish, since they are confined solely to registering births, marriages and deaths. The parish was served by visiting priests, paid by the patron, and sometimes their names are recorded, but more often the entries were made by the churchwardens. It is noticeable in the various other records that survive, namely, bonds, settlement certificates, settlement examinations, removal orders and bastardy bonds, that the Overseers of the Poor were also the Churchwardens, so that most of these documents only bear two signatures, whereas, many neighbouring parishes had two Overseers and two Churchwardens.

The earliest mention that I have found of the Church in Orcop was through reading an article entitled "Parish Life in the 14th Century" by Canon A.T. Bannister.[1] This was a fascinating article which gave details of Herefordshire Visitations to Churches in 1397 which the writer had completed from a 24 page manuscript in very poor condition in the archives of Hereford Cathedral. He tells of returns that laid gross charges against clergy who absented themselves from services, seven churches had had no services for months, even on festivals, while as many as thirty others were left for five or six weeks without Mass. Many churches reported that there were no lights in the chancel so that midday divine service could not be held. There was much said about the unsatisfactory condition of the churches, the roof and windows of the chancel being the most common part in disrepair. There were cases of the chancel being in ruins, and these were the churches which had religious houses as non-resident rectors. In some churches the incumbent allowed fences to be broken down, and pigs, geese and cattle to pasture freely around the churches. Part of one tower had been turned into a cowshed, and a rector had his corn threshed and winnowed, in the churchyard. One vicar sold the trees in the churchyard for his own profit, while another broke the branches for his own firewood. There were cases of forging of wills by incumbents who appointed themselves executors and administered estates to their own advantage. A very frequent complaint was that money, which had been levied in the form of a rent charge to provide a lamp to hang before the altar, or for some other recurring expense, had been misused. Even the Cathedral Chapter had not for some years supplied a lamp and corn for making bread at the Easter communion as they were bound to do to a Church appropriated to them. The clergy, in many cases, set a poor example to their parishioners; sick people died without the last offices, there was much frequenting of taverns and revealing of the secrets of the confessional, as well as sexual promiscuity among the parish priests. Canon Bannister states –

*"We must remember that these are the shadows only, not the lights of parochial life 530 years ago. The dark side of life in the 14th century so fiercely denounced by Langland, and described with such kindly tolerance by Chaucer, is here detailed with all its crudeness."*

***Church Cottage. At one time the Cross Keys Inn at the gate of the Church. where people came to pay their tithes. Also the home of a succession of sextons and grave-diggers as well as innkeepers and shopkeepers. The Rev Arthur Gray planned to build his vicarage here before ultimately settling on the Grange.***

***Church Cottage 1992.***

Following upon the reading of this article I was fortunate enough, with the help of Mr. F.C. Morgan, the Cathedral Archivist, to find the actual visitations in question, which had been bound many years ago to preserve them. There was an entry from Orcop which, unfortunately, was at the bottom of a page, and had both sides torn away so that it was not possible to obtain a full translation. It would seem that the Orcop font was in need of repair, and that there was much immorality in the parish; people were living in open adultery, including the priest who resided in another village nearby, and who kept a concubine in Orcop. This was probably Richard Orcop who was Rector of Llandinabo in 1391.

***Farmers were responsible for keeping a portion of the churchyard wall in repair; the picture shows the division between two such sections.***

The Cathedral Archives are rich in Articles of Enquiry and Visitations which date back to the 17th century, but these are uncatalogued though grouped in years. In order to find any information it meant a random search; the years I covered were from 1660 to 1686, from 1701 to 1736, 1762-1769, 1780-83, 1819-21 and 1860 to 1904. When the Visitation comprised a printed form requiring answers, there was constant repetition of one word answers which gave no information which was worthwhile. Apart from the years mentioned, I also checked through a dozen boxes of citations, marriage licences, church-wardens' accounts and presentments which were not always grouped or dated.

The following items represent the results of several weeks research which, although a rewarding experience, did not yield very much information about Orcop.

***1671. Presentment.***[2]

*Answering questions in Articles of Enquiry.*

1. *Concerning the church with its furniture we have nothing to present.*

2. *Concerning the churchyard it is likewise kept in due order.*

3. *And as concerning our minister he is for aught we know qualified and performing his duties as in the articles required.*

4. *For our parishioners we have these parties to present for papists, Joan, the wife of Philip Beavan.*
   *John Watkins.*
   *Roger Lambert and his wife Elizabeth.*
   *And for other things concerned with the articles we have nothing to present.*

5. *For our clerk he is responsible and doth his business as the articles required.*

*And lastly our churchwardens are duly chosen and all things therein performed as we conceive and we have consorted with our minister in these articles.*

*Signed David Llewellyn, Churchwarden*

***1671. Churchwarden's Accounts.***[3]

*John Jones, Old Warden.*
*David Powell. New Warden.*
*Elected our Wardens. Paid 4d. and 3s.6d. churchwardens Calls and Fees.*

***1674. Letter.***

*"These are to certify that Joan Parry and Thomas Symons have constantly come to church since and a little before I received this precept and citation. Symons is a poor and sickly man which was the cause of his former absenting himself, but his wife comes not at all, and as for Joan Parry she is but a child and on the parish charge who as soon as her father died, who was a papist, she came to Church. I pray, therefore, proceed not any further against them for fees less they are driven from the church again because it is not to be had. If you forebear, I will use my endeavour with them to send you some if possible. If not, we must certify the Chancellor's Worship to take it off, but I hope this will not prevail with you, being the truth, and the humble wish of your loving friend, Jere. Jackson".*

Jeremy Jackson was the Vicar of Garway, and his name appears several times in the Orcop Registers.

***1676. Presentment.***[4]

*"We, the Minister, Churchwarden and others of the parish of Orcop knowing that the bearer, hereof, George Powell and his wife have been presented for absentors from Church and excommunication, proceeded against them for their contempt of the Court, and with all that they are very willing to return and be conformable to the Church of England, and the commands of their Ordinary, do hereby certify that they are very poor people having a great charge of children, and their absenting from church was most for want of clothes, therefore humbly desire their absolution may be granted freely, we remain your humble servants.*

| | |
|---|---|
| *Jere. Jackson.* | *John Rogers, Churchwarden.* |
| *John Morgan.* | *John Lambert.* |
| *Thomas Powell.* | *Gilbert Jones.* |
| *John Lambert, Jun.* | *John Gunter.* |
| *Henry Hughes.* | *John Gething.* |

***1680.***[5]

*14th October. Thomas Lambert of Horcopp will certify to the Court upon his oath that the Churchyard rails there are in sufficient repairs.*

*I do certify that the Churchyard of Horcopp is sufficiently fenced with rails so that neither swine nor other cattle may annoy it. This I certify upon my own view and sight of it.*

*8th January 1680.*

Both these visitations are signed by John Willin, curate.

***4th December 1689.***[6]

*A summons as a result of a Visitation.*

*"Thomas Lambert and Thomas Griffiths. For not repairing the Church."*

1701. Articles of Presentment.

***19th January 1701.***

*William Stringer presented for not keeping his fence belonging to the Churchyard sufficiently repaired.*

I also found a marriage licence dated 1679 as follows.[7]

***1679.***

*To all persons whom this may or shall concern. I do certify that William Stringer and Mary Abrill, both of the parish of Orcobs in the county of Hereford were lawfully married the 26th day of July A.D. 1679 in the parish of Langatock Vibonanoll in the County of Monmouth by me John Nicholls, Vicar of the aforesaid parish.*

Mary Abrill's name was probably Abrahall, a very well-known Orcop family for many generations. William Stringer is mentioned on several Marriage Settlement documents of the Mynde Estate as occupying a cottage belonging to the estate. It is possible that later on the name got corrupted to "Stringham" since there is a small footpath on Orcop Hill called "Stringhams Green" which had a cottage built alongside it, which has now been demolished.

The following are extracts from Articles of Enquiry.[8]

***1859.***

*"The Prayer books are decent, but the Bible is not in good order. The Psalmody is fairly well performed for a village.*

***1870.***

*The Church is not large enough for the Parish. Only an oak box for a Parish chest.*

***1882.***

*Parish pays the expenses of laundering surplices. Holy Communion is held 156 times a year. In answer to the question "Have the last Churchwardens given a just account to Minister and Parishioners", the reply is "There is no account, everything has been voluntary."*

***1901.***

*Roof and tower need repairing. Services 11 and 6.30."*

The 1851 Census figures from Returns of all Churches and Chapels gives the following details of the Church.

*"Deanery of Archenfield and Abbey Dore. Date of Consecration not known. Supposed ancient parish church. Curate is paid by the day. Impropriator to whom all tithes belong.*

| | |
|---|---|
| *Free Seats.* | *82* |
| *Other seats.* | *31 = 113* |
| *Estimated number attending on 30th March 1851. Morning only.* | *80* |
| *No Sunday School.* | |
| *Average number for 12 months preceding 30th March 1851.* | *90* |
| *Signed by Hy. Prosser. Curate of Garway and Skenfrith."* | |

The Rev. N. Dredge states in his notes that cottage services were held about 1893 at Garway Hill in the Pigeon House, and at Ebenezer House, Orcop Hill. The latter was the home of Charles Burleigh who, after being active in the Baptist cause for many years, joined the Church, and was at one time, a Churchwarden.

The social life of the parish in the 19th century was closely bound up with the Church as can be gathered from the following extracts from Parish Magazines.[9]

***"May 1888.***

> *A village concert promoted by the School Board took place on Easter Monday evening. It proved very successful and was well attended. Several performers, vocal and instrumental from the neighbourhood kindly gave their services. Some of the Llanwarne Band were present."*

***"November 1888.***

> *The Harvest Festival took place here on Monday the 15th October. The Church was prettily decorated by the Vicar's daughter and the parishioners. Four fine sheaves of wheat were sent by Mr. Jones of the Moat farm, and also a pretty miniature wheat stack was placed on the Communion Table. Wreaths, crosses and flowers were sent from various quarters. An excellent tea was provided,and the lads had a good game of football during the afternoon. The evening was wound up with a dance in the schoolroom. Collections amounting to £2 were made which are to be applied to some needful repairs to the Churchyard wall and fence."*

The Vicar in 1890, the Rev. J.B. Davey Hopgood, successor to the Rev. A. Gray, was not very popular, and the following extract from the magazine shows that the Church was going through an unhappy phase.

***"December 1890.***

> *On Christmas Day, the parishioners showed that this is a thoroughly heathen parish, for not one of them received Holy Communion, but all marched out after Church Militant Prayer, thus despising their Lord's birthday, and insulting him by turning their backs on his Holy altar."*

With the next Vicar, the Rev. Norris Dredge, there seems to have been an upsurge in Church worship and social activities. A photograph of him can be seen on page 129. I have been in correspondence with his only surviving child, Miss Genevieve Dredge, who now lives in Suffolk, and who, in 1966, was aged 84. She used to play the organ in church for nearly 10 years during her father's ministry.

***"January 1896.***

> *A Christmas tree for the Sunday School children was held at the Grange on Tuesday January 14th 1896. After some games the children were admitted to see the Christmas tree, and receive their*

*prizes and presents. Among the prizes were a pair of boots, several shirts, pinafores, pairs of braces and several useful articles. A few toys, sweets, crackers and nuts were distributed. At Miss Dredge's request, cheers were given for the many subscribers and friends who were present. A sum of £4.17.0. was collected and a balance of 5/11d. remains in hand.*

***May 1896.***

*At the Vestry Meeting held on April 20th 1896, Mr. Charles Burleigh, Ebenezer House, was reappointed Vicar's Warden, and Mr. Frank Raymond, the Green, was elected Parish Warden. On Monday April 13th there was a Concert and Dance in the Schoolroom. This was arranged by Miss Dredge with the view to raising funds for a childrens' treat. The following programme was ably rendered and well received.*

*Pianoforte duets.*
*Song, "The Flight of Ages", Miss Wood, Hereford.*
*Song, "The Anchor's Weighed". Mr. T.C. Lewis, Ewyas Harold.*
*Song, "It was a dream". Miss Waite, Orcop.*
*Song. "Mona", Mr. Atkinson from Ireland.*
*Song, "We saved it for the Lodger". Dr. Jennings, Ewyas Harold.*
*Songs. "Dear Heart", "Good Company", "Slatterly's Mounted Foot", and "The River of Life".*

With regard to administration of the Church there are no old Church Accounts in existence, but the Rev. Dredge's notes which were written about 1907 contain copies of two old accounts for 1746 and possibly 1747/8 which were in existence then. These are as follows:-

**The Accounts for the year 1746**

| | £ | s | d | q |
|---|---|---|---|---|
| Payd. Ellenner Perce, 6 weeks. | | 4 | 6 | |
| Payd. David Morgan 8 weeks. | | 8 | 0 | |
| Payd. Walter Powell 8 weeks. | | 6 | 0 | |
| For 3 sesments (assessments) | | 3 | 0 | |
| Payd for the book for cattell | | | 6 | |
| For 2 weeks for William Lambert | | 4 | 0 | |
| For the affidavit for Peter Pew | | 1 | 0 | |
| Quarter pay | | 9 | 5 | |
| Payd Fillip Wibbey | | 6 | 0 | |
| Corte fees presentment, going to the visitation | | 6 | 10 | |
| Payd for glass in the windows | | 2 | 0 | |

| | | | | |
|---|---|---|---|---|
| For bred and wine | | 2 | 8 | |
| Payd Walter Williams for going to the visitation | | 1 | 0 | |
| For 3 urchins 4 cites | | 1 | 2 | |
| For putting in the trance grip (transcript) | | | 4 | |
| For my troubell for serving the ofis for the last half year | | 8 | 0 | |
| Wm. Prichet not payd | | | 2 | 2 |
| Thomas Grindall not payd | | | | |
| | 3 | 5 | 3 | 2 |

| | | | | |
|---|---|---|---|---|
| On the back the figures | 2 | 16 | 3 | 2 |
| | | 8 | 0 | |
| | 3 | 4 | 3 | 2 |

The above indicates that the Accounts of the Churchwardens and Overseers were kept together, possibly because the two offices were served by the same two men. Perhaps when the account was balanced it was one shilling deficient. The word "urchins" refers to hedgehogs, and the word "cities" might be "Kites" taken from the Anglo Saxon "cyta". I have seen kites in Orcop, and I understand they have been known to attack lambs. Since the following account mentions the same people, the first account might be a 6 monthly one. The account below was presented to a parish meeting on the 21st April 1746.

| | £ | s | d | |
|---|---|---|---|---|
| Py. Ellenner Pearce 52 weeks | 1 | 19 | 0 | |
| Py. Walter Powell, 48 weeks, sixpence a week | 1 | 4 | 0 | |
| Py. Walter Powell, 4 weeks 9d a week | | 3 | 0 | |
| Py. Shousan Nicklos | | 3 | 0 | |
| Py quarter pay | | 9 | 5 | |
| Spent at a parish meeting | | 2 | 6 | |
| Stopt by Tobias Bevan for a house | | 12 | 0 | 16/-? |
| Py. David Morgan 4 weeks twelve pence a week | | 4 | 0 | |
| F. Watkins not collected | | | 5 | |
| William Davis not collected | | | 10 | |
| Py Mr. Gof for mending the parish tools | | 3 | 7 | |
| Py Thos. Gough, paid for a warant | | 1 | 0 | |
| (This is 4/- more than it should be, Rev. Dredge suggests 12/- should be 16/- | | | | |
| | 5 | 6 | 9 | |

The remaining account was undated, but appears to be for a year in which Tobias Bevan was Churchwarden and Overseer, and this was 1747/8.

| | £ | s | d |
|---|---|---|---|
| Corte fees going to the vissitatyon and presentment | | 5 | 2 |
| 3 fichhogs, 5 urchins, 1 wilecat, 1 cite | | 5 | 0 |
| transgrip and going with him | | 2 | 0 |
| 2 books and paper | | 2 | 4 |
| Doing the bels 2 days work | | 2 | 8 |
| 3 pennyworth of ayle (ale or oil) | | | 3 |
| for tymber | | | 6 |
| nayls 3 pennyworth | | | 3 |
| Washin the shurplus | | 3 | 0 |
| Tobias Bevan going to the vissitatyon | | 1 | 0 |
| the book of fast | | 1 | 0 |
| one fichhog | | | 4 |
| one penny for paper on the Church dore | | | 1 |
| | 1 | 1 | 7 |

The second item on the account is, I think, again payment for animals classed as vermin. A fichhog would be a polecat since "fitch" is the dialect English word for such an animal. The Herefordshire word for the polecat was "fitchhocks", (Old English Dictionary), and these were recorded as being common in the county as recently as 1840.

Another statement of Accounts was for the year 1889 to 1890 in the Archenfield magazine.[10]

| **Receipts** | **£** | **s** | **d** |
|---|---|---|---|
| Per offertories, Easter 1889 to 1890 | 4 | 4 | 6½ |
| Proceeds of Concert, Whitsun Monday. | 1 | 9 | 4 |
| Proceeds of Tea etc., Harvest. | 1 | 10 | 0 |
| | 7 | 3 | 10½ |
| Balance due to Vicar | 1 | 11 | 2½ |
| | 8 | 15 | 1 |

| **Expenses** | **£** | **s** | **d** |
|---|---|---|---|
| New lamps, glasses and oil, | | 12 | 6 |
| Candles, broom, parcels | | 15 | 2½ |
| Hymn books and postage | | 11 | 7 |
| Burial Register and postage | 1 | 1 | 10½ |
| Wedding Churchyard | | 3 | 0 |
| Wick | | | 11 |
| Mending Bell | | 1 | 6 |
| Wine for Sick Poor | | 2 | 0 |
| Wine for Holy Comminion | | 5 | 0 |
| Washing surplices and altar linen | | 10 | 0 |
| Coke £1.2.6 Hauling 7/6d | 1 | 10 | 0 |
| Brandy for poor | | 2 | 6 |
| Poor | | 4 | 0 |
| Cleaning Church | 2 | 0 | 0 |
| Saunders for lighting fires | | 17 | 0 |
| | 8 | 15 | 1 |

An interesting entry occurs in the Parish Minute Book dated April 22nd 1889.[11]

> *"At the Easter Vestry Meeting the Parish Clerk having resigned, it was stated that as now people were able to read and join in the responses, they did not require a man to read for them, and so the office of clerk is abolished."*

The Church today is but a shadow of the past; in common with the rest of the country, the number of people who attend is small for the one service that is held weekly. The church is cleaned voluntarily by a few helpers who take their turn at flower arranging also, and the fact that the Vicar is not resident in the parish tends to make visiting non existent. The day of the Harvest Dance, the Tithe Dinner (held in the schoolroom) and Garden Fete has gone since the number of helpers are few, and the support insufficient to cover expenses. The Church itself is in a very reasonable state of maintenance having electric lighting and heating, as well as gas wall heaters, and simple, but new, altar furnishings which were made a few years ago to replace the worn items that had been there for a great many years. In the last few years the only services that have seen a full church were services which were held at the end of the School year when the older children would be responsible for the entire music of the service with their recorder playing, and the Harvest Services. Now that the school has closed the former services are but a memory, while the Harvest Services are not so well attended as they were in the past. One of the remarks put on the articles of enquiry in 1870 was that the church was not large enough; at that time the population of the parish was 637, and often a condition of work was that one attended church, (this was told to me by a parishioner, since dead, whose husband was a gamekeeper on a local estate), today the population is still decreasing, and is probably about 340. The collections at Orcop barely cover expenses, and of late years the Church has been unable to meet its commitments to the Diocesan Funds by way of Quota. When the Church year closes, whatever is in hand, which is never more than £15, an amount of £5 is left in the Church account, and the balance sent to the Diocesan authorities; there is no reserve. Whenever possible we return to worship there, but often the congregation numbers less than five. It is difficult to assess what the position of the Church will be in the coming years, particularly in view of the fact that the suggestion has been put, and is being considered by the Diocesan authorities, that redundant churches should be either sold or demolished.

***The Grange.***

***Built on the site of the old Tithing Barn by the Rev. Arthur Gray.***

# Chapter Twelve

## REFERENCES


| | | |
|---|---|---|
| 1. | A.T. Bannister | English National History Review 1927. Article, "Parish Life in the 14th C." Hereford City Library. |
| 2. | – | Hereford Cathedral Archives. Presentments. Box 18. |
| 3. | – | Hereford Cathedral Archives. Churchwardens Accounts etc., Box 5. |
| 4. | – | Hereford Cathedral Archives. Presentments. Box 1. |
| 5. | – | Hereford Cathedral Archives. Box 1. |
| 6. | – | Hereford Cathedral Archives. Box 23. |
| 7. | – | Hereford Cathedral Archives. Marriage Licences. Box 12. |
| 8. | – | Hereford Cathedral Archives. Articles of Enquiry. 1859, 1870, 1882 and 1901. These are in chronological and alphabetical order. |
| 9. | – | Archenfield Magazines. 1888. Hereford County Library. |
| 10. | – | Archenfield Magazines. Hereford County Library. |
| 11. | – | Orcop Parish Minute Book. 1886 to 1913. Loaned by Mr. A.J. Morgan, Pontrilas. Clerk to the Parish Council. |

# Chapter Thirteen

## CHARITIES AND THE POOR LAW

The Benefactions Board which is in the tower of the Parish Church, (see photograph overleaf) lists six Charities, of which only three are still distributed. They are as follows:-

| | £ | s | d |
|---|---|---|---|
| William Bridges, left charged on Tiberton Estate, due on Good Friday | 3 | 0 | 0 |
| William Pye left charged on Thruxton Estate, due on Good Friday | 1 | 0 | 0 |
| Thomas Powell, late of Stradway, left | 1 | 0 | 0 |
| Mrs. Elizabeth Morse, Spinster, left charged on the Rock Farm in Llanwarn | | 10 | 0 |
| Mr. William Powell of Pengethly left charged on the Whitehouse in Sellack, due at Christmas | 1 | 0 | 0 |

Left from the Moat Farm in this parish 1 acre of land for the use of the Sacraments in this Church

The Bridges, Pye and Powell of Pengethley Charities are still paid annually and amount to £4.17.0.

The Bridges Charity of £3.0.0. is paid by the Trustees of the Tiberton Estate near Madley in Herefordshire, and is of long standing as proved by receipts from the Churchwardens and Overseers of Orcop which run from 1648 to 1657. Before the Estate was bought by William Brydges in 1652 it was owned by the Delabere family[1] who had a connection with the Mynde through the marriages of John Pye (died 1547) with Anne Delabere and Anne Brydges.

The Pye Charity was granted by William Pye, one of the first Sir Walter's seven sons, in his Will dated 24th August 1689. He bequeathed an annuity of £20 from his manor of Thruxton, near Kingstone, in Herefordshire, to be paid to 26 parishes of which Orcop was one, benefiting to the value of £1 per year in common with several other parishes, smaller villages receiving 5/–, 6/8d and 10/–.[2]

The Thomas Powell charity is no longer paid. The donor lived at Stradway

Farm, Orcop, and the gift was made by Deed in 1721, the year he died.[3] The original donation was £20, and the parish later added £5 in order to produce an annual income of £1. The money was lent to a Hereford solicitor. Mr Thomas Bird on security of some property, who paid 5% interest. The Charity Commissioners recommended that the money should be invested in the Monmouth Savings Bank, but attempts to redeem the money failed since Mr Bird was bankrupt.

*Charity Board in Belfry of Orcop Church.*

The Morse Charity was to be paid from Rock Farm in Llanwarne, a neighbouring village. The farm ceased to exist before the beginning of this century, and payment has not been made since the early 19th century. The Morse family owned property in Orcop, and paid a chief rent to the Manor.[4]

The Powell Charity of Pengethley is referred to as the William Powell Charity, but was really John Powell's Charity. John Powell of Fulham, was the father of William Powell, later Sir William Powell, patron of the living of Orcop. A copy of John's will is to be found in the oldest Parish Register of Much Dewchurch. It was dated 27th May 1606, and reads as follows:-[5]

> *"John Powell of Fulham, Middlesex, in his Will dated 27th May 1606, 4th James I, gave to the poor of the parishes of Sellack, Hentland, Kings Caple, Llanwarne, Orcop and Much Dewchurch, one year's rent of Twenty shillings, and to the poor of the parishes of Llandinabo and Pencoyd, ten shillings to be payable for ever unto the said poor of the aforesaid parishes out of a farm situated in the parish of Sellack called the White House in Baysham. The yearly sum of twenty shillings and ten shillings to be paid at the feast of All Saints to the Churchwardens for the time being, and to be distributed unto the poor, half yearly by equal portions against the Feasts of Christmas and Easter."*

This charity is still paid today through the agents of Mr Charles Clore who bought this farm as part of the Guy's Hospital Estates.

The last Charity is worded thus –

> *Left from the Moat Farm in this parish 1 acre of land for the use of the Sacraments in this Church".*

The Charity Commissioners report that several old parishioners recollect bread and wine being distributed, but could not remember when this last occurred.[6] The old lady referred to in the chapter on Folk Lore and Superstition (see page 277) was the first person who refused to pay the charity. In later years when the farm was owned by Major Abraham Whittaker, early 1800's, agitation in the parish due to non payment of the charity caused him to inspect the Charity List. He is reported to have said "Left from the Moat Farm, then it is no longer there, it was left from it" and on this ground refused payment, no payments having been made since.

Charity Lists were available in the Church records for 1815 when £7.12.3. was distributed, and for 1820, £5.9.6. and 1821 £6.2.6. but these do not exist today.[7] Lists remain from 1895 to 1913 which show that between 17 and 20 people were in receipt of amounts from 2/6d. to 9/-. Today the Charities are paid by two Trustees appointed by the Parish Council.

In addition to the Charities which were given to those in need, the Church from the time of the two main Poor Law Acts of 1597 and 1601, appointed

Overseers or Guardians of the Poor who, together with the Churchwardens were responsible for the relief of those in distressed circumstances. Each parish was expected to look after its poor, and settlement Acts were passed whereby anyone leaving his place of birth or his usual residence could be sent back officially to that parish which was regarded as his legal settlement. A Removal order could be made by two Justices of the Peace at the request of the overseers, and any signs that a new inhabitant might become a pauper was sufficient for the order to be made out and executed until a more humane act in 1795 restricted removal to those actually applying for relief. Before such an order was made the persons concerned were examined by the magistrates who endeavoured to find out, if the person had not produced a Settlement Certificate, just where his parish of legal settlement was. If a person had hired himself for twelve months, worked the twelve months and received his wages, this ensured him a settlement in the parish in which he had lived and carried out this work. Orcop Church records are rich in documents of Poor Law Administration, possessing 23 Settlement Certificates dated from 1709-1778, 29 Settlement Examinations from 1739-1826, 26 Removal orders from 1705-1827, and other miscellaneous papers regarding settlements, indemnity and bastardy bonds. Some specimen items are detailed in the following pages.

***"Settlement Certificate. Dated 13th day of February 1778.***

*We, the Churchwardens and Overseers of the Poor of the Parish of Sellack in the County of Hereford aforesaid do hereby acknowledge James Treherne and Phillis his wife, and four children, Sarah 8 years, Thomas 6 years, James 4 years and Elizabeth 2 years, to be Inhabitants legally settled in our said Parish.*

*Signed by the Church Wardens and Overseers".*

James Treherne settled in Orcop, and a cottage remains to this day which is called Treherne Cottage. Either he or his son, James, was presented at a Court Baron as follows:-[8]

***"Court Baron held Monday 24th day of October 1808.***

*And we present James Treherne for digging and suffering a certain quarry upon Coneygare Hill to remain open, such quarry being made upon a certain team road leading from late Betham's farm to a parcel of land belonging to such farm, and we order the said James Treherne to fill up such quarry within one month from this Court under the penalty of thirty nine shillings".*

Treherne cottage is built on common land which I have identified as being Coneygar Hill. The Betham family were connected with Orcop in 1650, when an Edward Betham was the priest mentioned in a Parliamentary Survey of that date as receiving the small tithes. A descendant whose will I have perused,[9] yet another Edward Betham of Ross, possessed 14 acres on Orcop Hill, and had a nephew, John Abrahall, whose name appears on the Deeds of a property belonging to Mr Alan Thomas named "New House Farm". This building is situated on Coneygar Hill, although for nearly 150 years past it has been called Little Hill. I think that the land farmed by the various Bethams probably stretched from Orcop Hill to Coneygar Hill. An Edward Betham was Vicar of Hentland and Monmouth in 1678, and Vicar of Whitchurch in 1680,[10] and had 3 sons, named Rudhall, John and Edward. There exists in the Mynde Collection a Bond for the performance of covenants between Rudhall Betham of Orcop and Edward Betham, his son and heir, dated 1711.[11] The latter died in March 1732, and in addition to an inventory of his goods I have traced the lease of his farm, which will be mentioned in a later chapter dealing with agriculture.[12] James Treherne was buried at Orcop on the 1st February 1811.[13]

The following three documents show the way that the Poor Law administration worked in the case of one unfortunate woman who was single and pregnant.[14]

*"The examination of Hester Walters, singlewoman, touching the place of her last legal settlement taken upon oath before us whose hands are hereunto set, two of His Majesty's Justices of the Peace for the County of Hereford.*

*This examinant deposeth, and upon oath saith that she was born in the parish of Llanwarne, and about Two years and a half ago she went and lived with William Cook in the parish of Orcopp, but was not hired there nor hath not gained any settlement in the parish of Orcopp or elsewhere.*

*Signed with the Mark of Hester Walters."*

*9th January 1756 sworn and examined before us.*
*T. Gwillim.*
*W. Hoskyns.*

After this examination by the magistrates, a Removal Order was made out which stated that –

*"Hester Walters, singlewoman, lately came and intruded into the Parish of Orcopp, endeavouring there to settle as inhabitant thereof, contrary to Law, not having anyways acquired or obtained any legal settlement in, and is likely to become chargeable thereunto . . .*

*Therefore in His Majesty's name, we command you, the said Churchwardens and Overseers of the Poor of the Parish of Orcopp to remove and convey the said Hester Walters from the said parish of Orcopp unto the Parish of Llanwarne, and to deliver her over to the*

*Churchwardens and Overseers of the Poor there who are required to receive and provide for her as the Law directs".*

This order was made out on the same day as the examination, 9th January 1756. The next form is dated 31st January 1756 –

*"To the Churchwardens and Overseers of the poor of the parish of Orcopp in the county of Hereford.*

*We, the Churchwardens and Overseers of the poor of the parish of Llanwarne in the County aforesaid do hereby own and acknowledge Hester Walters, singlewoman, who is now with child of a base child, to be a parishioner legally settled in our said parish of Llanwarne, and do hereby promise to provide for her and the sayd child or children she now goeth withall (when born) as our parishioners".*

Since the Order of Removal is not signed as having been carried out as are most of the documents, it seems that since her legal parish would provide for her, she was allowed to remain in Orcop. This is borne out by the sad entry in the Church Register which reads –

*"Hester Walters of Llanwarne buried July 18th 1756".*

By the next century the Settlement Laws had been relaxed somewhat in that paupers under threat of removal could not be taken to their legal parish if they were not fit to travel. In the past, unfortunates had been bundled out of parishes with all speed to avoid expenses involved with illness and death. One instance of this is shown by the following Order of Removal dated 15th October 1825.[15] The removal of Mary Morgan, singlewoman, from Orcop to Madley had been ordered by the Magistrates. On the back of the Order are three statements, each signed by two magistrates.

1. *"Whereas it appears unto us Kedgwin Hoskins (Lord of Wormelow) and Jasper Farmer Esq., the justices within mentioned, that the within named Mary Morgan is at present unable to travel by reason of sickness and infirmity of body, we, the said justices, do therefore, in pursuance of the Statute in that behalf made and provided, hereby suspend the execution of the within written Order of Removal; and you, the Churchwardens and Overseers of the poor of the parish of Orcop are hereby commanded to desist from conveying the within named Mary Morgan until you shall make it appear unto us that the said Mary Morgan hath recovered from her said illness and may without danger be conveyed from the said parish of Orcop to the said parish of Madley.*

   *15th October 1825".*

2. *"Whereas it duly appears unto us Kedgwin Hoskins and Jasper Farmer Esq., two of His Majesty's Justices of the Peace for the said County of Hereford, that the above named Mary Morgan is wholly recovered from sickness and infirmity of body under which she lately laboured, and that she may therefore be conveyed from the within named parish of Orcop to the within named parish of Madley without danger. These are therefore to authorise and require you, the Churchwardens and Overseers of the said Parish of Orcop forthwith to convey the said Mary Morgan from and out of your said parish of Orcop to the said parish of Madley and deliver her to the Churchwardens and Overseers of the Poor as you are within directed to do.*

*22nd day of November 1825".*

3. *"Whereas it hath been proved upon Oath before us the Justices whose names are hereunto subscribed, and who signed the within written Order of Removal, that the charges incurred by the suspension of the said Order of Removal amounted to the sum of £2.1.1½ and which charges appear to us to be just and reasonable, we, the said Justices, do in pursuance of the Statute in that case made hereby, order and direct the Churchwardens and Overseers of the Poor of the Parish of Madley in the County of Hereford to where the within named pauper is to be removed, to pay the said charges to the Churchwardens and Overseers of the Poor of the said Parish of Orcop or to such of them as shall demand the same.*

*22nd day of November 1825".*

Another examination dated 23rd March 1797 is of John Scudamore, a pauper.[16]

*"Who saith he hath heard and believes he was born in the parish of Holmer in the said County, that he is twenty three years of age or thereabouts, that between four or five years ago he hired himself by the year with Thomas Webb of the parish of Vowchurch, served him a year and received his wages for such his services, that between three and four years ago he hired himself by the year with William Williams of the parish of Vowchurch aforesaid, that he lived from May till Candlemas in Vowchurch with his master, that his master then went to live in the parish of Kingston in the said County where this deponant served the remainder of his year and received his wages for such his service. That about Christmas last he was married in the parish Church of Orcop in the said County to Mary, his now wife, by whom he hath no child, and he hath done no act whereby to obtain a settlement elsewhere since.*

*Signed the mark of John Scudamore".*

The Church Register shows that John Scudamore married Mary Vail on the 29th December 1796. Mary was buried at Orcop on the 21st April 1825 aged 57 years, and John was buried on the 30th June 1834 aged 69 years. They had 6 children, 4 girls and 2 boys, the boys both died when young. John Scudamore was presented at a Court Baron in 1801 for erecting a cottage and enclosing a garden on Orcop Hill, amerced five shillings, and ordered to pull down the cottage and throw open the enclosure.[17] By 1828 he appears to be working for the Lord of the Manor, Thomas Hampton Symons, since an account has been rendered for work he has done quarrying tiles.[18]

***"December 10th 1828.***

*T.H. Symons Esq.,*

*To John Scydemore for rising tyles at Sadelbow quarey to go to Sadelbow for the Barne and Shed.*

| | £ | s | d |
|---|---|---|---|
| For rising 10,600 of tyles at 10s.0d for thousand | 5 | 7 | 6 |
| Do for 125 yards of paving at 4d for yard. | 2 | 1 | 8 |
| tyles before they could come to the tyles at 6d. | 1 | 13 | 0 |
| Do for rising 530 feet of paving at the Buts quarey at 7s.0d for hundred. | 1 | 16 | 11½ |
| | 10 | 19 | 1½ |
| Nov. 3rd paving to Ridby's Mill 179 ft. 12 4) | | | |
| Dec. 4th paving to Hendre, Orcop. 161 ft. 11 2) | 2 | 5 | 0 |
| Do paving to Sadelbow 310 ft. 1 1 9) | | | |
| Paving gone to Farm. | | | |
| | 8 | 14 | 1½ |

Settled December 14th 1828.
Thomas Parry."

The Butts quarry mentioned above at that time had a building in it named simply "ye Butts". Later on two further cottages were built named Lower Butts, (originally Rock Cottage), and Upper Butts. These are adjacent to the present road which took the place of the ancient team road lower down. Subsidence is a frequent problem here. When I first came to Orcop I assumed the name "butts" had a connection with local tradition that the finest archers at Agincourt were recruited from Archenfield, but I soon realised that the land is so named because it abutts on to the Saddlebow, and the parish boundary.

*The Lower Butts. (Rock Cottage).*

To return to the account of John Scudamore, Thomas Parry apparently paid for the paving which went to farms direct amounting to £2.5.0. leaving the remaining account for T.H. Symons to settle. Thomas Parry appears in Estate Books as being one of the masons who carried out work for the maintenance and improvement of the Mynde farms. John Scudamore by agreement with T.H. Symons in 1830 was renting a cottage on Orcop Hill at £1.2.6. per annum, (possibly the cottage he built himself on the waste), and had taken over 3½ acres of land which had a building on it from another tenant at an added rental of £1.15.0. making his yearly outlay £2.17.6.[19] Photograph of his cottage on p. 214.

Another newcomer to Orcop in 1720 was Thomas Grindon who produced proof of his Legal Settlement, (see page 162), and was presented at a Court Baron in 1738 for building a house, and enclosing a garden and orchard.[20] The Church Registers show that by 1741 he was a Churchwarden and Overseer, while in 1788 a descendant of the same name was sworn at the Court Baron of that year, and was also appointed Parish Constable for the ensuing year.

These are some happier examples perhaps of those who came into the parish of Orcop, and appear to have made a living there. There are other Removal Orders which show from the entries made on the reverse side that the unfortunate paupers were speedily removed to the parish of legal settlement, often on the same day that the Order was given. One instance was the following –[21]

> *"Recd. of and by ye hand of Mr J. Williams, Overseer of the Parish of Orcop in ye county of Hereford, by an Order of Removal dated 13th May 1799, Evan Prosser and Mary, his wife, whom I acknowledge and accept to*

*be parishioners legally settled in ye Parish of Llowes in the County of Radnor and at ye request of Mary Prosser I suffered her and her husband to return to their own house, and gave ye said Mary one guinea towards discharging Evan and Mary's rent and likewise I paid Mr Williams 7/6, 3 weeks pay as he advanced to said Evan and Mary Prosser.*

*16th May 1799.*

*Signed Lewis Williams.* *Overseer of ye Poor."*

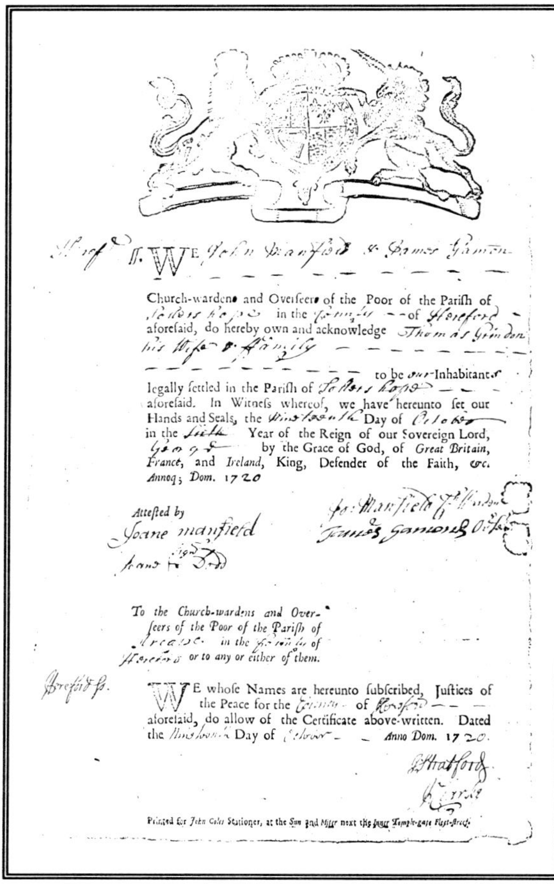

ss. WE John Manfield & James Gamon

Church-wardens and Overseers of the Poor of the Parish of [illegible] in the County of Hereford aforesaid, do hereby own and acknowledge Thomas Grindon his Wife & Family to be our Inhabitants legally settled in the Parish of [illegible] aforesaid. In Witness whereof, we have hereunto set our Hands and Seals, the [illegible] Day of October in the Sixth Year of the Reign of our Sovereign Lord, George by the Grace of God, of *Great Britain, France,* and *Ireland,* King, Defender of the Faith, *&c. Annoq; Dom.* 1720

*Attested by* Joane manfield

To the Church-wardens and Overseers of the Poor of the Parish of Orcop in the County of Hereford or to any or either of them.

WE whose Names are hereunto subscribed, Justices of the Peace for the County of Hereford aforesaid, do allow of the Certificate above-written. Dated the [illegible] Day of October *Anno Dom.* 1720.

Printed for *John Coles* Stationer, at the Sun and Mitre next the Inner Temple-gate Fleet-street.

***Settlement Certificate of Thomas Grindon, 1720.***

Another type of document which exists in the Parish records is a Bond which was executed in the case of an illegitimate child being chargeable to the Parish. The near relatives of the child's mother, or the father, if known, by a signed Agreement with the Churchwardens and Overseers of the Parish concerned, paid a sum of money, (in the case of the Orcop documents £40.0.0.) which was to be used by the Overseers to provide for the child. An order could also be made by the Magistrates for the maintenance of such children if they were to be chargeable to the Parish. One document of this nature ordered the father of the child to pay a sum of £2.13.4. "for and towards the lying-in of the said Mary Farr", and in addition ordered him to pay 1/4d weekly towards "the keeping, sustentation and maintenance of the child".[22] The mother was also ordered to pay 8d. per week to the Overseers until such time as the child was no longer chargeable. There is one instance in the Quarter Session Rolls where I noted that Thomas Gwatkin, farmer, of Orcop, was summoned to answer a complaint of a carpenter from Bridstow, that he had brought two children under the age of 7 years and left them at his house.[23] As so often happened with information that I found relating to Orcop in the Rolls, when checking the Rolls of the following sessions, nothing appeared to have been followed up from the original complaint. Possibly Thomas Gwatkin who was Churchwarden and Overseer in that year was seeking to apprentice the two children who were a charge on the parish.

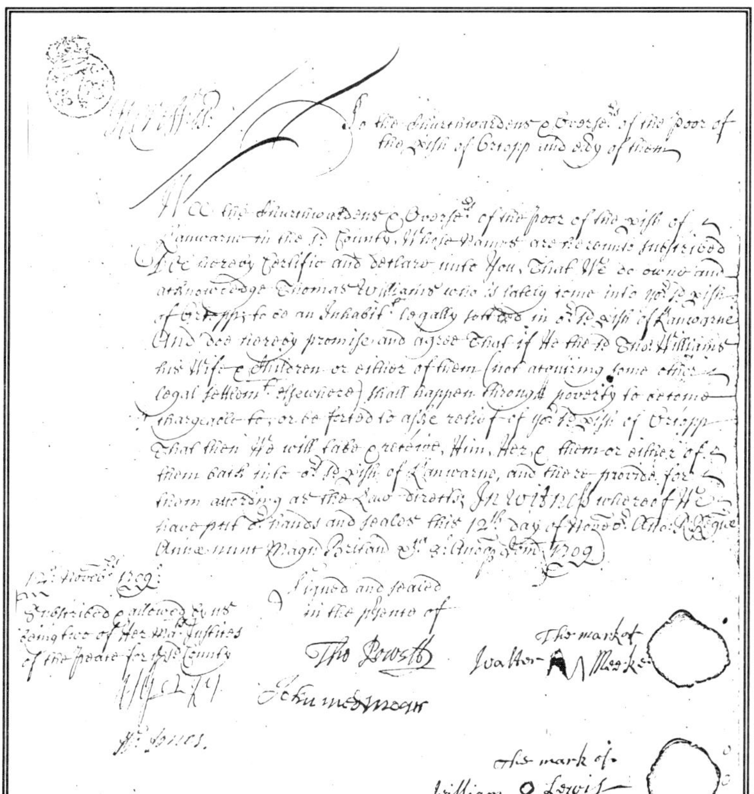
To the Churchwardens & Overseers of the poor of the parish of Orcopp and every of them

Wee the Churchwardens & Overseers of the poor of the parish of Llanwarne in the sd County whose names are hereunto subscribed Doe hereby Certifie and declare unto You, That Wee doe owne and acknowledge Thomas Williams who is lately come into yor parish of Orcopp to be an Inhabit legally settled in or parish of Llanwarne And doe hereby promise and agree That if He the sd Thos: Williams his Wife & Children or either of them (not attaining some other legal settlemt elsewhere) shall happen through poverty to become chargeable to, or be forced to aske relief of yor parish of Orcopp That then Wee will take & receive Him, Her, & them or either of them back into or parish of Llanwarne, and there provide for them according as the Law directs; In Witness whereof Wee have put or hands and seales this 12th day of Novembr Ano: Regni Annae nunc Magn Brittan &c 8: Anno Dom 1709

12o Novembr 1709
Subscribed & allowed by us being two of Her Ma: Justices of the peace for the sd County

Signed and sealed in the presence of

Tho Powell

John Medmore

The mark of Walter Meeke

His mark of William Lewis

*Copy of Settlement Certificate for Thomas Williams. Note the signature of one of the Justices, Henry Gorges of the Mynde, also the signature of one of the Orcop Overseers, John Medmore, (Meadmore).*

The Overseers often went to great lengths to ascertain the place of settlement for a pauper as instanced by one set of documents where the person concerned had been brought up by her uncle, a certificated person from another parish, until she was 13 years old, and then went to another parish as a servant for 2 years where her payment was her clothes and keep only, no wages being paid. Her uncle had 2 sons to whom he made over his cottage, one of whom hired himself for a year in another parish, returning later to his mother and father in Orcop. This son asked the girl, Ann James to come back to Orcop and look after his parents, offering her twenty shillings a year wages. She returned and after 11 months, the son was called to the Militia, but paid her twenty shillings wages. She continued in service for 2 years, only receiving 6/- from the other brother which was all he could afford. The question that worried the Overseers was –

> *"Did Ann James by this hiring and service to the son of a certificated person, mentioned in the certificate, who had gained a settlement in another parish, gain a settlement in Orcop?"*

The girl's uncle was examined by the magistrates, so also was she, and then a Counsel's opinion was sought, the expenses totalling £1.17.8. The opinion was –

> *"I think Ann James, under the circumstances of her hiring and service to William James, the son, gained a settlement in the parish of Orcop; the Certificate I conceive was discharged as to William James, by his having acquired a settlement in a third parish under his hiring and service in the parish of Garway. Therefore the pauper Ann James having been hired by him for a year in Orcop the certificated parish, and served for 2 years there, under the same hiring for ought that appears to the contrary, the service being chiefly for the purpose of looking after his father and mother, the master's absence, I apprehend will make no difference; or the master's paying her full wages a little before the expiration of the first year, there being no dissolution of the contract, will amount to a dispensation of the service, even tho' she had not completed her first year.*
>
> *Signed R. Phillips.*
>
> *24th August, 1801.*[24]

If an Order for Removal was appealed against by the parish to whom the paupers were to be sent, the case was taken to the Quarter Sessions in Hereford where a decision was arrived at; costs were sometimes awarded of ten shillings as under:-[25]

> *"Easter 1800. Removal Order St. Deveraux and Orcop. Thomas Embrey, Sara his wife, Ursula aged 6 years, and Maria, aged 3 years. To remove*

*from Orcop to St. Deveraux. On the appeal of the latter, the court do quash the order, and order the Churchwardens and Overseers of Orcop to pay to St. Deveraux the sum of ten shillings for their costs".*

Although the passing of the Workhouse Test Act of 1723 enabled parishes to unite together to build workhouses, the district around Orcop did not do so, relief being given through the Overseers in the parish, and parish houses being provided for the desperate cases. The Poor Law Act of 1834 put the administration on a national basis, and Orcop, with other neighbouring villages, joined the Dore Union.

The Boards of Guardians, which were constituted by the Poor Law Amendment Act of 1834 continued until they were abolished as from the 1st April 1930. The Dore Union consisted of 29 parishes, and was divided into 3 districts, Orcop belonging to the Kentchurch District. Each relieving officer or guardian had a book in which to record applications for relief and information about the applicant which was transferred to a report form to be put to the Board of Guardians which met weekly. On their report would be the following:-

*Name, age and occupation of applicant.*

*Opinion as to settlement.*

*Names, ages of family.*

*State of the house, which had to be visited by the local overseer to satisfy himself that the children lived with the pauper.*

*The earnings of family, any pensions or annuities.*

*Whether any relations were able to maintain the applicant.*

*Whether their condition was superior to a labourer.*

*Amount of rent paid, any lodgers, and whether any relief was being given to anyone else in the family.*

Each guardian was told to be very thorough in his check of his parish to see that no cases of real destitution existed. Out relief was not to exceed 2/6d per week, but 1/- to 2/- was allowed extra if attention of others was required as in the case of the totally disabled or infirm. This out relief was paid in advance weekly, in the Kentchurch district this was at Abbeydore (Dore), Wormbridge and Kentchurch, and applicants had to apply weekly. Extra nourishment could be authorised by medical officers who were appointed for each district. The salary of the medical officer for the Madley district was £60 per annum, plus 10/- for each midwifery case. At this time, 1837, the 4 lb. loaf was estimated to be equivalent to 8d. and mutton was 6½d. per lb.

The workhouse for the Dore Union was at Abbeydore (see photograph on page

168) and was built on just under 2 acres of land which cost £200. The cost of the building was in the region of £1580 since the original tender was for £1498 and a stable for 20 horses was later added at a cost of £78.[26] The type of out relief given was as follows, the instances quoted all refer to Orcop inhabitants.

| | |
|---|---|
| *Mary Rowbree.* | *Allowed 2/- weekly and bread value 2/- weekly.* |
| *Lucy Medmore.* | *1 lb. of mutton weekly being ill.* |
| *Sarah Hill.* | *2/- for 1 week, sons to show cause why they do not wish to support her, and later,* |
| *Sarah Hill.* | *Pay to be continued until sons appear before magistrates.* |
| *Lettice Hill.* | *To be allowed a pair of shoes.* |
| *Elizabeth Hill.* | *2/- for one week and 2 lbs. of mutton.* |
| *Thomas Morris.* | *15/- allowed for a shirt and a pair of boots.* |
| *Lucy Medmore.* | *4/- for fuel and 2 yards of flannel.* |

With regard to conditions in the workhouse itself, the Guardians tried to discharge their duties with as much humanity as possible. There are instances of bed clothing being delivered which was pronounced to be of inferior quality and ordered to be returned, and when tenders were advertised for 24 smock frocks, 24 coarse grey flannel waistcoats with sleeves and 24 trousers, the committee insisted on seeing the quality of the clothes before ordering. When the master reported that the butter supplied was of poor quality, the contractor was told his contract would be forfeit if the fault was not remedied. Those suffering from debility were allowed a pint of ale a day, and on one occasion the auditor took the committee to task for authorising a bottle of wine a week for 4 men suffering from malnutrition. Allowances were sometimes given for apprenticing pauper boys to master shoemakers, or for work on farms. Women and children were employed in knitting stockings of various sizes for the inmates for which they were paid 4d. to 6d. per pair. The first master and matron had a joint salary of £45 per annum, and were both to be capable of educating the boys and girls in useful knowledge and household works. Vagrants who were admitted and were journeying from one workhouse to another were given work to do in payment for shelter; the women cleaned the tramps ward while the men had to break up 1 cwt. of stone. They were not set to work on Sundays or wet days. One pauper who had been helping to instruct the children when leaving the workhouse was given clothes in lieu of wages which comprised 2 shirts, 1 hat, 1 neckerchief, 2 pairs of stockings, 1 pair shoes, coat, waistcoat and trousers. A check was kept on the way overseers discharged their duties; there was a pathetic case of the overseer from Madley being summoned before the Board for neglecting his duty in a case where a mother was found with her dead child lying destitute in a barn for 5 days without receiving relief, although he had been informed of her case.

Furniture and equipment which was ordered with a view to strength and durability consisted of wrought iron beds, flock mattresses and pillows, ash chairs, deal tables, iron pots and kettles, wooden trenchers, iron spoons, pint and half pint tin cans and knives and forks with "common bone handles". There were nine different types of diet, (children under 9 years to be dieted at discretion), and 3 meals per day. Old people of 60 and upwards were allowed 1 oz. of tea, 5 ozs. of butter, 7 ozs. sugar per week in lieu of gruel for breakfast. The bread ordered for a week for the out relief in the 3 districts and for the workhouse was in the region of 700 loaves. The menu for a week is set out below.

**Diet for Able Bodied men and women**

| | **Breakfast** | | **Dinner** | | | |
|---|---|---|---|---|---|---|
| | *Bread* ozs | *Gruel.* pts. | *Meat* ozs. | *Potatoes* lbs | *Soup* pts. | *Suet or Rice Pudg* ozs |
| ***Days of week*** | | | | | | |
| Sunday | 7 | 1½ | 5 | 1 | | |
| Monday | 7 | 1½ | | ½ | 1½ | |
| Tuesday | 7 | 1½ | | | | 14 |
| Wednesday | 7 | 1½ | | | | 14 |
| Thursday | 7 | 1½ | 5 | 1 | | |
| Friday | 7 | 1½ | | | | 14 |
| Saturday | 7 | 1½ | | ½ | 1½ | |

Women had 1 oz. less Bread for breakfast, and 2 ozs. less pudding.

| | **Supper** | | | |
|---|---|---|---|---|
| | *Bread.* ozs. | *Cheese.* ozs. | *Broth.* pts. | *Potatoes.* lbs. |
| ***Days of week*** | | | | |
| Sunday | | | 1½ | 1 |
| Monday | 6 | 1½ | | |
| Tuesday | 6 | 1½ | | |
| Wednesday | 6 | 1½ | | |
| Thursday | | | 1½ | 1 |
| Friday | 6 | 1½ | | |
| Saturday | | | 1½ | 1 |

Women had 1 oz. less Bread for supper.

Poverty in the district existed where there were large families; there are many instances of mothers with up to 6 children being admitted to the workhouse and remaining there for many weeks. In the books I checked through there were not many cases of Orcopians being admitted to the workhouse, and those that were, were usually elderly people. In the parish there were many Removal Orders which do not appear to have been enforced, and the rents charged by the Lord of the Manor for some of the cottages erected on the common were as low as 6d. or even 2d. per year, with some cases of several years in arrear before action was taken. Possibly Orcop's facilities for quarrying, coupled with the woodland and commonland enabled the poor to eke out an existence without frequent recourse to the Overseers and Guardians of the Poor Law.

***The Workhouse at Abbeydore, 1967. It is now converted into several dwellings.***

# Chapter Thirteen

## REFERENCES


| | | |
|---|---|---|
| 1. | – | Brydges Collection. Hereford City Library. |
| 2. | – | Charity Commissioners Reports. 1819-1837. Also Analytical Digest of Reports made by the Commissioners of Inquiry into Charities, 1841. |
| 3. | – | As Reference 2. |
| 4. | C.J. Robinson. | Manors and Mansions of Herefordshire. Also List of Orcop Chief Rents. Mynde Collection 5153. |
| 5. | – | Parish Register of Much Dewchurch. Years 1558-1745. |
| 6. | – | As Reference 2. |
| 7. | – | Amounts quoted in MSS notes of the Rev. N. Dredge. Lists from 1895 to 1913 in Parish Minute Book. In possession of Mr A.J. Morgan, Registrar, Pontrilas. |
| 8. | – | Copy of Court Roll dated 24th October 1808. Private Collection. |
| 9. | – | Index of Wills. Hereford City Library. |
| 10. | – | Visitations. Cathedral Archives, Hereford Cathedral. |
| 11. | – | Mynde Collection. 1123. |
| 12. | – | Mynde Collection. 961. |
| 13. | – | Parish Register of Orcop. From 1796 to 1812. |
| 14. | – | Orcop Church records. |
| 15. | – | Orcop Church records. |
| 16. | – | Orcop Church records. |
| 17. | – | Copy of Court Roll. 23rd October 1801. Private Collection. |
| 18. | – | Account found loose in Estate Rental book. Private Collection. |

19. – Mynde Rental book. Private Collection.

20. – Copy of Court Roll 4th November 1738. Private Collection.

21. – Orcop Church records.

22. – Orcop Church records.

23. – Quarter Session Rolls. May 1778. H.C.R.O.

24. – Orcop Church records.

25. – Quarter Session Rolls; Easter 1800. H.C.R.O.

26. – Minute Books of the Dore Union. April 1837 to March 1839. March 1839 to 1842. Vagrants Admission Register 1887-1888. Admission Register 1875-1877. Hereford County Record Office.

All the information quoted about the Dore Union Workhouse was taken from these books.

# Chapter Fourteen

## ASPECTS OF AGRICULTURE

Little is known of the agricultural history of the Archenfield district, although Marshall's "Rural Economy" of 1789 states that –[1]

> *"Herefordshire has been celebrated from time immemorial for a peculiar breed of sheep called the Ryeland sheep, from an indeterminent district named Archenfield in the southern quarter of the county. The Ryeland sheep are remarkable for the sweetness of their mutton, but still more for the fineness of their wool which may be said to rival that of the growth of Spain. If the Spaniards improved their wool by any breed of English sheep, it was most probably by that of the Ryeland of Herefordshire, not by that of the Cotswolds of Gloucestershire."*

The Wormelow manuscript states that the soil in Archenfield is generally sandy, and best adapted to the production of barley. This certainly does not apply to Orcop since the soil in many parts has up to 5 inches of heavy loam, with a clay sub soil. Certain parts of the parish, notably the Green and Lower Mill Farms, up to recent years, were considered the best corn farms since the soil was lighter, but the average soil is a heavy clay, best adapted for grass and wheat. The first chapter gave two indications of the quality and usage of the land at the end of the 18th and commencement of the 19th century. It had –

> *". . . a mixture of pretty large fields and small woods." (Cobbett, see page 19)*
>
> *It was also "cold and bare, and was probably cultivated but in a small degree a few centuries ago, being almost secluded from the rest of the world by high hills surrounding it on all sides, and on which cultivation seems to have been making a slow and laboured progress since it first commenced in the vale. There is very little coppice or meadow, and the latter is very inferior. The soil is a stiff reddish clay, and wheat the best adapted grain." (Wormelow MSS, see page 19).*

The Tithe Award Schedule of 1842 gives the apportionment of land as under:-

| | *Acres.* | *Roods.* | *Perches.* |
|---|---|---|---|
| *Arable Land* | *1000* | – | – |
| *Meadow and Pasture* | *934* | *2* | *38* |
| *Coppice Woods* | *165* | *2* | *37* |

***Mr and Mrs George Meadmore taken on the occasion of their Diamond Wedding anniversary, Sunday 30th April 1967.***

***The Meadmore family in 1959. The males, all resident in Orcop, represent four generations.***

Mr George Meadmore, who has lived in the village all his life, and was employed as a stone mason on the Mynde Estate for many years, before owning his own farm, Stradway, is in his late eighties, and has an excellent memory which has provided much information for this study. He tells me that before the turn of the century there was a great deal more land under the plough than today since farmers grew more corn for domestic needs and for their animals, whereas today imported grain is the general rule. He also remembers scything a 4 acre field of hay which took four days, and earned him 10/- for his labour! When working for the Estate he spent much of his time keeping the wall round the Mynde Deer Park intact, the stone coming, as it had always in the past, from quarries at the Saddlebow. Today, a great deal of the coppice wood has been reclaimed and used for pasture, whereas in the 1800s and up to the time of the Mynde Sale in 1916, the woodlands on most farms were reserved in the lease for the use of the Lord of the Manor. Coppice wood used to be in great demand, and was grown with a view to sale for hop-poles, fencing and fuel. The coppice on the Orcop part of the state was felled in rotation every 14 years, and usually comprised hazel, birch and alder; hazel and alder being very useful for hedging and making hurdles. A letter from the agent of the Estate in 1900 mentions that the Old Hall woods were due for felling, adding that the demand at that time was poor, so that it would be necessary to offer adjacent timber with it.[2] He was in negotiation for its sale, and hoped to obtain a sum of £200 which he suggested should be used for alterations to the mansion. This had been let on a long lease of 12 to 22 years, with the tenant paying a half share towards installation of heating, new bathroom, and considerable re-decoration of the hall, bedrooms, passages, kitchen etc. When the Estate was sold up in 1916, many of the farms had to honour agreements made for shooting rights at Orcop, and the timber valuation was assessed as part of the value of the farm.

*Stradway. The farm viewed from the back (north).*
*The least changed house and farm in the whole parish.*

The old leases in the Mynde Collection offer very little detail concerning size of farms, and it is only occasionally that the land is classified, but, where it is noted, the land mentioned is usually described as pasture and meadow. I feel that no definite conclusion can be reached by comparing land usage on farms in 1842, the date of the Tithe map, with the same land today, since it would appear from the old farm agreements and cottage agreements that the Estate was run efficiently with an eye to ensuring that the latest developments in convertible husbandry were carried out. Today, a field that is arable one year, will be pasture the next, so I have merely included two examples of farms for comparison. The Stradway farm which is one of the earliest farms mentioned by name in the Mynde collection, and which never belonged to the Mynde, (paying a Chief Rent instead to the Lord of the Manor), has varied very little from 130 years ago, its fields and hedges remaining almost the same, although the farmhouse is now disused. The Brooklands Farm or Old Shop as it used to be called, on the other hand, has expanded to take in the Bank and Pennant Farms, the farmhouses of which are now also empty and derelict, with many hedges being removed, maps on page 222.

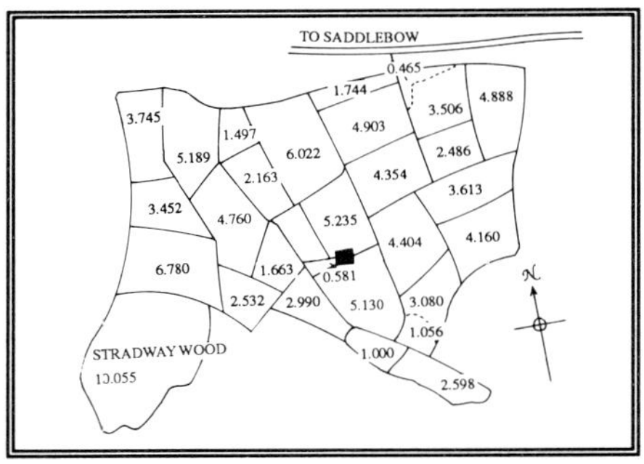


*Stradway Farm.*

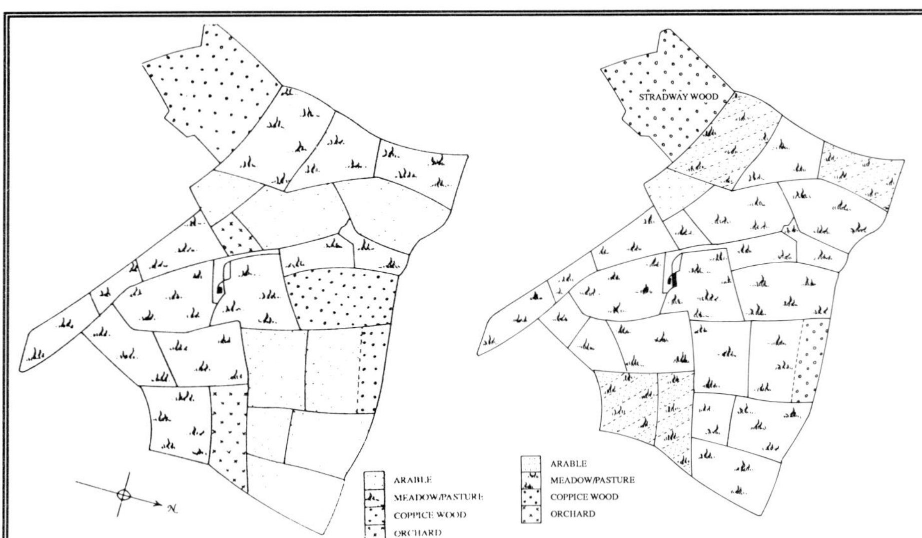


*Stradway as it is 1967 and as it was 1843.*

All these disused buildings are situated away from the road, with no amenities; they are extremely difficult of access in bad weather when the fields are waterlogged or snow comes. The farms, as sold in 1916, were larger than they are today, but partition came about in the 1920s when owners exchanged fields to make their holdings even more compact, and more equality in size was achieved. At the time of the Tithe Schedule the holdings were as follows:-

**Landowners Acreages**

| *Under 20.* | *20 to 50.* | *50 to 100* | *100 to 150* | *150 to 200.* | *Over 1000.* |
|---|---|---|---|---|---|
| 28 | 4 | 7 | 1 | 2 | 1 |

**Tenants**

| *1 to 5.* | *5 to 10* | *10 to 25.* | *25 to 50.* | *50 to 75.* | *75 to 100.* | *100 to 150* |
|---|---|---|---|---|---|---|
| 54 | 2 | 10 | 7 | 3 | 2 | 6 |

The process of piecemeal enclosure, as has been seen from the encroachments presented to the Court Barons, date back to 1663, and gathered momentum in the 18th century so that the only land that remained to be enclosed was 275 acres which is described as Common Land. This was allocated in 125 parcels of land as detailed on the schedules on pages 196/199. An authority has stated that there is little trace of the open field system in the county, and mentions the prevalence of several hamlets in most Herefordshire parishes, which would assist the amicable enclosure of fields much earlier than in other counties.[3] Orcop today is a village of scattered groups of dwellings, a pattern which has probably changed little from the past. It is difficult today to visualise that prior to the Enclosure Act of 1814/1824, the area of Coneygar Hill/Little Hill across Orcop Hill to Saddlebow was common or waste ground with very few buildings. When checking the Tithe Map I noticed that none of the fields is very large except two on the Cold Nose (White House) farm of 22 and 33 acres respectively, while some of the plots allotted on Garway Hill were very small. Much of the land was bought by the tenants of the Estate, and the land that was allocated to T.S.Symons was also divided into smallholdings and rented. It is a reasonable assumption that the old tradition of gavelkind persisted in the area which would also account for the constant breaking up of farm lands.

Some idea of the background to agriculture in the 18th century can be gained from the agreements made for leasing farms. One of these, which indicates the improved methods of farming, is between Sir Richard Symons and William Abrahall who took over land, of Edward Betham when he died in 1732 (see page 101).[4]

*"Land late of Betham, including messuage and farm with houses, outhouses,stables, gardens, orchards, folds, arable land and meadow, quarries of stone.*

*Abrahall must carry 90 lbs. of clover seed from the market and sow same at the rate of 9 lbs. of clover seed to each acre, 10 acres of clover to be sown.*

*Abrahall must from the New Year spread on the arable land 8 dozen barrels of lime in every year of the first three years.*

*Ten acres are to be ploughed for barley.*

*Allowance of £5 made out of the first year's rent in consideration of the poverty of the land.*

*Symons retained the right to stone from the quarry on the land as and when required.*

*Abrahall must manure the arable land, trench damp ground where needed, and keep it free from bushes, brambles and molehills.*

*He must use hay and straw and fodder produced in a proper and husbandlike manner. Reserve all fruit trees and plant crabstocks and graft same with good sorts of cider fruit in place of all that shall die on the said premises.*

*He must preserve all timber, trees, and trees likely to become timber.*

*The corn left on the farm at the takeover was to be threshed and kept by Richard Symons."*

This was a seven year lease at a rental of £28 per annum, and was sealed with Sir Richard's signet ring.

A farm agreement of 117 years later dated 27th October 1849, for the Old Hall Farm between Thomas George Symons, and Charles and John Barrell also makes interesting reading.[5]

*"The yearly rent of the farm which comprised 172 acres and 21 perches to be £85 payable half yearly.*

*The said Charles and John Barrell to use, manure and cultivate and crop the said farm and lands in a good husbandlike manner according to the custom of the County, and spend and consume the produce thereon, and to keep and leave the hedges, ditches and fences in good order and condition in all respects.*

*The said Charles and John Barrell to haul annually one load of çoals from the Forest of Dean, or two loads from the Tram House, at the option of the said Thomas George Symons, charging only the prime costs of the coals and turnpikes.*

*Also to keep one dog for the said Thomas George Symons without making any charge for same.*

*The said T.G. Symons reserves the exclusive right to the game on the said Estate, and further the said Charles and John Barrell agree to pay the sum of £20 as compensation for his allowing them the privilige of sowing at the present seeding time twenty acres of the arable land with wheat, such £20 to be paid on the 20th April next.*

*Lastly, it is agreed that Charles and John Barrell are to have the privilige on quitting the said farm of sowing one third of the arable lands with wheat as an offering crop with the usual privilige of harvesting and threshing out the same according to the custom of the county."*

An agreement, dated 1783, for the lease of Gillow Manor near Ross-on-Wye, from Sir Richard Symons (a farm which in recent years was one of the finest in South West Herefordshire, and which changed hands in 1964 for more than £100,000), showed that the value of coal at that time was £2.10.0. a wagon load since it stated the rent to be £200 per year, plus 2 good wagon loads of coal, or £5 in lieu thereof.[6] The turnpike fees from the Forest of Dean were about 6/- on a load. Tenants of cottage holdings also guaranteed to cultivate and manure their gardens in a proper and husbandlike manner, to keep the fences, hedges and the glass windows in good repair.

***Old Hall Farm***

***Cruck Barn at the Old Hall Farm***

The Quarter Sessions Order Books give details of the wages payable each year to workers in agriculture. The following are the wages appointed for the year commencing Easter 1735.[7]

| | | | |
|---|---|---|---|
| Every servant waggoner or bayliff in husbandry by the year | £4 | 10 | 0 |
| Every second servant in husbandry | 3 | 10 | 0 |
| Every servant boy from 11 to 14 years of age | 1 | 0 | 0 |
| Every servant boy from 14 to 18 years of age | 1 | 10 | 0 |
| Every Head servant maid in dairy or cookery | 2 | 10 | 0 |

| | | | |
|---|---|---|---|
| Every Head servant maid in dairy or cookery | 2 | 10 | 0 |
| Every second servant maid | 2 | 0 | 0 |
| Labourers by the day | | | 8 |
| Every mower or keeper in Hay in Corn Harvest | | 1 | 0 |
| And without drink | | 1 | 2 |
| Weeders of Corn with drink | | | 4 |
| And without drink | | | 5 |
| Every woman in corn harvest with drink | | | 5 |
| And without drink | | | 6 |
| Every woman in haymaking, sorting beans or picking fruit with drink | | | 5 |
| And without drink | | | 6 |
| Every carpenter, wheelwright, plasterer, mason and thatcher with drink, winter and summer | | 1 | 0 |
| And without drink | | 1 | 2 |

In the 1880s wages for agricultural labourers were about 12/- per week as quoted by the Rev. Arthur Gray (page 249), and by 1901 the average wage of Herefordshire agricultural workers was 13/11d which had increased to 14/2½d. in 1912. The hours of labourers were from 6.0 a.m. to 6.0 p.m. with 1½ hrs. for 2 meals, breakfast and dinner. Waggoner's hours were generally from 5.0 a.m. to 7.0 p.m. during the winter to enable the horses to be fed and cleaned ready for work at 7.0 a.m. By 1914 the following schedule had been drawn up due to the establishment of branches of the National Agricultural Workers Union founded in 1872 by Joseph Arch, who was an agricultural worker, and a non-conformist preacher. His grace ran –

*"O, Heavenly Father, bless us,*

*And keep us all alive,*

*There are ten of us to dinner,*

*And food for only five."*

A Branch of the Union was formed at Orcop, but I do not know at what date. At neighbouring St. Weonards, the Vicar took the chair at a general meeting and urged the agricultural workers to unite as the only effective way of improving their conditions.

***1914. Schedule of wages.***

*Hours for general workers should be 6 weeks before Christmas and 6 weeks after, work from 7.0 a.m. to 5.0 p.m,. with hour for dinner, 54 hour week, wages 18/- per week.*

*Summer hours, the rest of the year, work from 6.0 a.m. to 6.0 p.m. with 1½ hours for meals. Wages 20/- per week. Waggoners 75 hours a week summer, 59 hours in winter, including Sundays. Half holiday weekly. Cowmen and Shepherds, 59 hours per week, winter and summer.*

Prior to 1914, some labourers had allocations of potato ground in the farmer's field, perhaps a quart of skimmed milk, two or three quarts of cider per day and a load of wood calculated to be worth 2/- to 3/- per week. Cottages were usually "free" to stockmen, but they had to work one or two hours extra daily, and part of Sunday, for no extra pay, in many cases. The ordinary labourer paid 1/6d to 2/6d per week rent out of his wages, but he was not legally acknowledged by law as the tenant.[8]

Tea in the early 1900s was a great luxury, loaves of bread were usually of the 4 lb. variety, butter was very salt to enable it to be kept through the winter, and lard on bread was a common meal. Those working in the fields took toast and cider with them for sustenance. Most farms and larger cottages had cider mills, and many of the houses in Orcop still show traces of the old bake ovens; one can be seen on the end wall of the chapel house at Orcop Hill, (see photograph page 230). A photograph of a cider mill can be seen on page 206. This is situated at the Stradway farm, and was in use until the early 1950s. The farmhouse was finally vacated in 1956.

Mr George Meadmore built many brick ovens in the cottages of the Mynde Estate. These ovens were beautifully constructed with a domed arch of bricks, and much skill was required to enable them to survive so many firings. The oven had to be heated by burning the fuel inside it; apart from the door there is no outlet in the brick oven; the chimney is at the front, just outside the oven door and when the fuel is burning the door is left open for the smoke to escape. It would take about an hour for a brick oven to become properly heated for the dough, and the housewife could tell, by either throwing a little flour against the side of the oven which would blaze up, or by just putting her hand above the ashes, when it was ready. Before the dough went into the oven, the ash would be scraped out and stowed in a hole beneath.

***A line drawing of the old brick fire oven at Stradway Farm built by George Meadmore.***

The Estate employed its agent who reported on repairs needed to farms, on the general state of the land, and also on enclosures. There exists in the Mynde collection a list of repairs which has been attributed to the 18th century, and from which one gains some idea of the buildings which were an important part of farming at that time, but which have now disappeared or been utilised for other purposes.[9]

| | |
|---|---|
| *"Hendrie (Hendre).* | *Dairy window wants wiring, granary wants flooring, tiling and pointing. Malt kiln wants repairs, cyder mill wants repairs.* |
| *Burnet Farm.* | *House – one end of roof of house quite rotten, to be repaired and the floors also. Granary wants tiles here and there. Stone stairs to be repaired. Barn, thatched roof to be repaired. Wainhouse wants thatching. Beast house wants a door. Wagonhouse very much out of repairs as well as barn.* |

***The Burnet Farm, 1992. The original building was mentioned in an old Lease at the time of Henry VII when the rent was 9/6d. per year, the tenant paying suit to the Manor Court, and a heriot to the Lord. This farm as it stands today was probably the farm which Thomas Abrahall built with stones taken from the quarry without the leave of the Lord of the Manor. It stands on Orcop Hill.***

| | |
|---|---|
| *Green Farm (Page 193)* | *Wagon house roof to be repaired. Beast shed wants tiling. Goose and pig cot wanted.* |
| *Saddlebow Farm (Adjacent to the parish).* | *North foundation tumbling. Davies will do his part for £4.10.0. the mason will do his part for £3.6.0. and the thatcher will do his part for £8.0.0."* |

The Saddlebow Farm was farmed by James Pugh in 1851. The Census shows that, at that time, he farmed 250 acres, and employed 50 labourers, although it is possible that this figure would include those employed on casual labour at harvest and sowing periods, since even allowing for non-mechanisation, this seems a very high number of employees. An old account exists, dated 1828, from a haulier who had been hauling materials required for repairs at the Saddlebow Farm. His charges were as follows:-[10]

| | | | |
|---|---|---|---|
| Halling lath stuff out of Penstone Wood (Much Dewchurch) 2 days at 12/- per day | £1 | 4 | 0 |
| 520 feet of paving, about 9 cart loads at 3/6d per load | 1 | 11 | 6 |
| 12 tons of timber from different parts of the farm to the sawpit at 8/- per ton. | 4 | 16 | 0 |
| 165 yards of stone from the Butts Quarry at 2/-per yard. | 16 | 10 | 0 |
| 4 wagon loads of lime from the Doward Hills at £1.12.0.per load, turnpike included. | 6 | 8 | 0 |
| 5 card loads of strong stuff for the granary steps at 3/6d per load. | | 17 | 6 |

In 1864 stone was still being risen from the Quarry Farm at Orcop, and I have found two fragments of accounts which were rendered to the Estate by the mason and labourer respectively.[11]

***1864 April 27.***

*(The labourer's account).*

*An account of stone rose by Thomas Evans at Quarry Farm.*

| | | | |
|---|---|---|---|
| 1632 feet of paving sills and blocks at 8/- per 100 | 6 | 10 | 6 |
| 3 quarters of Tile at 9/- per 1000 | | 6 | 9 |
| Wallstone 45 yards at 9/- per yard. | 1 | 13 | 9 |
| Making road, 1 day. | | 2 | 0 |
| Recd. May 7th 1864. | £8 | 13 | 0 |

The mark of Thomas Evans.

The other account has been torn, but the 1632 feet of paving sills and blocks risen by Thomas Evans was dressed, (pointed and measured) by the mason, James Phillips, at a cost of 4/- per 100 feet.

*The photograph taken from 'X' on map below. The field in foreground covers the quarry from whence was raised the paving stones and flagstones.*

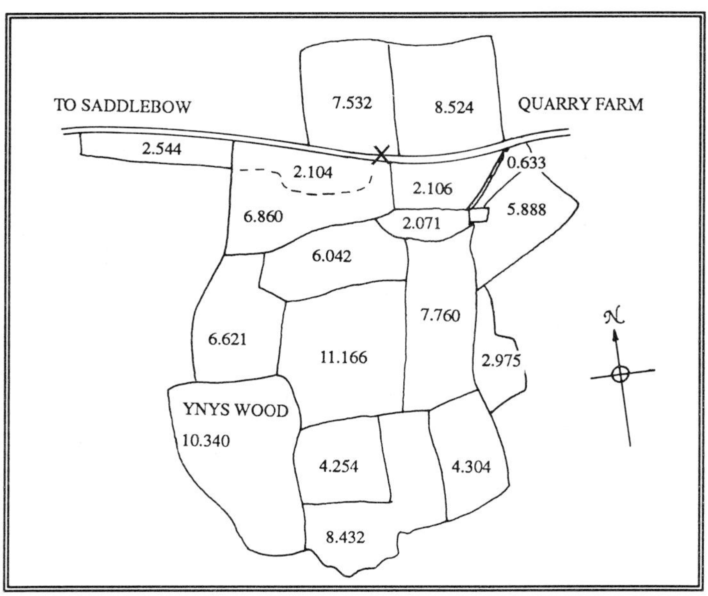


*Quarry Farm, 1843.*

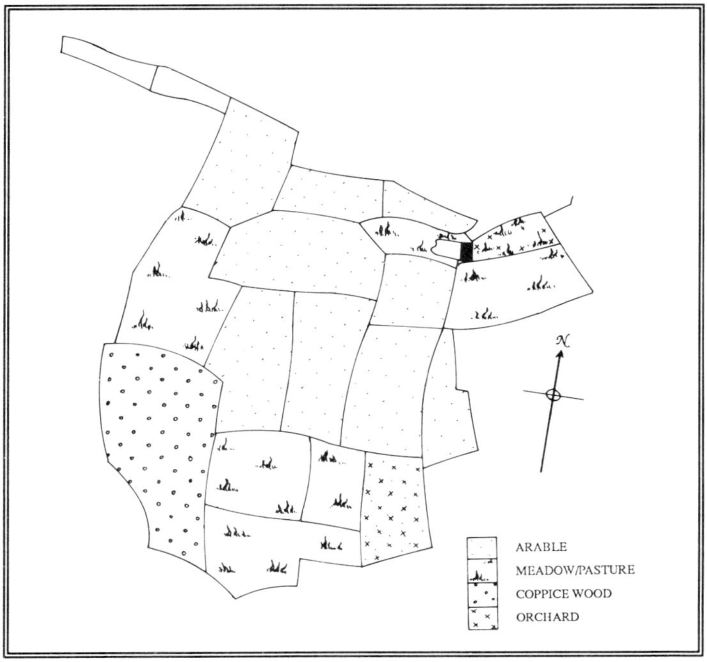


*Quarry Farm, 1967.*

*Quarry Farm, 1992.*

Allowances were given in lieu of rent by the Estate for drainage using stone and turf at 1/- and 6d a perch respectively, for white-washing buildings, for grafting fruit trees and hauling bark to the Mynde, for turnpike fees and property tax.

In 1830 the price of hurdles was 14/- per dozen, and the price of hop poles 9/- per hundred.[12] Other prices in the 1820s for repairs at farms are as follows:-

| | £ | s | d |
|---|---|---|---|
| Thatching a shed | | 12 | 0 |
| Making 10 new gates | 1 | 5 | 0 |
| Hanging 11 gates | 1 | 7 | 6 |
| A cider Mill | 10 | 4 | 0 |
| New press for a cider mill | 1 | 0 | 0 |
| Planting 3 dozen crabstocks | 3 | 0 | 0 |

On the death of a tenant or expiration of lease the Estate often bought certain fittings to go with the cottage, some are instanced below:-[13]

| | | | |
|---|---|---|---|
| Bacon cratch (a type of suspended crib for hanging bacon) | | 4 | 0 |
| Dresser and shelves | | 2 | 0 |
| Salting stone | | 6 | 0 |
| Bucket and chain for well | | 4 | 0 |
| Furnace | | 10 | 0 |
| Ironing Stove | | 6 | 0 |
| 4 door locks | | 5 | 0 |
| For fruit trees, planting and grafting | 2 | 6 | 0 |
| Pigs cot | 5 | 0 | 0 |
| 3 iron bolts | | 2 | 3 |
| A new grate and fixing | 2 | 0 | 0 |

I have checked through a book which deals with repairs and improvements made to farms in Orcop from 1894 to 1904, and this shows the costs of materials and wages paid. A few instances are quoted below.[14]

*The Bank Farm.* (see photograph, page 185). Now disused.

***1894***

*Fold yard wall rebuilt. Granary steps repaired. New goose cubs, foundations, timber built and covered with enamelled plates. General repairs to roofs of barn, open shed, stable and house*

*Labour 47 days* *£8 4 6*

*(Goose cubs meant pens for geese).*

| | | | |
|---|---|---|---|
| *Barn roof part stripped and covered with galvanised iron. 10 sheets.* | *1* | *0* | *0* |
| *New granary floor and rails to steps, new partition for house (see plan page 186)* | | | |
| *New stable door 6/8d new fold gate and posts 23/-* | *1* | *9* | *8* |
| *2 new gates 28/- 3 posts 14/-* | *2* | *2* | *0* |

***1901.***

| | | | |
|---|---|---|---|
| *2 new five barred gates* | *1* | *10* | *0* |
| *Kitchen ceiling and bedroom ceilings plastered, kitchen and bedrooms white-washed, barn roof repaired.* | | | |
| *Labour. H. Hartwell 14 days at 3/6d.* | *2* | *9* | *0* |
| *G. Meadmore 13 days at 2/4d.* | *1* | *11* | *4* |

***1903.***

| | | |
|---|---|---|
| *Bedroom windows repaired.* | | |
| *6 panes glass = 10" square, 4 ft. at 3½d.* | *1* | *2* |
| *6 panes glass = 9" square, 3 ft. at 3½d.* | | *9* |
| *30 feet deal 1¾ x ¼" for repairing casements.* | *1* | *3* |
| *W. Davies, 2 days at 3/-* | *6* | *0* |

***Bank Farm. All that remains of the farm houses and buildings. The last occupant of both was William Trotman Smith. Now forms part of Brooklands Farm.***

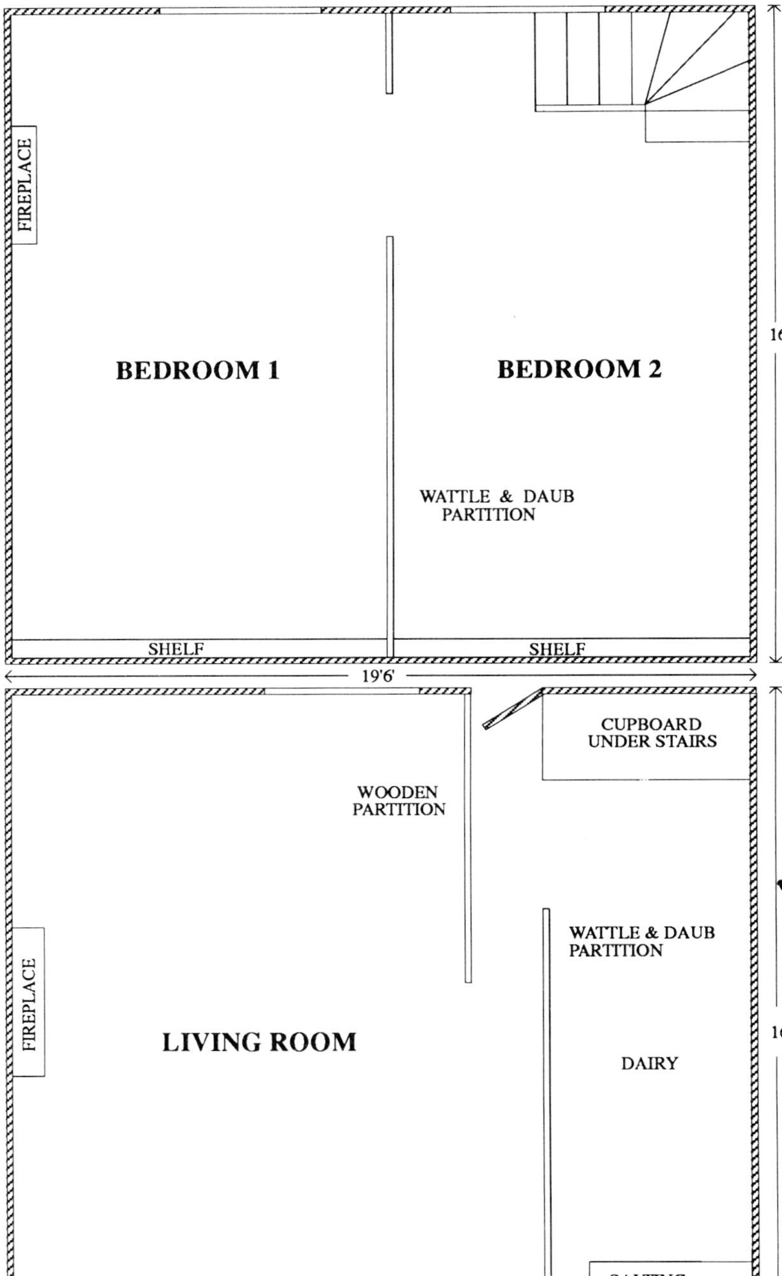


*Plan of Bank Farm.*

*The Cave, Orcop.* (see photograph page 215). Now disused.

***1900***

| | | |
|---|---|---|
| *1 falling post for garden gate* | *2* | *6* |
| *3 red deal boards 7' long x 1'9" at 2d ft.* | *3* | *6* |
| *Stuff for 2 window frames 2' x 2' each* | *2* | *0* |

***1902***

| | | |
|---|---|---|
| *Sides fixed to porch, 2 larch uprights 7' x 4' 3"* | *1* | *2* |
| *6' 6" run matchboarding* | *2* | *5* |

*The Pennant,* (see photograph page 188). Now disused.

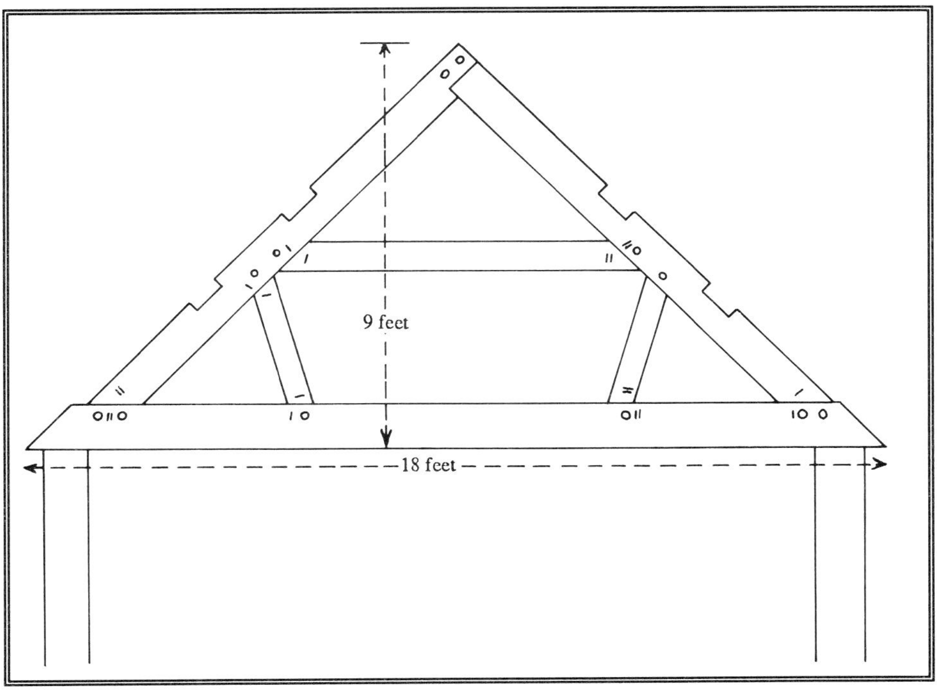


***The barn at the Pennant made of adze-hewn timber, tied with wooden pegs. The assembly marks of the carpenter can be seen quite clearly; a series of matching chisel cuts I and II in pairs. The whole structure is a perfect right angled triangle. There are two sets, one at the east end, and one in the middle, the other end being supported on stone walling.***

***1895***

*Pulled down old thatched ridge roof against house and put up galvanised iron lead to shed divided into coal house, pigscot and stable for horse and cow.*

| | | | |
|---|---|---|---|
| *Edwin Morgan, Labour.* | *5* | *0* | *0* |
| *16 – 7' sheets galvanised iron) 8 – 6' sheets )* | *2* | *2* | *10* |
| *Boards, 3 square 12/-* | *1* | *16* | *0* |
| *6 enamelled plates, 100 ft. of 3'/2", 6/3d. 3 doors 21/-, slabs 8/-, posts 18/- hinges 4/- nails 3/-* | *3* | *0* | *3* |

***The Pennant Farm – now forms part of Brooklands Farm.***

***1897***

*Both sides of roof of house stripped and covered with angular Bridgewater tiles, new timber in roof where necessary, walls rebuilt and repaired. Chimney rebuilt.*

| | | | |
|---|---|---|---|
| *J. Davies and boy, 48 days at 4/6d.* | *10* | *16* | *0* |
| *(Josiah Davies was one of the village blacksmiths).* | | | |
| *A. Hartwell 30 days at 3/6d.* | *5* | *5* | *0* |
| *J. Morris 45 days at 3/4d.* | *7* | *10* | *0* |
| *Materials for this work.* | *27* | *1* | *4* |

*(Included 20 plastering laths and 200 match board nails 5/-, oak sill 3' x 4" x 3½", 1/- and 900 red triangular tiles £7.10.9.)*

An interesting point here is that the stone for chimney and walls cost £2 and was brought from the original Lower Butts building which was, by this time, not in use.

***1893. Camdore Farm (see photogaphs, pages 218 and 219)***

| | | | |
|---|---|---|---|
| *Granary roof stripped and covered galvanised iron.* | | | |
| *Labour Mason 18/- Carpenter £1.7.6.* | *2* | *5* | *6* |
| *New granary floor 31' x 17' = 5' sq.ft at 14/- and handrail to steps, 1" red deal tongued and grooved.* | *3* | *13* | *0* |

| | | | |
|---|---|---|---|
| *Stripping large portion of barn roofs and covering with galvanised iron.* | | | |
| *Total iron used.* | *34* | *12* | *8* |
| *Carpenter's labour* | *9* | *7* | *0* |
| *Mason's labour, plastering granary, repairing roofs and spring* | *5* | *3* | *0* |

The size of the granary and barns can be seen by the aerial photograph. This farm remains obscure in its origins; it has the appearance of having, at one time, been a much larger residence. It has a walled garden, the remains of a huge fishpool, and fields bearing the names of Hopyard Orchard, Fishpond Orchard, The Lawn, Oldhouse Field and Shrubbery Orchard. The Deeds only date to 1916 when the Mynde Estate was sold.

With regard to prices of foodstuffs, Duncumb gives prices as follows:-

| | *1691* | *1740* | *1760* | *1804* |
|---|---|---|---|---|
| *Wheat per bushel of 10 gallons.* | *3/-* | *3/-* | *3/-* | *10/6* |
| *Butcher's Meat per lb.* | | *1½d* | *1½d* | *7d* |

A letter from the Mynde's agent, Thomas Harvey to Thomas Raymond Symons shows that prices in 1808 were very much higher, due, no doubt, to the war in Europe.[15]

***"23rd May 1808.***

> *I instructed Morgan to buy wheat and oats according to your order. Wheat is up to 30/- and 31/- a bushel of 10 gallons, and other grain nearly in proportion, and the meat market has advanced in price considerably, beef 7½d, mutton 8d, and veal 10d. per lb."*

Some more fragments of bills I have found show prices of hay and meal. I have given average prices as today for comparison.

| | *1864.* | *1966 (last harvest).* |
|---|---|---|
| *1 ton of Hay* | *£4* | *Average price £13 to £14* |
| *1 cwt of Bran* | *7/-* | *28/- to 29/-* |
| *1 sack of flour (usually 2½ cwts).* | *32/6d* | *£2 per cwt.* |

Another small account dated 18th April 1849 gives the following prices –

| | |
|---|---|
| *Wheat* | *14 bushels at 5/6d.* |
| *Potatoes* | *3 bushels at 3/-* |
| *Peas* | *½ bushel at 3/6d.* |

The yield of corn to the acre was as follows:-

| **1600**[16] | **1771**[17] | **1939** | **1967** |
|---|---|---|---|
| *8 to 10 bushels* | *24 bushels* | *40 bushels average* | *60 to 80 bushels average (depending on season.)* |

The increase in yield is due partly to better seed, but in the main to the excellence of fertilisers which are improving yearly.

The Enclosure Award for Orcop was officially completed on the 24th July 1824, although the first meeting had been held at the Mitre, Hereford on 23rd July 1814. The awards are listed on pages 196 to 199 together with maps showing the position of the land which was on Orcop and Garway Hills. Some of the Deeds of the land on Garway Hill give particulars of the amount paid to the Commissioners of Enclosure for the various awards.

| | a | r. | p |
|---|---|---|---|
| ***Plot*** *45* | | *3* | *28* |
| *56* | *1* | *1* | *20* |
| *119* | *3* | *2* | *12* |
| *120* | *6* | *2* | *0* |

***The grave of Abraham Baker, died 17th January 1827.***

These four plots were sold to Abraham Baker, (who, in his will, refers to himself as a yeoman), for £147.15.0. He also had 5 other plots which gave him a total of some 25 acres. He died on 17th January 1827. Later on, his son, another Abraham Baker, purchased plot 118 from James Probert, measuring 6 acres 1 rood 38 perches, for £50; this had been bought by his father John Probert on the 12th February 1820 for £66.0.0.[18]

An examination certificate in the Church records shows that William Ralph on 18th July 1826, made the following declaration:-

*". . . that he is sixty nine years of age or thereabouts, and that in the year 1817 he purchased two pieces of land about 3 acres of the Commissioners*

*of Enclosure of Common Land in the parish of Orcop at the sum of £63.0.0."*

This would be plot 64 measuring 3 acres 2 roods 30 perches. Entries in the book containing Cottage Agreements show that in 1829 William Ralph was occupying a cottage on Garway Hill, while on 1st August 1826 the following agreement reads –[19]

> *"I, Elizabeth Abrahams agree to rent the cottage, garden and plock of land, situated on Garway Hill, lately disputed between Old Ralph and myself, at the yearly rent of £3 per annum."*

The Estate Rent Book shows that 1842 was the last year in which "Old Ralph's" rent was recorded as "being paid by the Parish", and the rental of 5/- per year was 10 years in arrear. It appears that having paid quite a sum of money for his ground, old Ralph fell on hard times, and ended his life as a pauper.

Another examination certificate dated 22nd July 1824, and sworn before John Duncomb, the eminent Herefordshire historian, concerns Samuel Eames who was 31 years old at this time, and a stone mason. He was sufficiently ill to be a patient in the General Infirmary at Hereford, and since he had a wife and 3 children, was likely to be in need of help from the parish overseers. It was necessary for him to prove that he had a settlement in Orcop to be eligible for such help.

He related that his uncle, Samuel Watkins who was also a stone mason, had fetched him from Bristol about 1792 when he was a baby, and brought him to Orcop where he had lived ever since. Although he had not been apprenticed to Samuel, he had obviously learnt his trade from him. At the time of his illness he had been buying a piece of land and building a house on it. The plot was number 24 on the Orcop Hill Enclosure Map, and although it was allotted to him, another person took it over together with an adjoining plot so possibly his illness prevented him from completing the purchase. The purchase price was £29, of which he had paid £9, and the house was three parts completed.

Samuel and his wife stayed in the parish living mostly on Orcop Hill, but by 1835 he had built a cottage on Garway HIll, and was listed in the Register of Electors for that year as being the owner of a a freehold property there. This property is Dingle Cottage, previously called Suckling Dingle, and was built on a plot of land carved out from award number 102, originally allocated to Joseph Terret who owned the tithes (see page 135). In the 1851 Census it was occupied by JohnWatkins, Samuel's cousin, to whom he had leased it some years earlier.

Samuel Eames' wife died in 1855 aged 56, and sometime after that he emigrated to America with several of his children. A descendant for whom I was able to trace the above story, writes that he died 2 months after arrival, that the whole family were very much homesick, and several of his grandchildren died of smallpox. His uncle, Samuel Watkins, died at the grand old age of 94, at Garway Hill in 1849.

The prices of land do not appear to be based on a uniform rate per acre, so, presumably, the site and quality of land governed the price set. An interesting point here is that one of the Commissioners for the Inclosure was James Cranston of Kings Acre, Hereford, and I note on looking through one of the old Estate books that young trees were purchased from Cranston's Nurseries in 1895 for replenishing the woods on the Estate. On checking this, I find that the Cranston family ran the Kings Acre Nurseries at Whitecross, Hereford, for well over a century, the business changing hands in the early 1920's, and today, the Wyevale Nurseries use part of the old nursery land. The soil in that area is very fertile, particularly well suited to fruit trees, and the nursery gave its name to well known varieties of fruit, among them the "Kings Acre Pippin", and the owner's name is perpetuated, as gardeners will know, in the onion named "Cranston's Excelsior." Since the other Commissioner was a surveyor, the work of measuring presumably was his concern, while the "heart" of the land was valued by Mr Cranston. While the small enclosures, made by cottagers on the common, were formally presented to the Court Baron, and gradually became part of the rental of the Mynde Estate without recourse to law, there is one instance which shows that Thomas Symons did proceed against one of the freeholders. First, the letter written by the Agent to Mr Symons.[21]

***"23rd May 1808.***

*I have been over the common of Orcop with Brown. Mr Parry has just completed the fences of his last inclosure, and was seen to assist personally in making the fence. I think it may be advisable to commence the action of trespass against him for this offence, and to serve his tenant of the farm inclosure with a declaration. I had an interview with Parry on the subject, and informed him that if he did not immediately throw open his last inclosure an action would certainly be commenced without the least delay. He did not say positively that he would or would not do so, but proposed that all inclosures should be thrown open. We had a very calm conversation.*

*I find the inclosure made by the Farr's to be very detrimental to Powell's farm, and it should certainly be removed. Griffiths is willing to make an acknowledgement for his small additional inclosure at Saddlebow."*

A copy of Counsel's opinion reads as under:-[22]

*"No freeholder has a right to build or inclose on the commons without the permission of the Lord of the Soil who in this case, appears to be the Lord of the Manor. As to raising stones, the right claimed by Parry and the freeholders, may rest in point of law and the question will be a question of*

*evidence upon the usage. I think Mr Symons should put a stop to Parry's. In an action of trespass he may include the whole, the trees, the buildings, the inclosures and the stones, and therefore I think that action preferable to an ejectment. No advice can be given respecting the evidence till it is seen what plea Parry puts on the record to maintain what he has done, except that it will be necessary for Mr Symons to prove a possession of the wastes, which he may do by producing and proving his Court books, his letting the quarries and other acts of ownership on the waste.*

*No step is necessary to be taken previous to the commencement of proceedings against Parry, as Parry has, I presume an undoubted right of common of pasture over the wastes. He may throw down all inclosures made within these 20 years except they have been made under the authority of the Lord and can be protected under the Statute of Morton, a sufficiency of Common having been left."*

I am not certain where Parry lived as there were several in the parish at this time, but a certain Thomas Parry was presented at Court Barons in 1801, 1805 and 1808, for encroachments on the waste of Orcop and Garway Hills, for building 3 cottages, and for not keeping a certain footbridge in repair near the Lower House Farm on Garway Hill. If this was the same man, he must have been causing quite a nuisance to the Lord of the Manor! There is a Lower Moors farm on Garway Hill, but no Lower House Farm, although there is a High House farm, so perhaps this is another case of a homestead which has since disappeared.

***The Green Farm.***

The impact of mechanisation was making itself felt in farming methods before 1950. The first farm tractor in Orcop was bought by Mr Alan Thomas, of the Green Farm, in 1940. The Green Farm also had the first motor car, a famous T-model Ford. His farm of 112 acres, which 30 years before had been run by the owner with two workers and occasional casual labour, could now be run by the owner together with his son, later on by himself, with occasional casual labour at harvest time. The horse driven single furrow plough was replaced by the tractor drawing 3 and 4 furrow ploughs, and the enclosed fields have given way to the larger fields of between 10 and 15 acres by the rooting out of hedges enabling the tractor to turn more advantageously, reducing waste "headland" and completing its work far quicker and more efficiently. Many farmers in Orcop turned over to dairy farming, and later to general mixed farming when labour became harder to obtain, and electric milking machines made the milking routine far less onerous. Stock farming, i.e. the raising of cattle for beef, also gives the farmer more leisure because he can take the odd day off without the need to be present for milking. The lack of farm labour was due to several factors. Families over the last 20 years have been smaller, and the rising standard of living has enabled those young couples who wished to remain in the village to save more and buy or rent the smaller farms and smallholdings when the opportunity arose. Over the last 12 years these people, now in their late 30s or early 40s have become their own masters, and manage comfortably by skilful working of acreages of between 20 and 40 acres. The monthly milk cheque is a sheet anchor, while keeping of stock, even in the fluctuating price periods, still brings in a steady income. The introduction of government subsidies for farming also gave much incentive to all farmers.

*The War Memorial made of local sandstone and situated at the crossroads by the Green Farm. There was some dispute as to its siting when erected; church, chapel and secular interests being at loggerheads.*

*It was damaged in 1964, being broken in three places, and was repaired, ironically enough by a man of German nationality.*

The subsidies and introduction of mechanical ploughing resulted in the successful reclaiming of wood-land for pasture and crops. Orcop is a prosperous agricultural community, all farms or small holdings are run by their owners or tenants with family help, and the need for a permanent agricultural lab-ourer attached to the farm, is a thing of the past. The only farm that employs regular casual labour is one that specialises in prepacked poultry, the Ynys (see photograph page 216). The business commenced in 1955, has its own processing and refrigerating plant, and deals with about 2,000 birds per week, rising to a peak figure of 8,000 to 10,000 birds over the Christmas period. The labour for this work is supplied by housewives, and the wives of some of the small farmers who work on an hourly basis.

Agriculture today is worthwhile for the farmer working on his own, but for the agricultural labourer who 15 years ago was paid at the rate of £4.10.0. per week, and today still only receives £9.15.0. basic wage, it offers little incentive or reward. I should like to end this chapter with the following quotation relating to another part of the country, (East Anglia).[23]

*"Farming is the basic rural industry, and it is probable that when the history of the countryside in the twentieth century comes to be written, the revolution in agriculture especially the application*

*to it of the internal combustion engine, will be considered the chief agent in the final break up of the old community.*

*No farmworker of the present day would wish to go back to the old conditions, and no thinking person would advocate a return to the old domination of squire or near-squire, that most villagers have suffered in the past. But the fact has to be met that the old community was organic, at however low a level; and since its fragmentation, village life, and therefore, the life of the nation, has suffered because nothing comparable has taken its place."*

The writer, George Ewart Evans, is a Welshman who became a village headmaster in Suffolk some years ago. His books on the country scene make fascinating reading, and he has been instrumental in making present day historians aware of the importance of recording oral reminiscences before it is too late.

***A view taken from the Quarry Farm adjacent to Stradway Farm on Orcop Hill***

# ORCOP ENCLOSURE AWARD, 1814 TO 1824.

| *Name.* | *Plot Number.* | *Measurement.* | | |
|---|---|---|---|---|
| | | *a.* | *r.* | *p.* |
| Isaac Butts Price. | 1 | | 2 | 4 |
| Isaac Butts Price. | 2 | | 2 | 19 |
| David Widow. | 3 | | | 6 |
| Isaac Butts Price. | 4 | 1 | 1 | 28 |
| Thomas Powell. | 5 | | | 8 |
| Mrs Hanley. | 6 | | | 20 |
| T.H. Symons. | 7 | | | 37 |
| Nathaniel Prosser. | 8 | | | 11 |
| T.H. Symons. | 9 | | | 5 |
| John James. | 10 | | | 8 |
| James Price. | 11 | | | 30 |
| John Hughes. | 12 | | | 6 |
| James Elliott. | 13 | | | 7 |
| John Holly. | 14 | | | 35 |
| John Grindall. | 15 | 1 | 1 | 9 |
| James Williams. | 16 | | | 25 |
| Thomas Nash. | 17 | | 3 | 23 |
| T.H. Symons. | 18 | | | 34 |
| Abraham Whittaker. | 19 | | 1 | 3 |
| Abraham Whittaker. | 20 | | | 20 |
| William Griffiths. | 21 | 2 | 3 | 13 |
| T.H. Symons. | 22 | 1 | 1 | 9 |
| – Williams. | 23 | | 1 | 35 |
| Samuel Eames later Thomas Williams. | 24 | 2 | 2 | 0 |
| Simon Woodall and Jonathan Rudge. | 25 | | 2 | 35 |
| T.H. Symons. | 26 | 22 | 0 | 31 |
| T.H. Symons. | 27 | | 2 | 28 |
| T.H. Symons. | 28 | 1 | 3 | 34 |
| T.H. Symons. | 29 | 14 | 0 | 0 |
| T.H. Symons. | 30 | 1 | 0 | 8 |
| Rev. J. Basnett. | 31 | | | 15 |
| John Jones. | 32 | | | 8 |
| T.H. Symons. | 33 | 14 | 3 | 19 |
| T.H. Symons. | 34 | | | 16 |
| T.H. Symons. | 35 | | 1 | 10 |

| | | | | |
|---|---|---|---|---|
| Thomas Meadmore. | 36 | 1 | 2 | 14 |
| T.H. Symons. | 37 | 2 | 2 | 7 |
| Robert Wilcox. | 38 | 1 | 0 | 6 |
| T.H. Symons. | 39 | | | 20 |
| William Rogers. | 40 | | 1 | 0 |
| James Meadmore. | 41 | | | 8 |
| T.H. Symons. | 42 | 1 | 2 | 36 |
| John Probert. | 43 | | | 15 |
| Thomas Hill Jnr. | 44 | | | 28 |
| Abraham Baker. | 45 | | 3 | 28 |
| T.H. Symons. | 46 | 1 | 2 | 28 |
| William Rowberry. | 47 | | | 28 |
| Thomas Baker. | 48 | | | 16 |
| James Baker. | 49 | | | 12 |
| Thomas Evans. | 50 | | | 12 |
| William Powell. | 51 | | | 10 |
| William Bevan. | 52 | | | 30 |
| John Probert. | 53 | | | 13 |
| Thomas Hill, Snr. | 54 | | | 9 |
| Abraham Baker. | 55 | | | 20 |
| Abraham Baker. | 56 | 1 | 1 | 20 |
| Abraham Baker. | 57 | 2 | 1 | 20 |
| Thomas Baker. | 58 | | 2 | 0 |
| John Probert. | 59 | 1 | 0 | 30 |
| Thomas Evans. | 60 | | 1 | 24 |
| Thomas Baker. | 61 | 1 | 3 | 0 |
| Thomas Evans. | 62 | 1 | 1 | 32 |
| Abraham Baker. | 63 | 2 | 1 | 6 |
| William Ralph. | 64 | 3 | 2 | 30 |
| T.H. Symons. | 65 | 1 | 1 | 30 |
| James Baker. | 66 | 1 | 3 | 8 |
| Abraham Baker. | 67 | 5 | 2 | 0 |
| John Pritchard, Snr. | 68 | | 3 | 0 |
| Richard Hull. | 69 | | | 26 |
| Daniel Price. | 70 | 1 | 0 | 2 |
| Francis Lewis Bodenham. | 71 | 2 | 1 | 9 |
| Thomas Evans. | 72 | 5 | 0 | 7 |
| Daniel Price. | 73 | 8 | 0 | 0 |
| George Rowberry. | 74 | 2 | 0 | 33 |
| James Farr. | 75 | | 3 | 10 |
| Richard Watkins. | 76 | 1 | 3 | 26 |
| Richard Watkins. | 77 | | 1 | 20 |
| William Watkins. | 78 | | | 11 |
| James Hill. | 79 | | | 23 |
| John Cooke. | 80 | 5 | 3 | 3 |

| | | | | |
|---|---|---|---|---|
| William Pritchard. | 81 | 5 | 2 | 0 |
| John Cooke. | 82 | 11 | 0 | 0 |
| John Cooke. | 83 | 2 | 2 | 25 |
| John Cooke. | 84 | 1 | 0 | 33 |
| Elizabeth Pritchard | 85 | | | 35 |
| James Hill. | 86 | | | 14 |
| Benjamin Court. | 87 | 2 | 0 | 11 |
| John Donne. | 88 | | 2 | 26 |
| William Watkins. | 89 | 1 | 0 | 22 |
| William Watkins. | 90 | 3 | 0 | 0 |
| John Donne. | 91 | 1 | 0 | 12 |
| James Phillips. | 92 | 2 | 2 | 30 |
| Benjamin Court. | 93 | 1 | 1 | 24 |
| Samuel Watkins. | 94 | | | 15 |
| Thomas Hill, Jnr. | 95 | 2 | 1 | 0 |
| Edward Hill. | 96 | | 3 | 5 |
| John Cooke. | 97 | | 3 | 5 |
| Thomas Hill, Jnr. | 98 | 1 | 0 | 0 |
| John Cooke. | 99 | 2 | 0 | 0 |
| John Powell. | 100 | 12 | 0 | 36 |
| William Watkins. | 101 | | | 13 |
| Joseph Terrett. | 102 (in lieu of Tithes, surviving devisee) | 40 | 3 | 0 |
| Rev. Basnett. | 103 | 1 | 1 | 9 |
| A stone pit for repair of highways. | 104 | | 2 | 0 |
| Rev. John Herbert. | 105 | | 2 | 25 |
| Richard Hull. | 106 | | 2 | 0 |
| Ann Pritchard. | 107 | | 2 | 0 |
| John Bevan. | 108 | | 1 | 25 |
| Thomas Bevan. | 109 | | 1 | 24 |
| William Pritchard. | 110 | | 1 | 10 |
| John Pritchard, Jnr. | 111 | | | 32 |
| John Pritchard, Jnr. | 112 | | | 32 |
| William Powell. | 113 | 1 | 3 | 20 |
| Joseph Terrett. | 114 | 1 | 0 | 13 |
| John Cooke. | 115 | 5 | 0 | 0 |
| Abraham Baker. | 116 | 4 | 2 | 20 |
| Francis Lewis Bodenham. | 117 | 19 | 0 | 0 |
| John Probert. | 118 | 6 | 1 | 38 |
| Abraham Baker. | 119 | 3 | 2 | 12 |
| Abraham Baker. | 120 | 6 | 2 | 0 |
| Thomas Hill Jnr. | 121 | 2 | 1 | 30 |
| John Williams. | 122 | | | 4 |
| T.H. Symons. | 123 | | 1 | 23 |

| | | |
|---|---|---|
| Mary Powell. | 124 | 7 |
| George Rowberry. | 125 | 10 |

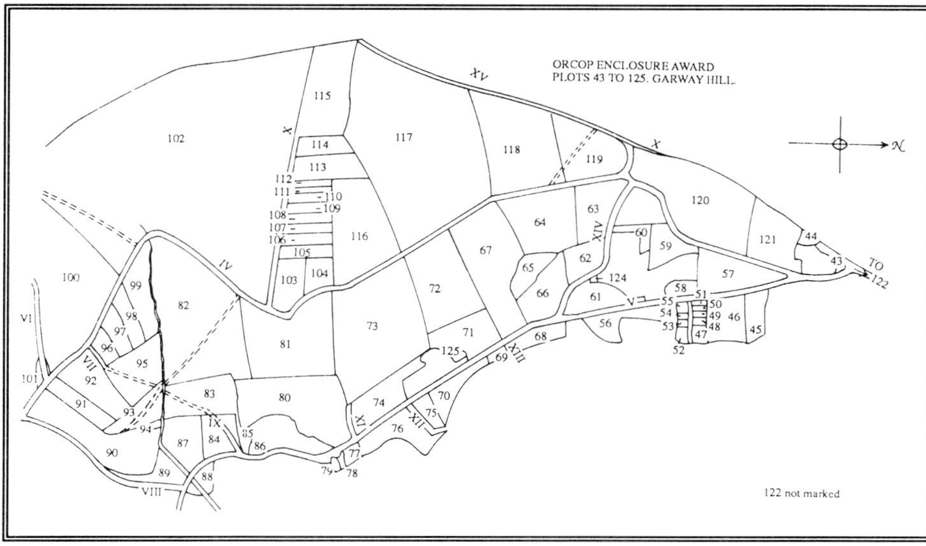


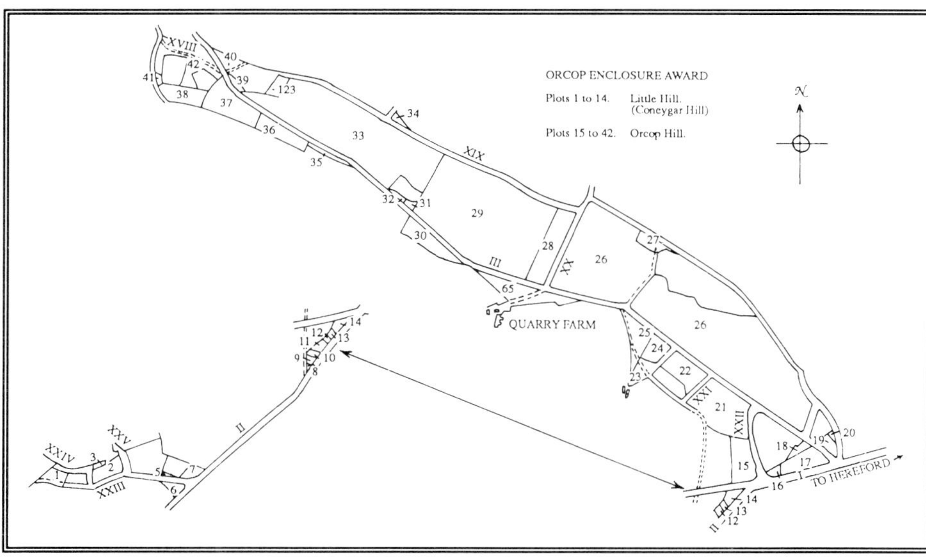


***Orcop Enclosure Awards***

# A Selection of Photographs of Farmhouses, Cottages, Farm Implements and Country Crafts

## relating to this chapter

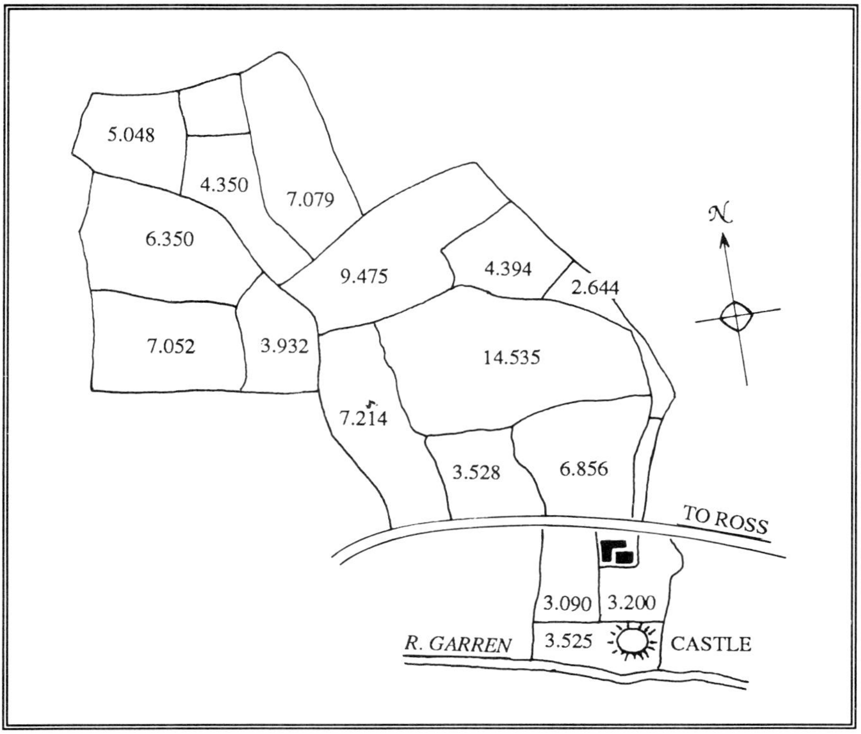


*Moat Farm, 1843.*

*The Moat Farm looking westwards along the road from Ross to Pontrilas. The castle mound is off this picture to the left.*

*Holly Cottage on Conyegar Hill – unoccupied. Probably named after one of the Holly family who were well known in the parish in the 19th century, and have descendants in America. A John Holly was connected with the Orcop Baptist Church.*

*Rose Cottage on Conyegar Hill, built in 1837 by James Williams*

*The farmhouse at Stoney, Garway Hill. The plaque to the right above the door bears the inscription, J. D. gent, 1805. (Probably John Donne).*

*The cruck beams in the barn at Stoney Farm*

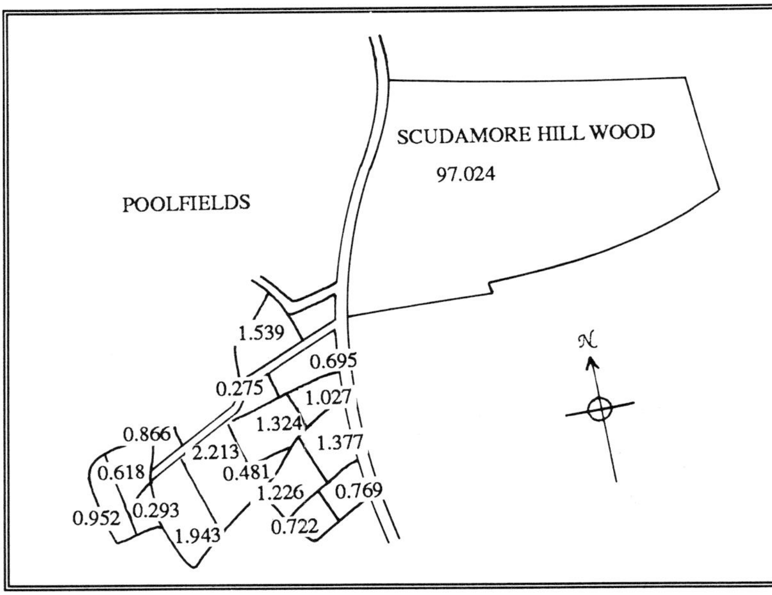


***Map of Poolfields Farm, 1843.***

***Poolfields Farm. The largest farm on Little Hill, (Conyegar Hill), the woodland, to the east of the road is in Llanwarne parish.***

*New House Farm. Little Hill (Coneygar Hill).*

***Rubbings of stamps from the Deeds. These showed that land belonging to the farm was known as the "Penmain", and that a John Abrahall owned it prior to 1755 when it passed to another old Orcop family, the Bethams.***

***(Left) Deed dated 30th August 1817.***

***(Middle) Deed dated 14th February 1755.***

***(Right) Deed dated 27th February 1782.***

***Stradway Farm.***
***The cider mill which is still complete, and in working order although the farm is now abandoned.***

***The banks of a small stream at Stradway, (bridge in foreground). The logs are laid and pegged to the banks to prevent churning up of the ground when cattle stop to drink.***

***A butter churn at Garrondale.***

***An old farm wagon at Garrondale Farm. The old farm on this land was named Three Chimneys, and a Manor Court was held there in 1676.***

*Hand operated seed drill at Stradway Farm*

*This shows the arrangement of "spoons" which, working on the dredger principle, lifts and puts seed into the chute leading to the drill.*

*The age old method of sowing seed by fiddle. John Porter photographed by his daughter, the late Sandra James, at White House Farm, Garway Hill.*

***The New Inn, Baggwyllydiart, as it apppears in 1967.***
***Part of the Mynde Estate in 1843 rental £2 per year. Hand operated petrol pumps.***

***The same Inn early in the century.***
***The horse, a stallion, was taken around the farms by the state groom to serve the mares in season.***

***How cruck beams were made in Herefordshire.***
***The word cruck was allied to the word "crutch".***

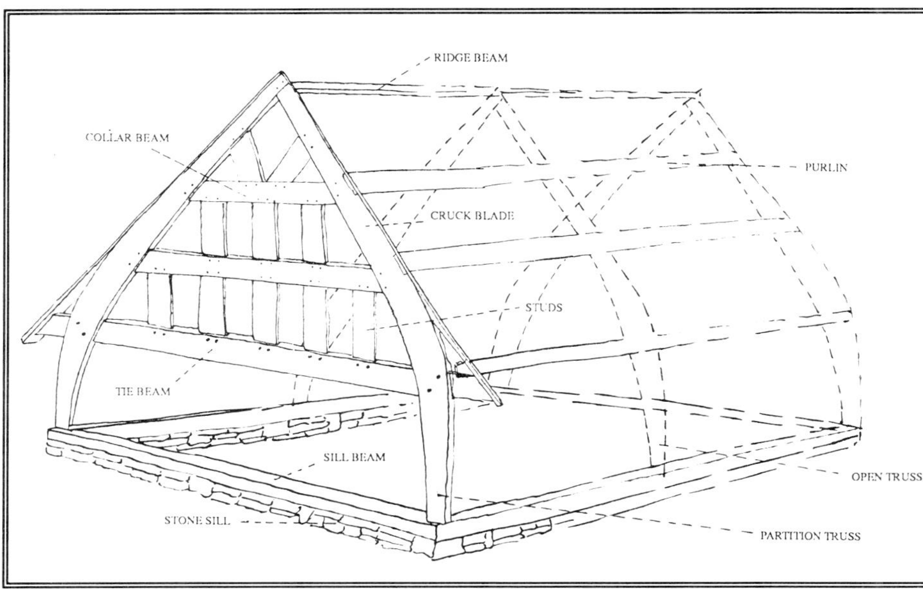


***Cruck beams.***
***Stoney Farm (p. 203) Old Hall Farm (p.177)***

*Little Stradway – better known locally as the Owl's Nest*

*Newcastle Farm from the southwest. Built on plot 21 of the Enclosure Award for Orcop Hill. Once used as a meeting house for religious dissenters.*

***The Meadows, adjacent to Newcastle Farm. The house remains although most of its original land has been absorbed by another neighbouring farm.***

***Ebenezer House, Orcop Hill, from the East. Built by Charles Burleigh. One time staging post for the Orcop carrier, and until 1964 the Post Office and only general store in the village.***

*Yew Tree Cottage on Little Hill, opposite Scudamore Wood, from the south.*

*The cottage built on John Scudamore's land (see page 161). The present occupant is a Meadmore.*

*Cave Cottage, near Newcastle Farm. Built on plot 22 of the Enclosure Award for Orcop Hill. Occupied until 1965. The only cottage at that date with its original beaten earth floor. Now used as a piggery.*

*The entrance to Green Lane at the back of the Lower Butts, still the northern boundary of the parish.*

*The Ynys Farm (from the west). At one time the stream from the Copywell flowed around the sides, probably giving rise to the name (Ynys – island – Welsh). 1967.*

*The Ynys Farm 1992. Note turkey rearing houses in foreground. Green Farm far middle left.*

*The Copywell (Probably derived from Coppice Well) near the Fountain Inn on Orcop Hill. Still the sole source of water for the inhabitants on Orcop Hill due to be replaced this year, (1967).*

Extracts from the Hereford Evening News, 27th July, 1965.

"What a way to live in 1965". Elizabeth Watkins.

"Until further notice consumers are advised to boil this water, reads the sign.

Nothing sinister about that, you might think, but to the householders in the Herefordshire village of Orcop it was the proverbial straw that broke the camel's back. The sign appeared over the communal village well a few months ago when there were drought conditions. No one knew why it was suddenly necessary to boil the water after generations of use. But they did know that it would make life one degree harder.

Orcop is one of those districts where the domestic water supply has to be seen to be believed. Houses two miles apart and scattered along country lanes depend on the well in the centre of the village for all their drinking water. The well, really a glorified spring, is situated under a hedge, at the foot of a steep grassy slope and two parts surrounded by nettles. Water is carried from the well to different homes each day in a variety of containers, buckets, tins and even bottles.

Dore and Bredwardine are responsible for the well at Orcop and their public health inspector told me . . . "Water is taken home from the well for drinking purposes in all types of receptacles. It could easily become contaminated and we decided, as a precautionary measure, to put up this sign . . . "

But the people of Orcop are not impressed. "They think we have straw in our hair. What we really want to know is when they are going to bring us a decent water supply", said one villager.

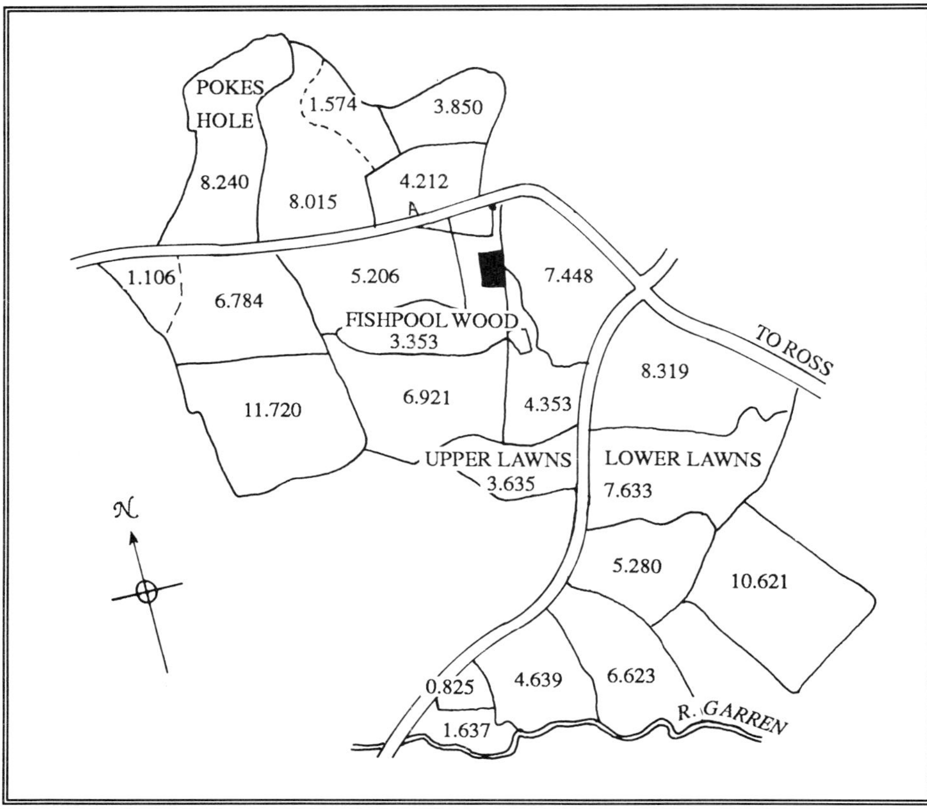


*Map of Camdore Farm, 1842.*

*These are old lime kilns on the roadside at "A". The farmhouse viewed from the south, 1992.*

*This aerial photograph shows the square layout of the farm buildings.*
*The lane (top left) is the entrance road to Little Camdore Farm.*

*White's Barn in Camdore Ground. This was built towards the end of the 18th century by Thomas Gwatkin, whose great grand-daughter recounted to the Rev N Dredge that her grand-mother remembered holding the trees while her father planted them in the orchard. Thomas Gwatkin served on the jury at the Manor court regularly, and was sworn in at one Court as as assessor. William White inhabited the cottage in the 19th century. It was demolished in the 1950's.*

*Outside the Lyons – photograph taken at the beginning of the century.*

*The Lyons. One time home of the Rev Norris Dredge, and earlier The Red Lion, a cider house.*

***The gravestone of John and Elizabeth Meadmore, possibly the last occupants of the Butts. A fine example of the stone mason's art.***

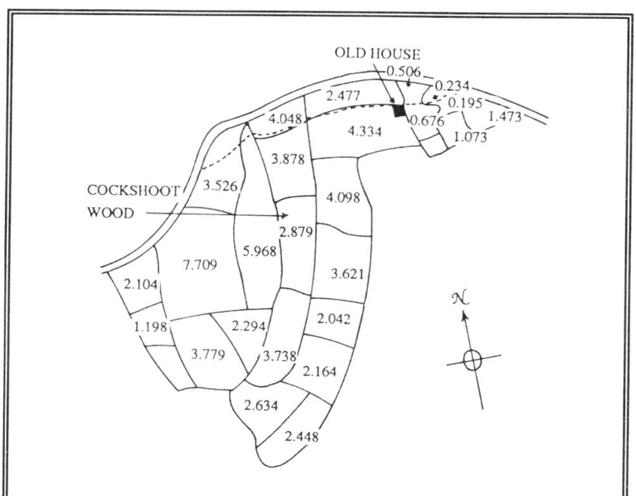


***1843. The plan of the original Lower Butts, known as "ye Butts". The old house has long since disappeared as has the original team road to the Butts quarry here marked below the present highway. The eastern boundary joins to Stradway farm. (see page 160).***

# *Changes in land usage*

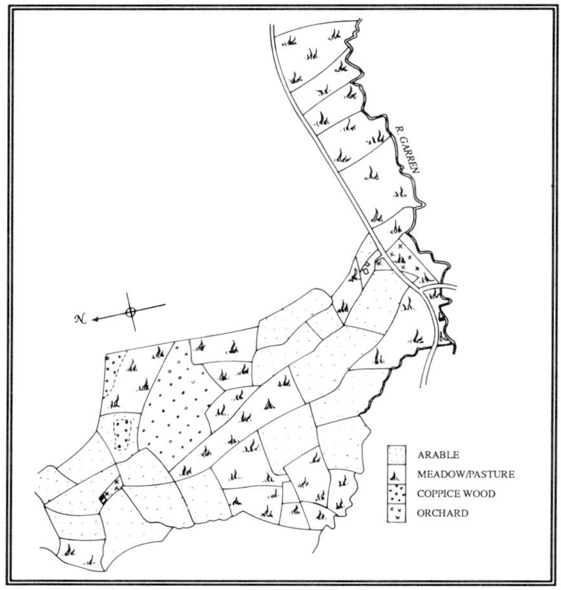


***Brooklands Farm, 1843.***

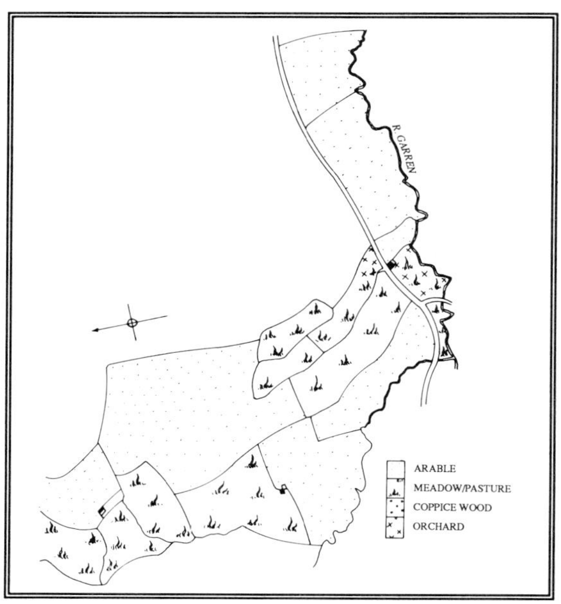


***Brooklands Farm, 1967.***

*Brooklands Farm. The farmhouse (and petrol filling station) seen from the East, 1966. Petrol pumps above and at the New Inn, Baggwydliart have now gone.*

*1992 Council houses adjacent to Fountain Inn.*

# Chapter Fourteen

## REFERENCES


| | | |
|---|---|---|
| 1. | – | Marshall's "Rural Economy" published 1789. Extracts noted in Wormelow Manuscript A. |
| 2. | – | Book of Estate Accounts. Private Collection. |
| 3. | H.L. Gray. | "English Field Systems." London. 1959. First printed 1915. p.140. |
| 4. | – | Mynde Collection. 961. |
| 5. | – | Book of Farm and Land agreements. Private Collection. |
| 6. | – | Mynde Collection. September 2nd 1783. |
| 7. | – | Quarter Session Order Books. 1733-1762. |
| 8. | Sidney Box. | The Good Old Days, then and now. Local printing. Hereford County Library, Local Collection. |
| 9. | – | Mynde Collection. 2699. |
| 10. | – | Book of Farm and Land Agreements. Private Collection. |
| 11. | – | Private Collection. Lying loose in old Account Book. |
| 12. | – | Private Collection. |
| 13. | – | Mynde Estate Rental Book 1843. Private Collection. |
| 14. | – | Book of Farm Repairs 1894 to 1904. Private Collection. pages 9, 53, 153, 267. |
| 15. | – | Mynde Collection. 2484. |
| 16. | L. Syson. | British Watermills. |
| 17. | | Prices of 1600 and 1771 quoted from Arthur Young. |
| 18. | – | Details taken from Deeds of Garway Hill property by kind permission of the owners. |

| | | |
|---|---|---|
| 19. | – | Book of Cottage Agreements. Private Collection. |
| 20. | – | Orcop Church Records. |
| 21. | – | Mynde Collection. 2521. |
| 22. | – | Mynde Collection. 3100. |
| 23. | George Ewart Evans | "Ask the Fellows who cut the Hay". Faber, 1956. |

Much information in this chapter regarding land usage and current prices was gained from the inhabitants of Orcop.

# Chapter Fifteen

## ORCOP HILL BAPTIST CHAPEL

The history of dissent in Orcop can be traced back to 1592.[1] There are 62 recusants recorded between 1592 and 1683 although I am unable to trace the source of this information which is recorded in "The Hundred of Wormelow". It is said that among the principal and most dangerous recusants of the diocese of Hereford were Richard Whiting alias Witting, gentleman of Orcop and his wife. There were three papists listed from 1704-10,[2] and the Bishop's Registers yield the following information:-[3]

*"**1813**.*

> *Dissenting Meeting House.*
>
> *I, Daniel Bullock, of New House, Cordwainer, (shoemaker) do hereby certify that a certain building or messuage, together with the garden adjoining thereunto where I reside at, and being my own premises, situated in the parish of Orcop and County of Hereford, is included forthwith to be used as a place of religious worship by an assembly or congregation of Protestants, and I do hereby require you to register the same according to the provisions of an Act passed in the 42nd year of the reign of George III, entitled "An Act to repeal certain Acts and accord other Acts relating to religious worship and assemblies and persons preaching therein." Certified 2nd August 1813.*

It is not possible to state where this dissenting house would have been since there were several dwellings called "New House" in the parish at that time, but the following similar entry can be verified more fully.[4]

*"**1820**.*

> *Dissenting Meeting House.*
>
> *A house in the occupation of William Griffiths, licensed as a place of Religious Worship for Protestant dissenters".*

William Griffiths was a weaver, and under the Enclosure Award he was allotted a piece of land number 21 of the Enclosure Award Map (see page 199) amounting to 2 acres 3 roods 15 perches. The land was allocated on the 23rd July 1814 at The Mitre Inn, Hereford, and the Offical Enclosure Act was dated the 24th July 1824, but an agreement dated 4th April 1823[5] shows that Griffiths had got into monetary difficulties, and that the Lord of the Manor bought the land from him for £195.0.0. which included rent arrears of £95. The land included Griffiths' dwelling house, lately erected, together with stable, barn and other buildings, and this farm, now named Newcastle (see photograph on page 212) remained a part of the Mynde Estate until the final sale of 1916. The sale agreement does not give the name of the farm, but the measurements given in the original award and in the later bill of sale coincide. Since another letter from Griffiths, dated 22nd July 1830, asks for his barn at Orcop to be "put in order, where I can have the weat safe", presumably he remained in possession, but as a tenant.[6] It is interesting to note that several past occupants, and the present occupants of Newcastle Farm are strong supporters of Orcop Hill Baptist Chapel.

*The chapel viewed from the west front, 1966.*

Another entry in the Bishop's Registers for 1834 states "a dwelling house in the occupation of John Grindle, situated in the parish of Orcop was licensed as a place of religious worship for Protestant dissenters."[7] John Grindall was allotted plot number 15 on the Enclosure Award Map (see page 199). This piece of land measured 1 acre 1 rood 9 perches, and is situated directly opposite the piece of land on which the Baptist Chapel was erected in 1826, this would indicate a meeting house of the Primitive Methodists who were meeting on Orcop Hill long before 1860 when their chapel was built on Garway Hill, (see page 233) However, the date of 1826 given in these returns cannot be verified since no Conveyance

***Gravestone of John Hayes Predgen.***
***Minister of Orcop Baptist Chapel.***

was made as will be seen in the following paragraphs.

These are the only references I have found regarding dissent from the Established Church. The Orcop Baptist Chapel has few records, but through the kindness of one of the Trustees I have been able to peruse the earlier documents which were forwarded from the Baptist Union Offices in London. The first minister at Orcop was William Rogers, who had an allocation of 1 rood of land under the Enclosure Act. This was plot number 40 on Orcop Hill, (see Enclosure Map page 199). The actual title of the Chapel begins with a Conveyance dated 23rd January 1858 which refers to land at Orcop Hill containing 91 square yards, and states that the chapel, or meeting house, and a dwelling house and premises were on the land, and contains the words –

*"which have for many years passed been used for purposes of religious worship by the Particular Baptist Church meeting there".*

The Chapel was in existence before Trustees, on behalf of the Church, had any ownership. It is built on 35 perches of land allocated to John Holly under the Enclosure Act, (plot number 14 on enclosure map page 199), and John Holly sold this parcel of land for £2.10.0. to William Rogers. The conveyance of 1858 states –

*"William Rogers many years since agreed with John Holly £2.10.0. for a parcel of land. No Conveyance was ever made. William Rogers out of his own and other monies collected by voluntary contribution hath erected on the site a Chapel or meeting house, and also a messuage or dwelling house for the use and benefit of the Particular Baptists now assembling there for religious worship in consideration for the love which he hath for the said Church."*

Prior to this Conveyance, on the 11th September 1841, there is a Conveyance between John Holly and John Sims, whereby the latter paid £118.0.0. purchase money for –

> *"a messuage or dwelling house containing 2 dwellings with garden thereto belonging on Orcop Hill in occupation of James Embrey and John Green."*

Between 1814 when the land was first allotted to John Holly and 1841 the Chapel had been built, together with a dwelling house on each side of it (see photograph on page 227). The cottage on the left of the picture has a door (now sealed) into the chapel, and the cottage on the right was used as a shop. Another Agreement made between John Sims and John Holly dated the 25th August 1841 states that John Sims was purchasing "all the stock and crops belonging to John Holly in his buildings and lands called Abels Yatt, together with 1 tenement and land, and all the stock in trade and business of the said John Holly as a shopkeeper and publican". On a List of Voters dated 1st November 1835, John Holly is noted as living in Much Dewchurch and owning a property called Chapel House in Orcop.[8] William Rogers, the first Baptist Minister, is also noted as living in, and owning, a freehold house on Orcop Hill. The house that is built on the piece of land he bought from the Commissioners of Enclosure is the Lower Butts, (see page 161). It appears that John Holly was not resident at the Chapel House, but owned the land and carried on a business in one of the dwelling houses. Parishioners tell me there was once a shoemaker working there, and the present occupier says she had always understood the cottage had once been a shop. John Holly's land and tenement mentioned were held of T.G. Symons, and were on the boundaries of the parish of Orcop and Much Dewchurch. The mention of land called "Abels Yatt" was of great interest to me since this name was mentioned in many leases and was one of the places which marked the bounds of the manor of Orcop which was so important in the law case over possession of cottages on the waste, (see pages 90/95). The original title was "Abrahall's Yatt" so named after the many Abrahalls who lived in Orcop in the 16th, 17th and 18th centuries. I had spent many hours endeavouring to find out just where this could be, and this mention was the first indication of its exact whereabouts.

Very little other documentary evidence is available regarding the history of the Chapel and its activities. By 1858 when the Chapel was formally conveyed to Trustees, William Rogers had become a Baptist Minister at Dudley, and the Minister then resident in Orcop was the Rev. John Hayes Predgen who is listed in the 1851 Census as the Baptist minister and schoolmaster. His signature appears as a witness on local wills about this time, and since there was no resident Vicar in the village until 1859, he probably had a strong influence on village affairs. He was buried in Orcop Churchyard, having died on the 23rd November 1860, aged 54 years (see page 228). A Trade Directory of 1851 mentions that the Baptist Chapel had a Day School attached.

The 1851 Census figures from Returns of all Churches and Chapels reveals that the Orcop Particular Baptist Chapel was erected in 1826, and was used exclusively as a place of worship. No mention is made of the day school. The details show that there were 200 free seats, with free space or standing room 30 feet by 3 feet. The numbers attending for the 12 months previous to 30th March 1851 were:-

| | Morning | Afternoon | Evening |
|---|---|---|---|
| *General Congregation* | *50* | *100* | *20* |
| *Sunday School* | *20* | *12* | - |

In 1863 a meeting held at Ewyas Harold was presided over by the Rev. C. Burleigh of Orcop, and it was resolved that "none but members of the Baptist Churches should be admitted to the Ordinance of the Lord's Supper, thereby making it a Strict or Close Communion Church."[9] Charles Burleigh was a well-known Orcop resident, preacher, carrier and sub-postmaster. He built Ebenezer House which for many years until very recently was the Post Office and village store. Today it still remains a shop, (see page 213). He is reputed to have walked to Hereford on his 90th birthday, to have traversed the old bridge as the clock was striking eight in the morning, and to have walked back again in the night. He was also a member of the Parish Council and the School Board. An extract from the Parish Council Minute Book dated 8th February 1892 mentions that when nominations were considered for the election of new members, it was stated that "Mr Burleigh was the most useful member and that new blood was needed".

***Orcop Hill Baptist Chapel. (Abrahall's Yat)***

By 1870 great stress came to be laid on Anniversary services, and each year the services of special preachers were obtained. In April 1876 the Chapel of Orcop, together with those of Garway and Ewyas Harold came under the pastorate of one minister. In August 1876 a great united service was held at a barn on Garway Hill when it was put on record that there were "500 souls present".[10]

Today the Chapel is ministered to by visiting preachers, and comes under the jurisdiction of the Hereford Baptist Union. It has a small Sunday School, and every year holds its Anniversary and seaside outing, but its supporters are few. This applies to the Church and to the Garway Hill Primitive Methodist Chapel also, but those who attend never fail, and whenever the need arises for capital improvements or general maintenance to the buildings, somehow support for money raising events is found. The Chapel also has a small burial ground.

# Chapter Fifteen

## REFERENCES


| | | |
|---|---|---|
| 1. | J.H. Matthews | p.106/7 |
| 2. | - | Account of Papists. 23746. Local Collection. Hereford City Library. |
| 3. | - | Hereford Diocesan Office. Bishop's Registers. 1791-1821. p.122. |
| 4. | - | Hereford Diocesan Office. Bishop's Registers. 1791-1821. p.217. |
| 5. | - | Mynde Collection. Number 986. |
| 6. | - | Mynde Collection. Number 2457. |
| 7. | - | Hereford Diocesan Office. Bishop's Registers. 1791-1821. P.223. |
| 8. | - | List of Voters,Wormelow Hundred. 1st November, 1835. H.C.R.O. |
| 9. | W. Penry Rowland Davies. | Pamphlet entitled "Centenary Celebrations 1862-1962". Ebenezer Baptist Church, Ewyas Harold. |
| 10. | W. Penry Rowland Davies | As above reference 9. |

All information regarding Conveyances taken from the following documents in possession of Mr F.H. Greening, Trustee of Orcop Baptist Chapel, Little Birch, Hereford, on loan from the Baptist Union Corporation Ltd., 4 Southampton Row, London, W.C.1.

| | | |
|---|---|---|
| Articles of Agreement. | 25th August 1841. | J.H. Holly and J. Sims. |
| Conveyance | 11th September 1841. | J. Holly and J. Sims. |
| Conveyance | 23rd January 1858. | J. Holly and Rev. Wm. Rogers to Edward Niblett and Others. |

# Chapter Sixteen

## GARWAY HILL PRIMITIVE METHODIST CHAPEL

The Primitive Methodists built their Chapel on Garway Hill sometime in 1860, but the 1851 Census figures from Returns of Churches and Chapels state that the Primitive Methodists were meeting for evening service every Sunday in Orcop at a house near to the Baptist Chapel on Orcop Hill.[1] This dwelling house had been built in 1849, and had 40 free seats, but no standing room. The average attendance for the previous 12 months had been 30. The person signing the return was William Williams. The 1851 Census returns list two men with the same name, one aged 75 and the other aged 42. The older man lived at "New House" which I am unable to trace since there were seven of these listed on the return, and today only one building retains that name. I happen to have seen the Deeds of this particular farm, and the occupant at that time was not William Williams. The other house in question is called the "Way Gate", and there is still a cottage of this name today near the Orcop Baptist Chapel standing on land allotted under the Enclosure Act, (plot 12 see page 199) The William Williams who lived there was an agricultural labourer, and his household consisted of his wife, 5 children and a niece.[2] The attached copy of the Primitive Methodist Preachers' Plan for 1850 lists him as Methodist Preacher, number 18, and shows that he preached at several villages in the vicinity of Orcop. It can also be seen that a Revival Meeting was to be held on Orcop Hill on the 21st July 1850 to be addressed by four preachers, three of whom lived in the parish. It is possible that the other William Williams mentioned lived on Garway Hill since a William Williams was buried on 9th May 1855 aged 80 which would correspond to the older man mentioned in the Census Returns.[3]

***The Chapel from North Front, 1966. Note the false chimnney.***

# PRIMITIVE METHODIST PREACHERS' PLAN

## FOR THE HEREFORD CIRCUIT, 1850.

"Speaking the truth in love."

| Places and Time. | | July 21 | July 28 | Aug. 4 | Aug. 11 | Aug. 18 | Aug. 25 | Sept. 1 | Sept. 8 | Sept. 15 | Sept. 22 | Sept. 29 | Oct. 6 | Oct. 13 |
|---|---|---|---|---|---|---|---|---|---|---|---|---|---|---|
| Hereford .......... | 2½ | 1 S | W | 1 T | 6 | 30 | 1 S | J P | 1 Q | 31 | 13 | 24 | 1 S | 30 |
| | 6½ | 1 | W | 31 | 19 | 30 | 1 | J P | 1 Q | 5 | 1 L | 9 | 1 | 6 |
| Open Air .......... | 9½ | 1 | 31 | 1 | 31 | 31 | 1 | 6 | 1 | 30 | 13 | 9 | 1 | 31 |
| | 5½ | 1 | | 31 | 6 | 30 | 1 | 6 | 1 | 5 | 1 | 6 | 1 | 6 |
| *Tuesday* ...... | | 1 | 1 | 17 | 1 | 1 C | 1 | 7 | 1 | 1 B | 1 | 15 | 1 C | 29 |
| *Friday*, P. M. | | 1 | 1 | 1 N | 29 | 1 | 1 | 1 N | 20 | 1 | 1 | 1 N | 6 | 15 |
| White Rocks ........ | 10½* | 8 | 33 | 36 P | 32 Q | 8 | 19 | 18 | 10 | 20 | 5 | 1 S | 35 | 12 |
| Penny Wink ........ | 2½ | 24 | 13 | 36 P | 32 Q | 8 | 19 | 18 | 10 | 20 | 5 | 1 S | 35 | 12 |
| *Wednesday* .. | | | | 1 | | | | 1 T | | | | 1 | | |
| Harewood's End .. | 10½* | 10 | 8 | 34 | 18 P | 12 Q | 5 | 35 | 24 | 1 | 33 | 20 | 36 | 26 |
| | 6* | 13 | 19 | 34 | 26 P | 13 Q | 10 | 35 | 24 | 1 S | 19 | 13 L | 36 | 8 |
| *Wednesday* .. | | 1 | | | | 1 | | | | 1 T | | | | 13 |
| Little Birch ...... | 2½ | 5 | 6 S | 35 | 7 P | 9 Q | 13 | C M | 18 | 12 | 16 | 31 | 34 | 10 |
| | 6 | 5 | 6 | 16 | 29 P | 9 Q | 13 | 1 L | 8 | 12 | 24 | 31 | 34 | 10 |
| *Thursday* .... | | 1 | | 1 + | | 1 | | 1 T | | 1 C | | 1 | | 19 |
| Kinnerstone ....... | 2½* | 19 | 21 | 23 | | 28 | 25 | 14 P | 23 Q | 11 | 21 | 25 | 14 | 23 |
| *Thursday* .... | | | 1 | | | | | | 1 T | | | | | |
| Broadmore .......... | 2½* | 33 | 20 | 25 | | 23 | 14 | 21 | 28 P | 9 Q | 25 | 23 | 33 | 7 |
| *Wednesday* .. | | | 1 T | | | | 1 + | | | | 21 | | | |
| Woolhope .......... | 6* | 19 | 20 | 25 | | 23 | 14 | 21 | 28 P | 9 Q | 25 | 23 | 33 | 29 |
| *Wednesday* .. | | | | | 1 | | | | 1 T | | | | 1 S | |
| Ridge Hill ...... | 10½ | 12 P | 18 Q | 29 | 10 | 31 | 24 | | R M | 6 | 1 S | 27 | 20 | 9 |
| | 2½ | 12 P | 18 Q | 7 | 10 | 31 | 24 | | 31 L | 6 | 30 | 5 | 20 | 9 |
| *Monday* ...... | | | 1 | | 30 | | 1 T | | 5 | | P | | 30 | |
| Shucknall Hill ...... | 6* | 7 | 1 L | 21 | 27 | 25 P | 23 Q | 4 | 14 | 29 | 23 | 3 | 25 | 20 |
| *Friday* ...... | | | | | 1 | | | | 1 T | | | | 1 S | |
| White Stone ........ | 6* | 23 | | 14 | 17 | 20 P | 25 Q | 27 | 21 | 23 | 3 | 29 | 17 | 31 |
| *Monday* ...... | | 1 | | | | 1 | | | | 1 T | | | | |
| Red Rail .......... | 2½* | 13 | 8 | 32 | 26 | 12 | 5 | | 24 P | 1 Q | 19 | 13 | 18 | 8 |
| Hampton .......... | 6 | 6 | 31 | 1 S | 15 | 14 P | 6 Q | 5 | 31 | 7 | 13 L | 24 | 23 | 30 |
| *Thursday* .... | | | | | | | 1 T | | | | 1 | | | |
| Orcop Hill .......... | 6* | 24 L | 13 | 5 | 18 | 10 P | 32 Q | 8 | 19 | 33 | 32 | 1 S | 8 | 18 |
| *Tuesday* ...... | | | | 1 | | | | 1 T | | | | 1 | | |
| Marcle ............ | 6* | 28 | 21 | 23 | 1 L | 11 | 25 | 14 P | 23 Q | 28 | 21 | 25 | 14 | 23 |
| *Thursday* .... | | | | | 1 | | | | | | | | 1 S | |
| Wormelow Tump .... | 6* | 32 | 16 | 35 | 10 | 33 | 19 | | 18 P | 24 Q | 33 | 20 | 18 | 5 |

*Preachers' Names & Residences.*

1 J. Best, Hereford
2 J. Lea, Hampton
3 A. Harris, Shucknall
4 T. Vaughan, Stoke Lacy
5 J. Thomas, Ridge Hill
6 T. Davies, Hereford
7 C. Jones, Hereford
8 J. Cowdall, Ridway
9 J. Rook, Hereford
10 G. Cross, Saddlebow
11 J. Davies, Marcle
12 G. Davies, Orcop Hill
13 J. King, Pencoyd
14 G. Davies, Broadmore
15 A. Burgoine, Hereford
16 R. Powell, Ridge Hill
17 C. Davies, Hereford
18 W. Williams, Orcop Hill
19 T. Porter, Birch
20 R. Davies, Hereford
21 J. Morgan, Broadmore
22 J. Prosser, Old Field
23 J. Ford, Bosbury
24 J. Morgan, Birch
25 R. Freeman, Bosbury
26 B. Watkins, Harewood
27 J. Tranter, Hereford
28 R. Perren, Kinnerstone
29 J. Jones, Hereford
30 G. Jones, Ridge Hill
31 S. Jones, Hereford

ON TRIAL.

32 A. Hammons, Birch

EXHORTER.

33 J. R.

*Pillawell Circuit Preachers.*

34 J. Williams
35 T. Morgan
36 T. Coney

REFERENCES—T. Tickets, L. Lovefeast, S. Lord's Supper, Q. Quarterly Collection, P. Publish, * Lead Class, N. Read Missionary Notices, C. Committee Meeting, + Teachers' Meeting, D. Leaders' Meeting, M. Missionary Collection.

NOTICES.

I. Mr. Lea, Circuit Steward, & 5, 6, 7, 9, 19, 24, 30, and 31, compose the Circuit & Sub-Missionary Committees.

II. The next QUARTERLY MEETING will be held at Hereford, September 23rd; to begin at Nine o'Clock in the Morning.

III. CAMP MEETINGS—Shucknall, July 28th; Preachers for the Morning, 1, 29, 4, 25; Afternoon, 23, 9, 14, 1. Marcle, August 11th; Preachers for the Morning, 1, 20, 24, 9; Afternoon, 5, 31, 13, 1. Birch, September 1st; Preachers for the Morning, 1, 8, 10, 26; Afternoon, 30, 31, 1. The Preachers to address the Meetings in the order they stand planned.

IV. REVIVAL MEETINGS—Orcop Hill, July 21st; by 24, 8, 10, 18. Ridge Hill, September 8th; by 31, 8, 5, 16.

REGULATIONS—*First.* No Person is allowed to Preach among us unless authorized by, and subject to the Circuit Authorities.
*Second.* Any Preacher who neglects an appointment, or to publish or make Collections, or lead Clas, when planned to do so shall, for the First and Second neglects be admonished, and for the Third, be removed from the Plan.
*Third.* No Tea Meeting must be held without the sanction of the Quarterly Meeting.
*Fourth.* All our Members are respectfully requested to subscribe their Class-pence Weekly, according to rule.

☞ HYMN BOOKS, &c., may be obtained, by applying to Mr. BEST, and must be paid for on delivery, as the Book Room Order is, "None to be Sold on Credit."

## GOSPEL TRUMPET.

1 Heralds blow the gospel trumpet,
Sound the notes of Jubilee,
Bid the slaves of sin and Satan,
From their galling yoke be free;
Present, free, and full salvation,
Spread abroad from shore to shore;
Satan's kingdom now is falling,
And shall fall to rise no more.

2 Go, unfold the cheering story,
Of the Saviour crucified,
In the cross be all your glory,
All is useless dross beside;
Fix the blood besprinkled banner,
Where it ne'er was fix'd before;
Satan's kingdom now is falling,
And shall fall to rise no more.

3 Go, where heathen rites are practis'd—
Go, where error does prevail;
On the strength of Christ relying,
Now the gates of hell assail;
Pluck the brands out of the burning,
Pagans shall your God adore.
Satan's kingdom now is falling
And shall fall to rise no more.

4 See the fields are white to harvest,
Reapers now your work begin;
Gather precious souls to Jesus,
These who hate and leave their sin;
Harvest home we'll shout for ever,
On bright Canaan's peaceful shore;
Satan's kingdom now is falling,
And shall fall to rise no more.

5 Arm yourselves—the foe's advancing,
In one mighty phalanx join:
Blow your trumpets, break your pitchers,
Let your lamps with lustre shine;
In the contest eye your captain,
He, the Breaker, goes before;
Satan's kingdom now is falling,
And shall fall to rise no more.

6 Hear the watchword "forward, forward,"
On to glorious victory go;
Raise the war shout "glory, glory,"
And believing charge the foe.
Soon the contest will be ended,
War and strife will then be o'er;
Satan's kingdom now is falling,
And shall fall to rise no more. JUKES

F. AND A. MERRICK, PRINTERS, HIGH-STREET, HEREFORD.

*Primitive Methodist Preachers' Plan*

The Conveyance which is dated 1860 states –[4]

*"A parcel of land was procured from William Rowlands and £5 was paid for consideration money."*

The Conveyance is popularly supposed to have been buried somewhere in the foundation of the building; I cannot help wondering myself why a false chimney was added to the building apart from the possibility that it was considered to enhance the chapel, since a fire-place could never be built in such a position.

***Car used for the Wedding***

William Rowlands in 1860 was a mason aged 42, and he married the grand-daughter of Abraham Baker of Garway Hill who was allotted 9 parcels of land under the Enclosure Act which was finalised in 1824. It is on one of these pieces of land that the chapel is built, number 57 on the Enclosure Award Map (see page 199). A small lane running nearby to this day is still called Baker's Lane, although no one living on Garway Hill had realised why. Both William and Abigail Rowlands are buried in the small burial ground attached to the chapel, and Abigail's great grand-daughter whose husband farms the Brooklands farm, (see page 223) is one of the few regular worshippers at the chapel today.

***Wedding of Alfred Powell and Beatrice Woodhouse 1912.***
***Group taken in orchard at Adam's Plain, Baker's Lane. See end of chapter reference.***

The Primitive Methodist Preachers' Plan of 1845 attached shows that J. Cowdell of Penny Wink, which is a homestead about half a mile from Garway Hill chapel in Kentchurch parish was one of the travelling preachers of the day. His tombstone is also to be found in the burial ground. He died on the 27th September 1878 having been an office bearer in the Church for 50 years.

The Methodist Archives and Research Centre in London were able to trace the following account of the opening of the Chapel which was published in the Primitive Methodist Magazine for 1860.

5. GA[illegible] HILL, HEREFORD CIRCUIT [illegible] Hill is situated about [illegible] south-west of Hereford, [illegible] rather numerous though [illegible] population. At this place [illegible] have conducted religious worship during the last twenty-seven years, and have sometimes been much inconvenienced for want of a suitable sanctuary. During the [illegible] months the congregation [illegible] considerably increased, and [illegible] have been converted [illegible] added to the society. Hence it b[illegible] desirable to erect a suitable and more commodious place of worship, and arrangements were made for the erection which is now completed. The chapel is 30 feet by 20, and 13 feet from the floor to the ceiling. It is a substantial stone building, covered with blue slate, and has four circular-headed windows, a circular-headed door with fan-light, and will accommodate 130 persons. This sanctuary was opened for Divine worship on Sunday, September 30th, 1860. A sermon was preached in the morning and another in the evening by the superintendent of the circuit, and the Rev. J. Richards preached in the afternoon. The chapel was crowded, and many were unable to find access. A tea-meeting was held on the following day, and 300 people enjoyed the social repast, which was truly excellent, and partly gratuitous; after which addresses were delivered by the Revs. J. Oliver, J. Richards, W. Purley, of Orcop; and Mr. Williams, of Pontrilas. The opening services were continued on Sunday, October 14th. A sermon was preached by Mr. T. Hughes, of Hereford, at Pontrilas railway station, about four miles from the chapel (kindly offered by the station-master, who was present at the tea-meeting). The cost of the building is about £90, towards which we have raised by subscriptions £18 17s.; public collections, £8 3s.; proceeds of the tea-meeting, £10 10s.; total, £37 10s., and the sum of £12 10s. is proposed to be raised by Christmas, leaving a debt of £40 on the building.

THOMAS HOBSON.

One wonders if the Mr Williams of Pontrilas was the same William Williams who nine years ago had presided over the meetings at Orcop. One of the Anniversary meetings is depicted in the old photograph overleaf.

The Centenary Meeting of the Chapel was held at the Village Hall in Orcop on Monday, 11th July, 1960, and I remember well the lovely summer day and wonderful attendance that greeted the guest speaker who was Professor John Evans of Brecon, (now deceased) who was himself a centenarian. The field opposite the hall owned by Mrs E. Smith, the Chapel Superintendent, was full of cars which could not find room to park on the road.

The Chapel is still served by visiting preachers who work on a circuit basis, but there are no particular records of any age to be perused. There is a small Sunday School which is run by the descendants of the same family who built it. Contributions have to be raised by each Chapel on the circuit to make up the stipend of the Circuit Minister, and it is a real struggle often to reach the necessary figure. Electric light and heating have been installed in recent years, and now an attempt is being made to accumulate sufficient money to make concrete paths in the burial ground.

***The Chapel Anniversary of Garway Hill, early 1900's.***

# Chapter Sixteen

## References

1. - 1851 Returns of Churches and Chapels. Public Record Office. London. H.O.129.

2. - 1851 Census Returns.

3. - Orcop Church Registers. Burial Register 1813-1899. Entry No. 143.

4. The only details available about the Conveyance given to me by Mrs George Sayce, Brooklands Farm.

The Circuit Preachers' Plans were also loaned to me from relatives of Mrs Sayce.

The wedding took place in Orcop Church.

The groom was employed as a water bailiff by Mr.H. Moreland of England's Glory Matches, who loaned the car, complete with chauffeur and camera for the day.

Abraham Baker's daughter-in-law, Mrs. Lillian Baker is in the back row.

Back row. Miss 'Tiny' Badham, Miss Mary Barrel, Mrs. Beavan, Mrs. Benjamin, Groom, Miss Gladys Beavan, Mrs. Lillian Baker and baby Eva, Zacharias Castree, – Sawkins, Hedley Castree, Lewis Powell, Miss Fanny Robinson, Bert Woodhouse.

Front row. Mrs. Lizzie Powell, Miss Laura Castree, Miss Winnie Smith, Miss Nancy Castree, Bride, Miss Sarah Castree, Doris Benjamin, Mrs. Lydia Castree, Miss Alice Castree, Mrs. Martha Smith.

# Chapter Seventeen

## THE VILLAGE SCHOOL

### HEAD TEACHERS OF ORCOP SCHOOL 1858 to 1964

| **Name** | **Date** | **Length of Service** | **Qualifications** |
|---|---|---|---|
| | | | |
| *Cornelius Ramm* | *Noted in Trade Directories for years 1858 and 1862.* | | |
| | *No details known.* | | |
| | | | |
| *William Harding* | *Sept. 1864 to July 1865* | *10 mths* | *Ex.Pupil Teacher* |
| | *No entries in Log Book after July 1865 until 1867.* | | |
| | | | |
| *Mrs Cranham* | *Trade Directory, 1867.* | | |
| | | | |
| *Miss R. Prichard* | *Oct. 1867 to Oct. 1869.* | *2 years* | *Certificated* |
| | | | |
| *Miss Birland* | *Jan. 1870 to July 1871* | *18 months* | *Certificated* |
| | | | |
| *Mr Hill* | *Oct. 1871 to March 1873* | *18 months* | *Uncertificated* |
| | | | |
| *Mr James Jones* | *Oct. 1873 to Dec. 1873* | *2 months* | *Uncertificated* |
| | | | |
| *Miss R. Broughall* | *Jan. 1874 to Sept. 1874* | *9 months* | *Certificated* |
| | | | |
| *Mr Smith* | *Oct. 1874 to Dec. 1874* | *3 months* | *Uncertificated* |
| | | | |
| *Ebenezer Meredith* | *Jan. 1875 to July 1875.* | *7 months* | *Certificated* |
| | | | |
| *George Luxton* | *Sept. 1875 to Dec. 1875* | *3 months* | *Certificated* |
| | | | |
| | *School closed from December 1875 until May 1877.* | | |

| | | | |
|---|---|---|---|
| | *End of Voluntary School Period.* | | |
| | | | |
| *Thomas Ball* | *May 1877 to August 1880* | *3 years 3 months* | *Certificated* |
| | | | |
| *H.B. Hutchinson.* | *Sept. 1880 to August 1883* | *3 years* | *Certificated* |
| | | | |
| *Henry Sargent* | *Oct. 1883 to Dec. 1894* | *11 years 2 months* | *Certificated* |
| | | | |
| *Miss M. Sargent* | *Jan. 1895 to Oct. 1895* | *9 months* | *Certificated* |
| *(daughter of above).* | | | |
| | | | |
| *Robert Davies* | *Oct. 1895 to Feb. 1908.* | *12 years and 4 months* | *Certificated* |
| | | | |
| | *Orcop Board School becomes Orcop Council School, 4th May 1903.* | | |
| | *Robert Davies served 4 years and 9 months under the Herefordshire Education Committee.* | | |
| | | | |
| *William Thomas* | | | |
| *Jenkins* | *March 1908 to Apr. 1913* | *5 years 1 month* | *Certificated* |
| | | | |
| *John Davies* | *May 1913 to Jan. 1921* | | *Certificated* |
| | *Interrupted by War Service. Actual service 6 years* | | |
| *Supply teachers in charge from August 1917 until January 1919.* | | | |
| *George Gale* | *March 1921 to Oct. 1923* | *2 years 7 months* | *Certificated* |
| | *Died at Orcop.* | | |
| | | | |
| *Supply teacher in charge until January 1924* | | | |

| | | | |
|---|---|---|---|
| *Cyril Brook* | *Jan. 1924 to Dec. 1926* | *3 years* | *Certificated* |
| *Supply teacher in charge until June 1927* | | | |
| *Thomas Davies* | *June 1927 to Aug. 1929* | *2 years 2 months* | *Certificated* |
| *Supply teachers in charge until March 1930* | | | |
| *Henry Dale* | *Mar. 1930 to Dec. 1933* | *3 years 9 months* | *Certificated* |
| *Kenneth Nuttall* | *Jan. 1934 to Nov. 1941* | *7 yrs 11 months* | *Certificated* |
| *Eric Barker* | *Dec. 1941 to May 1947* | *5 years 5 months* | *Certificated* |
| *William Morgan* | *June 1947 to Dec. 1954* | *7½ years* | *Certificated* |
| *Eric Coleman* | *April 1955 to Dec. 1964* | *9 years 8 months* | *Certificated* |
| | *School re-organised from an all-age council school in April 1957 to Orcop County Primary School, Infant and Junior.* | | |

The village school was first envisaged in 1856 when Thomas George Symons of the Mynde conveyed, on the 27th December 1856 to the Minister and Churchwardens of Orcop, half an acre of meadow adjoining the Church, which was part of the Green Farm.[1] The Deed says –

> *"Under the Authority of the Acts of the fifth and eighth years of the Reign of Her Majesty for affording facilities for the Conveyance and Endowment of Sites for Schools, I do hereby freely and voluntarily and without valuable consideration, grant to the Minister and Churchwardens of the Parish of Orcop half an acre for the purpose of the said Acts, and upon trust to*

*permit the said premises and all buildings thereon erected to be for ever hereafter appropriated and used as and for a school for the Education of Children and Adults or Children only of the labouring and manufacturing and poorer classes in the parish of Orcop".*

The Deed goes on to state that the school shall be at all times open to the inspection of the Inspectors of Schools, and shall always be in union with, and conducted according to, the principles and in furtherance of the ends and designs of the National Society for promoting the education of the poor in the principles of the Established Church. The officiating Minister was to superintend the religious and moral instruction of all scholars. In all other respects the control and management of the school and premises, and of its staff, should be vested in a committee consisting of the Officiating Minister, and five other persons. These five committee members had to contribute at least twenty shillings to the funds of the school, to be communicants of the Church of England, and to have an estate situated in the parish or a parish adjoining. Any vacancies which occurred on the committee should be filled by persons qualified as aforesaid, who should be elected by the votes of contributors to the school of at least ten shillings per year, communicants and property holders. Each person had a right to vote for each sum of ten shillings paid to the school funds, but no one was entitled to more than six votes. The first five members of the Committee were –

| | |
|---|---|
| *Thomas George Symons.* | *The Mynde, Much Dewchurch.* |
| *Rev. Michael Hodsoll Miller.* | *Clerk. (see page 136).* |
| *Robert Maulkin Lingwood* | *Lystone. (Near Orcop).* |
| *James Phillips.* | *Bryngwyn, Much Dewchurch.* |
| *Abraham Whittaker.* | *St Weonards.* |

James Phillips is listed on the 1851 Census returns as follows:-

| | | | |
|---|---|---|---|
| *Bryngwyn* | *James Phillips* | *aged 52.* | *Magistrate* |
| | *Lucy, wife* | *aged 46* | |
| | *James, son* | *aged 23* | *No Profession* |
| | *Mary, daughter* | *aged 18* | |
| | *Harriet, daughter* | *aged 16* | |
| | *Laura, daughter* | *aged 13* | |
| | *Isabella, daughter* | *aged 12* | |
| | *Julia, daughter* | *aged 6* | |
| | *William, son* | *aged 3* | |
| | *Eliza Hughes* | *aged 26* | *Governess* |
| | *Mary Ann Edmonds* | *aged 23* | *Lady's maid* |
| | *Elizabeth Barrett* | *aged 66* | *General servant* |
| | *Elizabeth Harris* | *aged 13* | *Servant* |

| | | |
|---|---|---|
| *Elizabeth Patten* | *aged 32* | *Servant* |
| *Eliza Roberts* | *aged 20* | *Servant* |
| *Ellen Addis* | *aged 16* | *Servant* |
| *Daniel Price* | *aged 18* | *Footman* |

When looking through the Church Registers of Much Dewchurch I noted that the Rev. Arthur Gray of Orcop married Isabella Phillips on the 25th April 1867. They are both buried in Orcop Churchyard.

In 1851 the census figures show a population of 631 in Orcop, with a child population of 196 under 14 years of age. The records of the National Society show that the school was built to accommodate 80 to 100 children who were already attending a daily school organised at the beginning of 1857.[2] There are no records whatsoever to show where this was. Parishioners remember their parents telling them that there were two dame schools at one time, one on Garway Hill, and the other in the old Tithing Barn which the Rev. Arthur Gray bought, building his own residence, The Grange, on the site. The Baptist Chapel was used as a school, and the Rev. J. Predgen is listed in the 1851 Census as "Baptist minister and schoolmaster". A Trade Directory of 1851 states "Baptist Chapel with Day School attached".[3] Some children walked to attend a school in the neighbouring village of Llanwarne, which was also a dame school I should imagine, since its Church School, now closed, was not built until after Orcop's school.[4]

The Diocesan Inspector of Schools at that time, together with the Rev. Miller who held the tithes (see page 136), raised £336.13.0. by subscriptions and local collections, and the school was eventually opened on the 28th June 1858, and comprised one large classroom, 42 feet long x 18 feet wide, divided by a curtain to separate the boys and girls. The original cost had been estimated at £455.0.0. ;but as shown below the final figure was £675.3.0.[5]

| **Receipts** | **£** | **s** | **d** |
|---|---|---|---|
| Subscriptions and collections | 336 | 13 | 0 |
| Grant from Committee of Council. | 288 | 0 | 0 |
| Grant from Diocesan Society | 25 | 10 | 0 |
| Grant from National Society | 25 | 0 | 0 |
| | £675 | 3 | 0 |

| **Expenditure** | **£** | **s** | **d** |
|---|---|---|---|
| Cost of schoolroom | 200 | 0 | 0 |
| Cost of residence | 300 | 0 | 0 |
| Fixtures, fittings and sundries | 154 | 13 | 0 |
| Legal Expenses of conveyance | 20 | 10 | 0 |
| | £675 | 3 | 0 |

Orcop School started its existence as a Voluntary, or non-provided, Church of England School. It is unfortunate that the subscriptions and collection lists which made up the sum of £336.13.0d. cannot be traced since this was a sizeable figure to have been raised in those days. How much of it was given by wealthy landowners in the vicinity, or by the Lord of the Manor himself, and how much by parishioners, seems destined to remain unknown. It seems safe to assume that the Church was anxious to assume responsibility for education in the village, and it is possible that the Baptist chapel school was insufficient to deal with the number of children involved. Religious interests, I suspect, had much to do with the motives behind the foundation of the school. The Log Books do not commence until 1864, but are continuous from then on until the School's closure at the end of 1964. The school's administration suffered several changes which are listed below.

| | |
|---|---|
| *Orcop Voluntary School* | *June 1858 until May 1877.* |
| *Orcop Board School* | *May 1877 until April 1903.* |
| *Orcop Council School* | *May 1903 until April 1957. (All Age).* |
| *Orcop County Primary School* | *May 1957 until December 1964.* |

During the Voluntary School period so far as can be ascertained from Trade Directories and the Log Books, 11 teachers were appointed to take charge of the school, 5 of whom were certificated. There were often closures which lasted from 2 months up to 16 months due to illness or no staff. The attendance figures mentioned in the Log Books were very poor; the population in 1851 was **631**, in 1861, **583** and in 1871, **637**. The average number of children attending school was never more than 35 during this time, more often it was between 8 and 15. The financial problems of the school must have been great. The Revised Education Code of 1862 provided grants for the voluntary school in addition to local subscriptions which were based on attendance under a certificated teacher, and on the results of the examinations conducted by Government Inspectors in the three R's. Although there are no records at this stage to prove it, school fees were payable in voluntary schools. There is an entry in the Log Book stating that the wife of one of the managers of the school paid for two children to attend. There was much poverty in the village, and the whole county was suffering from a succession of poor harvests which were to ruin many farmers. This initiated a flow of emigrants to the mines and iron works in South Wales where there was steady employment. Orcop's population fluctuated little in the voluntary school period, but there are instances of children leaving school because their parents were emigrating to America. In the first few years that I lived at Orcop I can recall several Americans calling to see the school, and my husband showing them the old Log Books with the names of their relatives recorded. Unfortunately, I never noted their names and addresses, but there have also been occasions when in the absence or non appointment of a Vicar, I have checked up details from the Church Registers for descendants of Orcopians in America. Many agricultural labourers, who comprised the majority of the population, lived in small cottages built on less than a quarter of an acre of ground, on which they depended to provide them with much of their food. The possession of such plots led to the economic necessity of the whole family often being required to work on larger farms when various crops needed attention. This was often one of the reasons for non-attendance at school. Log book entries recorded, "Lydia and Hannah Jones returned to school after a long absence, principally through poverty".[6] "Harry Meadmore has been absent the whole week having no shoes to wear".[7]

Since education was not compulsory until 1876 when Lord Sandon's Act set up school attendance committees, parents were not obliged to send their children to school. Even the Act of 1876 could not be fully implemented because children who lived more than two miles from school were exempted from attending, and in rural areas they were allowed to help with agricultural work for a period of up to six weeks. The former distance stipulation provided a most convenient loophole for parents since the school was not ideally situated. As can be seen by the large aerial photograph (p.137), the school stands on a hill over a mile away from the village. Since Mr Symons owned over half of Orcop, it was unfortunate that another piece of land which was more centrally situated was not chosen, but no doubt its proximity to the Church, a quarry, and a well, were the determining factors. Also at this time there were several cottages in the vicinity of the proposed school and church which have now disappeared. This was a Church of England school, the pupils were taken to services in Church, and the Vicar had originally intended to build his residence nearby.[8] In those days, when children had to walk a long distance to school in all weathers, it is quite understandable that when the weather was poor, they did not attend. The children from Garway Hill had to struggle through muddy fields, often arriving at school with mud over their boots. Those who came from the village at Orcop Hill had to contend with the brook at the bottom of the school lane which frequently flooded over the road, particularly when the mill was operative. There are comments that "The water was up to the children's knees, and the boys had to carry the little ones through"[9] and "the brook is rising so school was abandoned so that the children could get home".[10] In the voluntary school days children were kept from home for apple and acorn picking, to make cider, to pull turnips, for crow scaring, to work in their gardens, to make hay, bind sheaves and gather corn, for bark stripping and potato planting, picking stones, poultry dressing (particularly near Christmas), hop picking, and beating for the keepers at the big local shoots. One headmaster tells of the difficulty in collecting school fees, many of the parents being out of work and very poor.[11]

The distance children had to travel in all weathers, the existence of much poverty, and the need to help their parents to supplement the family income, all had much to do with the poor attendance figures in the first forty years of the school's existence, together with the fact that the teachers appointed were often uncertificated; many were women who received good reports from visiting Inspectors,[12] but who often stayed for less than twelve months, possibly finding the life too lonely and not receiving sufficient support from the parents. One master who was appointed in 1874 made his first entry in the Log Book, copied verbatim, as follows:-

> *"Having the charge has master of Orcop School, I hereby gives a diaree of progress and attendance".*

He did not remain for long, leaving three months later. His successor, a certificated teacher from Caernarvon Training College stayed seven months, and encountered much opposition from parents as the following entry shows[14]

> *"Mr Benjamin Harris called and complained that his children were caned for not being clean. Was found fault with by a few parents before the Committee for trying to enforce cleanliness and discipline in school, and was recommended to do it very gradually as they were not accustomed to it. Mr Benjamin Harris has withdrawn his children in consequence."*

On 9th August 1877 the Voluntary School of 1858 was formally made into Orcop Elementary Board School, and came under the jurisdiction of the District Schools' Board.[15] I have endeavoured to trace correspondence for this period from County Archives, Diocesan records and from the local District Councils without success, but it would appear that the need for transfer came about due to the lack of annual subscribers to the school. It is not difficult to assess why this happened. The village had had dissenters for many years before 1858, and it had never had a wealthy family actually living within its confines. It is significant that the five members of the original committee were all gentlemen with estates outside the parish. By 1877, all the original members were dead or had moved from the immediate area, and the heir to the Symons' estate was still but a child. In addition, there was by this time, another chapel in the village, the Primitive Methodist, which had been built in 1860. The Ecclesiastical Census taken in 1851 of all places of Religious Worship showed that the number of people attending the Baptist and Methodist Chapel and meeting house was almost double that of the Church congregation, (see pages 145 and 230). The Rev. Gray's ministry was to last until 1889, and, judging by his remarks in correspondence, he was apt to assume a rather dictatorial attitude in his dealings with the parish. Of the 637 persons living in the parish in 1871 the greater proportion were agricultural labourers and their wives, and it seems unlikely that there were many families who were able or willing to subscribe to a village school. Although there was a need for a school, the more basic need for subsistence was uppermost in the mind of the agricultural workers; this being instanced by the work often undertaken by children. It also appears from the Log Books that the general standard of the school was not good, and that the qualifications of some of the staff employed were suspect. This would not lead to a feeling of confidence in the village which would be required for the financial support of the school.

The National Society have little correspondence regarding the school, but there does exist a letter from the Rev. A. Gray written in 1876 in answer to the Society's enquiry into the reason for the suggested transfer of the school.[16]

> *"I can assure you a School Board is no wish of mine, but circumstances have been drifting in that direction for a long while, and I do not at present see how it can be averted as we have to contend in this parish with much*

*poverty, ignorance and apathy as to education. The school is unfavourably placed, and if the School Board should choose to build another in a more central position, I fear it would be impossible for us to carry on a school."*

The Memorandum of Agreement provided that the Officiating Minister of the Parish should be present at all meetings of the Committee, and the Rev. Arthur Gray was also appointed correspondent to the School Board. The Agreement also made it perfectly clear that the original Managers and Trustees still owned the school, and had the right to use it after school hours and on Christmas Day, Ash Wednesday, Good Friday, Ascension Day, and one other day in each year. The Board School period is well documented. There exists a School Fees Book from 1877 to 1891 (when the fees were abolished), giving attendance figures, which show a distinct improvement on the Voluntary School period. The averages are as follows: [17]

| **Year** | **Average Yearly Attendance** |
|---|---|
| *1877* | *84 (8 months)* |
| *1878* | *90.5* |
| *1879* | *95* |
| *1880* | *80* |
| *1881* | *84.5* |
| *1882* | *81* |
| *1883* | *77.5* |
| *1884* | *81* |
| *1885* | *63* |
| *1886* | *50.5* |
| *1887* | *63* |
| *1888* | *68* |
| *1889* | *60.5* |
| *1890* | *55* |
| *1891* | *61.5 (8 months)* |
| | *Fees abolished 31.8.1891.* |

Although attendance had improved, and the Mundella Act of 1880 compelled all School Boards and School Attendance committees to enforce attendance, there was still much friction between the School Board and parents. An entry in the Log Book states: [18]

*"This week has closed the school year. It has been one of continual strife between the Board and the parents. The one endeavouring to get the children into school, and the other keeping them at home to work on the fields, in their gardens, or in their houses. In the case of those who have been summoned before the magistrates, the Board have failed to obtain*

*support, judgement going against them. The weather and sickness have also tended to make the attendance anything but satisfactory. A great number have left the parish during the year, and none have come to take their place."*

The latter sentence is borne out by the Census figures which show –

**1871** 637 **1881** 554 **1891** 474

# ORCOP

# SCHOOL BOARD.

In consequence of the present rate of Fees being lower at Orcop School than in any other School in the neighbourhood, and with a view to lessen the undue pressure upon those Ratepayers who have no occasion for using the School, the Board have determined that in future the Fees (which must in all cases be paid in advance), shall be as follows :—

For one child—Twopence a week ; or Sixpence a month ; or 1s. 4d. a quarter.

For two children—Threepence a week ; or Ninepence a month; or 2s. a quarter.

For three children—Fourpence a week ; or 1s. a month ; or 2s. 8d. a quarter.

Should there be more children than three, such additional child or children shall be admitted free.

In cases where peculiar poverty is proved, the Board may remit part of these Fees.

This change will take place on and after 2nd April, 1883.

S. Adams, Printer, 29. High Town, Hereford.

Other comments, although probably not intended to be in a humourous vein, cannot help but raise a smile.[19]

> *"One week has elapsed since the Government Examination.*
>
> *As a rule after the annual visit of Her Majesty's Inspector the attendance of the children is better, but in this parish it is the reverse."*
>
> *"The attendance this week is low, probably owing to the hot weather, for at Orcop School children are all affected, by cold, heat and rain. These are three of the chief causes for stopping at home."*

A letter from the Rev. Gray to the Board of Education also gives his reasons for the poor attendance at school.[20]

> *"I wish to bring before you one cause which, in my opinion, works against our efforts to get a better school attendance. I refer to the exceptional facilities for drinking given in Orcop, far in excess of any neighbouring parish. There are 5 places for the sale of liquor, three of them fully licensed, in a population of 554, which speaks for itself. The wages here are about 12/- a week, and even that is precarious, for the farmers, who are of a humble class, work hard themselves, and employ as little labour as possible. With so much diverted from the scanty wages by drink, one can easily understand that unprincipled parents are only too ready to use the children's labour to compensate for their own vice and improvidence. Little boys can often be seen here breaking stones on the road. The School Board is at present petitioning the Magistrates to refuse to renew the licence of one particular house which has been an evil to the neighbourhood."*

***The Seven Stars Inn which gave its name to Stars' Pitch, the climb from the Green Farm on the road to Ross. Also at one time named the Maltsters Arms.***

***Seabourne Cottage – at one time the Blue Boar Inn. Now unoccupied. 1967.***

***The Fountain Inn, 1992. The only remaining public house in the parish.***

In actual fact there were seven public houses in the parish, but two of these were situated in the Garway Hill area. From the Quarter Session Order Books of 1872 to 1880 which I inspected, nearly all the cases referring to Orcop dealt with drunkenness and assault, the other offences being trespass or to do with the Game Laws or Highway Act. This was the pattern of almost all the cases brought before the Magistrates, and was certainly not confined to Orcop judging by the Order Books. While not condoning such conduct, it is only reasonable to remember that with such low wages the public houses were the only meeting places, apart from places of worship, alcohol was cheap, and life must have been devoid of much opportunity to improve one's lot. The School Board did on many occasions sanction free schooling on grounds of poverty.

*The one time Globe Inn on Garway Hill.*

Among the school papers is a note of a proposal which must have taken place at a village meeting, to judge by the number present, namely forty. This paper is undated, but I think it likely that the School Board had come to the conclusion that to ensure a really good attendance it was necessary to have a more centrally placed school. The proposal reads –

*"That this meeting is of opinion that, if the Orcop School Board persist in their extravagant proposal to buy a new site and erect new schools, the present building being adequate for the wants of the parish, it becomes the duty of this Parish of Orcop to send a Memorial to the Council of Education praying them to stop such action on the part of the School Board."*

This proposal was defeated by a majority of four, and probably led to the decision to add an infants' room to the original building. The Orcop School Board borrowed £373.0.0. on the 16th December 1892 which was to be paid back over thirty years with interest at 3½%, the debt being cleared in 1923.[21] The classroom was first used on the 19th June 1893.[22] The architect's account throws an interesting light on the travelling expenses of the day; he came from Hereford to Orcop (10 miles).

*"Trap hire for twenty journeys at 7/6d.   £7.10.0."*

The School Board was elected triennially, very often en bloc, or, in order to avoid the expense of having an election; should there be too many nominations, certain candidates were asked to withdraw.[23]

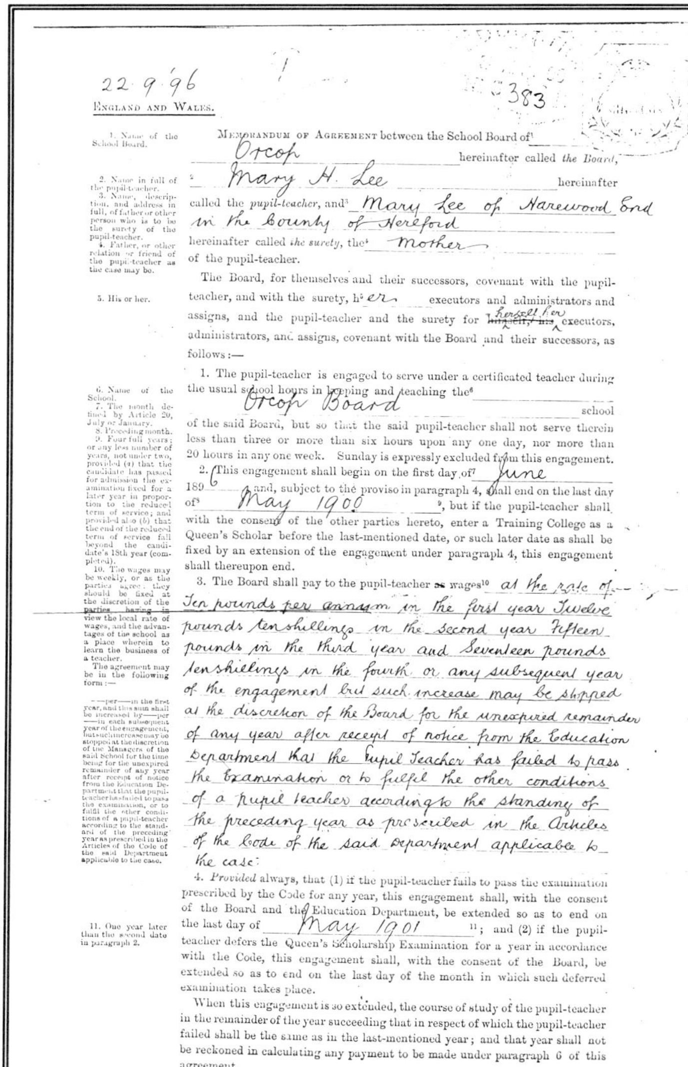

22·9·96

ENGLAND AND WALES.

383

MEMORANDUM OF AGREEMENT between the School Board of[1] Orcop hereinafter called *the Board*, [2] Mary H. Lee hereinafter called the *pupil-teacher*, and[3] Mary Lee of Harewood End in the County of Hereford hereinafter called *the surety*, the[4] Mother of the pupil-teacher.

The Board, for themselves and their successors, covenant with the pupil-teacher, and with the surety, h[5]er executors and administrators and assigns, and the pupil-teacher and the surety for ~~himself, his~~ herself, her executors, administrators, and assigns, covenant with the Board and their successors, as follows:—

1. The pupil-teacher is engaged to serve under a certificated teacher during the usual school hours in keeping and teaching the[6] Orcop Board school of the said Board, but so that the said pupil-teacher shall not serve therein less than three or more than six hours upon any one day, nor more than 20 hours in any one week. Sunday is expressly excluded from this engagement.

2. This engagement shall begin on the first day of[7] June 1896 and, subject to the proviso in paragraph 4, shall end on the last day of[8] May 1900 [9], but if the pupil-teacher shall with the consent of the other parties hereto, enter a Training College as a Queen's Scholar before the last-mentioned date, or such later date as shall be fixed by an extension of the engagement under paragraph 4, this engagement shall thereupon end.

3. The Board shall pay to the pupil-teacher ~~as~~ wages[10] at the rate of Ten pounds per annum in the first year Twelve pounds ten shillings in the second year Fifteen pounds in the third year and Seventeen pounds ten shillings in the fourth or any subsequent year of the engagement but such increase may be stopped at the discretion of the Board for the unexpired remainder of any year after receipt of notice from the Education Department that the Pupil Teacher has failed to pass the Examination or to fulfil the other conditions of a pupil teacher according to the standing of the preceding year as prescribed in the Articles of the Code of the said Department applicable to the case.

4. *Provided* always, that (1) if the pupil-teacher fails to pass the examination prescribed by the Code for any year, this engagement shall, with the consent of the Board and the Education Department, be extended so as to end on the last day of May 1901 [11]; and (2) if the pupil-teacher defers the Queen's Scholarship Examination for a year in accordance with the Code, this engagement shall, with the consent of the Board, be extended so as to end on the last day of the month in which such deferred examination takes place.

When this engagement is so extended, the course of study of the pupil-teacher in the remainder of the year succeeding that in respect of which the pupil-teacher failed shall be the same as in the last-mentioned year; and that year shall not be reckoned in calculating any payment to be made under paragraph 6 of this agreement.

1. Name of the School Board.
2. Name in full of the pupil-teacher.
3. Name, description, and address in full, of father or other person who is to be the surety of the pupil-teacher.
4. Father, or other relation or friend of the pupil-teacher as the case may be.
5. His or her.
6. Name of the School.
7. The month defined by Article 20, July or January.
8. Preceding month.
9. Four full years; or any less number of years, not under two, provided (*a*) that the candidate has passed for admission the examination fixed for a later year in proportion to the reduced term of service; and provided also (*b*) that the end of the reduced term of service fall beyond the candidate's 18th year (completed).
10. The wages may be weekly, or as the parties agree: they should be fixed at the discretion of the parties having in view the local rate of wages, and the advantages of the school as a place wherein to learn the business of a teacher. The agreement may be in the following form:— ——per——in the first year, and this sum shall be increased by——per——in each subsequent year of the engagement, but such increase may be stopped at the discretion of the Managers of the said School for the time being for the unexpired remainder of any year after receipt of notice from the Education Department that the pupil-teacher has failed to pass the examination, or to fulfil the other conditions of a pupil-teacher according to the standard of the preceding year as prescribed in the Articles of the Code of the said Department applicable to the case.
11. One year later than the second date in paragraph 2.

W B & L (503Y)—68817—3000-4-96

***Agreement for training of a pupil teacher.***

With regard to finance, the Board received the yearly grant from the Education Department which was based on the examination results in the 3 R's, plus a Needlework Grant, a 6d. grant for singing by ear, and a fixed grant of 4/6d. per pupil based on average attendance. From the examination schedules and schedules of grant for the years 1883 to 1890, when the grants for the 3 R's were abolished, the examination results of Orcop School varied from between 59% to 70% which was well above the average for the country in 1880. H.C. Barnard in *History of British Education* states that nationally only about 25% of those examined qualified for the 1d. per cent grant. It seems that in spite of the difference in the numbers on the register and those who actually attended, the three qualified head teachers who served the school up to 1895 did produce better results than had hitherto been achieved. A grant was also payable from the rates, plus school fees, although these were abolished in 1891. The average income of the school over these years was between £100 and £110 per annum. Since the salaries of the head teacher, plus an articled pupil teacher, with sometimes a temporary monitor, amounted to £90 or so, there was very little left for books and stationery, since fuel, light, cleaning and furniture replacements amounted to anything between £5 and £20 according to circumstances. In the light of these accounts it is understandable why the Board were at such pains to avoid election expenses, since, literally, every shilling saved was urgently needed to balance the account.

Pupil teachers were tested by the School Inspector each year of their four year agreement, and several failed. Judging from the following entry in the Log Book this is not surprising.[24]

> *"The pupil teacher's composition is still very poor and careless as the following work will show. The subject was Admiral Lord Nelson.*
>
> *'General Nelson fought the French at Alexander, he then travelled up the Levant but missed the French. From this we may date his glorious career'"*

See previous page for a copy of a Memorandum of Agreement between the School Board and one pupil teacher who successfully completed the four year period.

On the 21st October, 1895, Robert Davies, a former pupil teacher, trained at Chester Diocesan College, commenced duties together with his wife, Kate Amelia, who had served four years as a pupil teacher. The Inspector's reports from this time on, all testify to the great improvement in the school.[25] Robert Davies and his wife raised the standard throughout the school by, as an Inspector termed it, "intelligent teaching". Within two months of his arrival, natural history pictures were ordered for the infants class, a globe, compasses and material for varied occupations arrived for the upper school. The Vicar was persuaded to loan the organ from Church for the teaching of hymns. School notice boards were procured on which local and national events were posted and discussed. Above all, the children were given incentive to learn. A summer treat was organised and prizes procured by the sale of needlework completed in school. Sports took place after a village tea party which was superintended by Mrs Davies at which prizes were presented for winners of races and for good attendance. Discipline was extremely firm, but fair. Bad language, playing truant and misbehaviour were punished with two strokes of the cane. In order to build up a school fund for prizes, a school concert was organised. Children were sent home after lunch to get ready for the evening's festivities. At last, the activities of the school began to reach out into the village. This was also the time of the Rev. Dredge's ministry in Orcop, and one feels that there was a happier spirit of co-operation between, school, church and village than had existed for many years. In addition to the fixed grant, the school qualified for grants of 1/- for singing by note, 2/- for elementary science and history, geography and needlework, and 1/9d. for drawing.

From the Minutes of the Technical Instruction Committee of the Herefordshire County Council I noted that Robert Davies held evening classes, or Continuation School classes at Orcop on agriculture and commercial geography.[26] The Minutes recorded that only eighteen schools in the county held these classes; the report on Orcop states –

*"This little school has been very earnestly and carefully taught".*

*"This school is conducted with success in face of great difficulties."*

***Robert Davies with his class, approximately the turn of the century.***

During this period practical lessons in pruning and budding were given to the villagers, and also a series of lectures on "Manures and Feeding Stuffs" and "Fruit and Horticulture".[27] Robert Davies and his wife were to stay at Orcop for thirteen years; their twin boys were born at the school house, (one of whom visited the School in 1958), and their infant daughter died there. He became a Churchwarden and remained so for many years, whilst his wife organised many social events mainly for the children, but in which the parents were able to participate.

The next event in the school's history came with the 1902 Education Act by which all schools were placed under the direct care of the County Council by the setting up of Local Education Committees. At the time of the change-over there were 183 schools in the county of Herefordshire, with an average attendance in 1899 of 13,069 children.[28]

**1902. Elementary Schools in the County of Herefordshire.**

| Voluntary Schools | | 1899 Average Attendance |
|---|---|---|
| Church of England | 142 | |
| Undenominational | 7 | |
| Roman Catholic | 3 | |
| | **152** | **9790** |
| Board Schools | **31** | **3279** |
| | **183** | **13069** |

On April 30th 1903, Orcop Board School ceased its existence, and from then on came under the control of the Herefordshire Education Committee. Robert and Kate Davies did not leave Orcop until 1908, and I learnt from their son that his parents died in 1957 in their late eighties. They are remembered with gratitude by many of the older parishioners of Orcop, and a more permanent, although unseen, memorial is to be found in the belfry of Orcop Church. Here, in addition to the peal of four bells dating from 1663 to 1731, a fifth bell was added in 1907 which bears the name of the Churchwardens, of whom one was Robert Davies. The inscription on the bell reads, "God Bless Orcop".

At the first meeting of the Herefordshire Education Authority on the 7th February 1903, Sir James Rankin was elected Chairman. He was a Trustee and Manager of Orcop School until his death in 1915, living in the large mansion of Bryngwyn at Much Dewchurch, which was built by his father, a Liverpool merchant. He was Member of Parliament for South Herefordshire for many years, and endowed the Museum and City Library of Hereford. He was an enthusiastic worker for all educational and social good works, in which he was ably supported by Lady Rankin who took a great interest, together with Miss Marallier, one of the daughters of the then Vicar of Much Dewchurch, in the children of Orcop School. Both Sir James and Lady Rankin, and the Marillier family are buried at Much Dewchurch. At the same time, the Northgate, a large mansion situated near Orcop, but in St Weonards parish, was owned by the Capper family, and here again, this family for many years, until the 1930's, took an active part in the affairs of the school, serving as Managers. Parishioners tell me that they were conveyed in farm wagons to the Northgate for an annual outing where teas and games were arranged, and prizes distributed by Sir James Rankin.

***Sir James Rankin. Hereford City Library.***

The improved state of the school obviously made an impact on those in the village who previously had shown little interest in its affairs. In 1904, a Mr Field who lived at the Grange (the Rev. Gray's late home), purchased and donated eighty books for the purpose of providing the school and village with a lending library, and a few months later a Savings Bank Scheme was also started.[29] In 1906 cottage gardening became part of the syllabus, and a set of garden tools was delivered. Attendance continued to improve, and the figures available from the copy of returns made to the Local Education Authority show that for the years 1905 to 1908 the attendance figures were approximately 81%, the number of children on roll varying between 85 to 90.

Robert and Kate Davies set the pattern of staffing for many years, that of husband and wife, usually with another assistant certificated mistress. They were followed by William Jenkins and his wife Margaret, (1908-1913). I was very fortunate in being able to trace Mrs Jenkins who now lives at Blackwood in Monmouthshire, and is in her nineties. Mr Jenkins was a fellow of the Royal

Horticultural Society, and did evening school work at Orcop. There is mention of a pruning demonstration held at a local farm for the evening school. [31]

Mrs Jenkins told me that, when first at Orcop, she and her husband were mystified at the apparent dullness of the children in the afternoons until they discovered that they brought raw cider to school for drinking with their lunch! Mr Jenkins prevailed upon several farmers to take it in turns to bring milk to school for which the children paid 1d. per week, and in cold weather this was either boiled or made into cocoa. The health of the children was far from good, and chest ailments were common. Wages were still about 12/- per week; the school cleaner was paid 1/6d. extra per week to empty the toilet buckets, (this continued to be a separate pay cheque until closure, the final figure in 1964 being £1.8.4d. per month!)

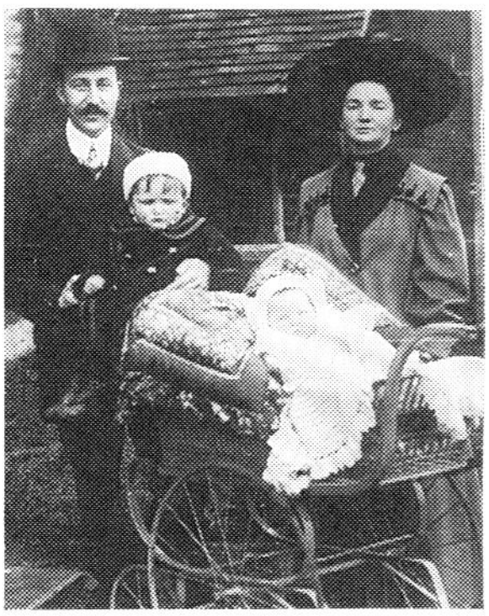

***Mr and Mrs W. Jenkins and family. The first appointment made by Herefordshire Education Committee.***

The feudal atmosphere of the village still remained. I was told how Lady Rankin would often call at the school followed by her footman bringing books and magazines on a cushion for the use of the school, and the headmaster had to contend with absentees who were engaged on tapping and beating operations for the local shoots held by the big landowners, among them Sir James Rankin, who, although a manager seemed to disregard absenteeism when it came to the shooting season.

Another landmark was reached on November 2nd 1911. The Log Book states –

*"65 children present, 100%. The occasion is unique. The time table was departed from to mark the occasion, and various children entertained the others with speeches and songs, etc.,"*

By a remarkable coincidence, the baby girl in the pram grew up to be a Medical Officer in the second World War at H.M.S. Heron, Yeovilton, at the time my husband was stationed there.

This is also interesting in that it bears out the census figures which show a drop of 14% in population, and the consequent drop in the number of children on roll.

The last Inspector's report before Mr and Mrs Jenkins left Orcop read:[32]

*"This school continues to supply a capital training. As indicating the soundness of the education in a matter often deficient in rural schools, it may be mentioned that the children show a remarkable development in capacity to read intelligently, to reproduce the substance of what they are reading, and to study effectively.*

*Such development is the more gratifying considering that the village is one of the most isolated in the county, and without training, the expressive powers of the children are extremely meagre. This success tends to show how much more sound training can do for rural children than is often supposed."*

***The Last appointment to Orcop made by the Herefordshire Education Committee. Mr E J Coleman and family. April 1955, photographed in the same place as the Jenkins' family.***

There is little change in the routine of the school over the next few years, but a significant entry in the log book of 1917 shows that there was still poverty in the parish,[33] remembering also that this was during the first World War.

*"Having practically completed sowing the school garden, work commenced today upon a plot of ground kindly granted by Mr Symons of the Hendre, for potato growing for poor people in the parish who have not sufficient ground to grow enough potatoes for their own use.*

*One row a-piece is allotted to each child of such poor parents, the ground will be worked by the gardening boys. Manure is given free by the farmer while the seed is found by the parents, Mr Robertson kindly supplying them with Scotch seed at reduced prices. Through the kind influence of Mrs Capper a further gift of twelve rows for potato planting has been offered by Mr Bowen."*

During these years there was much trouble about the supply of drinking water which was to bedevil the school right up to the 1960s, the only supply being an open well set across a field near the school which was open to all contamination. Although the educational standard of the school had greatly improved, the building was the subject of many requests to the managers to see that repairs were put in hand, plastering of walls, leaking pipes (for rainwater tanks), and the bad state of the playground and bucket toilets being particularly mentioned. The village at this time had no village hall, and the school room was used for dances which meant that it was often left in a dirty state, that holes were made in the floor, windows broken and desks damaged. One of the recent school managers recalls that horses were often tethered to the playground fence all night until their owners were turned out in the early hours of the morning.

The building was also used as a polling station for very many years. When a General Election was pending it was often booked by the prospective candidates for election meetings. On one occasion, I well remember the sitting M.P. Mr J.P.L. Thomas, who was at one time First Lord of the Admiralty, arriving to face a meeting of three; a retired doctor, my husband, and the school caretaker. After a short round of pleasantries he asked the latter if he had any questions, and was told, "I'm just waiting for you to go so that I can lock up". Mr Thomas obligingly took the hint and adjourned to school house for a cup of tea. He was re-elected!

On the lst March 1921 G.B. Gale and his wife took charge of the school, and it is remembered that Mr Gale was a churchwarden, a member of the Football Club and a very keen follower of village activities. He died suddenly of quinsy, after only three days illness, in 1923, and a tablet to his memory remains to this day in the large schoolroom. His widow became headmistress of Stretton Grandison in the county until her retirement when she moved away, and on the death of the sexton some years ago who had tended his grave my husband took over this charge.

From this time until ten years later in 1934 although there was a series of relatively short appointments, the school continued to provide a good education for its scholars. A Boot Club was formed for the poorer children by one head teacher, and 1924 saw the introduction of wireless to the children when a firm from Peterborough was responsible for providing several programmes for them. From 1934 to 1955 the school was served by three head teachers assisted by their wives, during which time classes in dairy work, cookery and poultry dressing were held in the village hall, the National Milk scheme was commenced in 1936, a school wireless was procured, and thirty children from London came to stay at Orcop for a holiday under the Country Holiday Fund Scheme. The first meeting of the Herefordshire Teachers' Study Circle was held at Orcop in 1937 when it was addressed by the then Director of Education, Mr A. P. Whitehead, who always showed great interest in the village and its school. On one occasion he visited the school bringing with him a telephone demonstration set, and on another opened the Sports and Carnival. He was also present at the First Area Village Halls Conference (see page 273) being himself Chairman of the Village Halls Committee of the Herefordshire Community Council.

During the war years the school became the focal point for all collections for the war effort, a few details of which are given below.

***February 1941***

*War Weapons Week. Target £300. Amount subscribed £1,089. Total of £2.13.3. per head of population.*[34]

***March 1943***

*Wings for Victory Week. Target £750. Amount subscribed £2,380. Total of £4.18.7. per head of population.*[35]

***June 1944.***

*Salute the Soldier Week. Amount subscribed £4,078. Total of £10.0.7. per head of population.*[36]

***During the summer months the playgrounds were used as often as possible as classrooms. May 1955.***

The roll of the school mounted to 125 in 1941 with the addition of thirty evacuee children from Bootle, and the using of the village hall as a classroom. The children arrived on the 10th June 1941, and returned home on the 2nd April 1942. The school water supply was still inadequate, a new reservoir and well which had been built, proving a failure.[37]

June 1947 saw the appointment of Mr William Morgan and his wife to Orcop.

The school was still without an adequate water supply, had approximately 90 children on roll, with only bucket toilets and no dining facilities other than on the desks in three crowded classrooms. The school house was also devoid of a bathroom or inside toilet. In 1951 Mr Morgan took 41 children to the Festival of Britain where they toured London by coach seeing places of interest. They slept in the Clapham South deep air raid shelters, and the following day went to the Royal Docks, were shown over a ship, and completed their visit with a trip to the Tower of London. In 1953, 87 children were taken to see the film of the Coronation.

*The walk to school. Jan 1963.*

The last headmaster of Orcop School, Eric John Coleman, broke the tradition of almost forty years of joint appointments when he was appointed in April 1955. His term of service was to last for nearly ten years which saw many changes in the school and village. The school at this time had 110 children on roll. A new water supply had been found which gave fresh impetus for plans to install a kitchen for cooking meals on the premises, flush toilets for school, and a bathroom for the school house. These plans were shelved several times due to lack of money, and later on because the supply became polluted and was condemned. April 1957 saw the re-organisation of the school from an all age school into an Infant and Junior School. There was at the time some opposition in the village to this change, many parents not wishing their children to travel eleven miles each day to Kingstone County Secondary School. A visit was arranged to Kingstone, and accompanied by Eric Coleman, a coach load of parents toured the school, spoke with the staff, and were so impressed with the facilities that would be available that the change over was effected smoothly and happily.

*The School Centenary. William Trotman Smith, one of the Managers and the oldest living ex-pupil of the school cuts the birthday cake with the assistance of Geraldine Skyrme, the youngest pupil, July 1958.*

*Some of the children, and their parents at the party.*

The Centenary of the School was celebrated in July, 1958, this being marked by an exhibition of work in school and by sports and games, followed by a party attended by over 100 children. The cake which sported 100 candles was cut by the oldest ex-pupil in the village, and the youngest, (see page 261). The following day a special church service was held when lessons were read by ex-pupils attending Ross Grammar and Kingstone County Secondary Schools, and by pupils of Orcop Primary School. Extra seating had been arranged in the belfry, but even this was not sufficient for the numbers of people wishing to join the congregation. Chairs were fetched from the school house and neighbouring cottages, and still people were standing in the church, and outside in the porch. Several hundred people visited the school afterwards to see the work displayed, and exchange reminiscences remarking that it was the largest village gathering within living memory.

After reorganisation the number on roll at Orcop was 68, and in 1959 a report in the *Hereford Times* stated that the Education Authority had decided to amend the Educational Development plan which planned closure of many village schools, and that it was proposed, because of its geographical position, that Orcop School should be retained, St Weonards School should be closed, and a new school built at Garway to accommodate pupils from St Weonards and Garway.

A new water supply from a private source was turned on in 1959, and this was quite satisfactory with regard to purity. New negotiations took place for a kitchen block, flush toilets, extended playground and many improvements. However, the supplier of the water, a Londoner and a local transport contractor-cum-farmer who had bought the Vicarage, decided that this would take too much water, and was not prepared to sanction extra supplies so the scheme was shelved once more. 1961 saw the arrival of mains electricity which was switched on for the first time on April 13th. An entry in the Log Book reads,

> *"Wiring of the school was completed today, and current switched on at 1.30 pm. Russia sent the first man into space today also."*

*Orcop School and School House. The flower beds in the lane were made by the children.*

In July 1962 the *Hereford Times* gave details of the latest plans for Primary reorganisation in Herefordshire which proposed that 79 schools were to be closed and 25 new schools were planned. Orcop was included in the list of closures. By this time de-population had continued in the village, and the number on roll was 45. August, 1963, saw the bringing of a main water supply to the school, and several houses nearby. The supply was not taken to the main part of the village since this involved extra pumping equipment. The coming of this supply was too late to be advantageous since by this time the Local Education Authority had decided that de-population, difficulties over water, and the fact that the school was a leasehold property which they could not own, did not warrant its retention. They, therefore, decided to build a new school at St Weonards, and eventually to divide the Orcop children between the schools of Garway and St Weonards. This would not take effect for several years, and in the meantime they proposed to modernise the school house with bathroom and toilet facilities, to decorate the school putting in a hot water system, but not to spend money on a toilet installation. This caused a storm of criticism from the local Medical Officer of Health, district Council, local newspapers, and the school managers, which reached the national press and the radio. My husband, knowing nothing of this, returned from holiday to find headlines on the placards of the local Hereford Times announcing –

*"Flush toilets for the head, buckets for pupils. The 45 pupils whose ages range from 5 to 11 years at Orcop School are likely to be without water sanitation for at least 2 or 3 more years. But Herefordshire Education Authority say they propose to install flush toilets and a bathroom in the school house for the benefit of the headmaster. Mr Edge said that the Education Committee propose to close the school at some future date, but the proposal would have to wait until a new school could be provided at St. Weonards."*

**Village schoolmasters**

Lots of things are bringing about the enormous changes taking place in the countryside, but not the least important of them is the process by which many village schools are being closed. In fact 58 primary schools – most of them in the countryside – have been closed in Herefordshire since 1946 and there are proposals to close another 68.

This has many consequences but one of them is the removal from village communities of the schoolmaster who in many cases contributes more to the life of the village than anyone else.

Orcop is one of the villages with a school due for closure and Mr Eric Coleman, headmaster of the school there, is an outstanding example of just how important the schoolmaster can be to the life of the village.

He is talking about his job in a Midland region radio programme "In the Country" at 9.30 am tomorrow.

The reduction in the total number of schools is expected to result in economies of staffing and maintenance, and, by siting new school buildings within the principal rural centres, their social and intellectual activities should be enhanced. On the other hand, the loss of the village school may well be detrimental to life within the smaller villages. With infants and juniors being transported away from the village from early youth, their local ties are weakened and the possibility of emigration is increased. The loss of the village school teacher may sadly affect parish activities to the detriment of rural life.

***(Left) Extract from the Hereford Times, 31st January, 1964.***
***(Right) Extract from the County Development Plan of 1951.***

These rather disturbing events caused the premature decision to close the school as soon as convenient, and to spend no further money on improvements whatsoever. The Chairman of the Herefordshire Water Board criticised this decision stating that £3,000 had been spent to bring water to the School in the belief that it would be open for a reasonable period. Petitions were signed by villagers, and a petition from the Dore and Bredwardine Rural District Council was sent to the Local Education Authority and to the Ministry of Education, but since the school numbers were still falling, it was clearly economically desirable that the school should be closed.

CAROL SERVICE

ORCOP CHURCH

SUNDAY, 17th DECEMBER, 1961

The children will play one verse of each carol as an introduction.

THE PLAYERS

Treble Recorders

| | |
|---|---|
| Sheila Vallance | Albert Robinson |
| Patricia Thomas | Ivor Jones |
| Pearl Whistance | Robert Roden |
| Jennifer Davies | David Kaye |
| Joyce Panniers | Vivian Morgan |
| Gillian Gatfield | Owen Sterry |
| Fiona Price | Margaret Davies |

Descant Recorders

| | |
|---|---|
| Philip Jones | Keith Morris |
| Francis Williams | Robin Coleman |

THE READERS

| | |
|---|---|
| Francis Williams | Alison Grice |
| Pearl Whistance | Philip Jones |
| Robin Coleman | Joyce Panniers |

ORDER OF SERVICE

CAROL – O Come All ye Faithful (Congregation and Organ)

Service as usual to end of Third Collect – omitting Lessons. Psalm 23.

| | | | |
|---|---|---|---|
| CAROL | – | Christians Awake | (61) |
| READING | – | Isaiah Chapter 9 verses 2, 6 and 7 | |
| CAROL | – | O Little Town of Bethlehem | (642) |
| READING | – | St. Luke Chapter 1, verses 26-33 | |
| CAROL | – | While Shepherds Watched | (62) |
| READING | – | St. Luke Chapter 2, verses 1-7 | |
| CAROL | – | Once in Royal David's City | (329) |
| READING | – | St. Luke Chapter 2, verses 8-16 | |
| CAROL | – | Away in a Manger | (Red Book 1) |
| READING | – | St. Matthew Chapter 2, verses 1-11 | |
| CAROL | – | The First Nowell | (Blue Book 8) |
| READING | – | St. Luke Chapter 2, verses 25-30 | |
| CAROL | – | Silent Night | (Blue Book 7) |

VICAR'S ADDRESS

CLOSING HYMN – Hark the Herald Angels Sing (60)

(Collection by the children)

CLOSING PRAYER

VOLUNTARY – The Holly and The Ivy

Despite the difficulties that attended the last years of the life of the school, its educational standards never dropped. Children continued to gain entrance to Ross Grammar School, and those attending Kingstone Secondary School were invariably placed in the G.C.E. class and A and B streams. The Senior Mathematics prize and Art prize at the Grammar School have been won by Orcop children, and the Head Girl at Kingstone in 1966 was from Orcop. The curriculum was varied, and a timetable, as such, did not exist. If children were thoroughly engrossed they were not interrupted at a given time to change to another subject. Bee-keeping was amongst the practical subjects undertaken by top juniors. Recorder players performed at musical festivals and accompanied the Annual

Carol Service in Church, and at Anniversaries in the village chapels. The guiding principle was "learning by doing".

When the school closed in December 1964 there were only 28 children on roll. Perhaps the best ending to this chapter is the last entry in the Log Book.

> *"School closed at 3.15 for the last time. I cease duty today as Headmaster of this school with the deepest regret, the last of a long line, since the opening on 28th June 1858. I calculate that during its lifetime some 2,000 children have attended here."*

# Chapter Seventeen

## References


| | | |
|---|---|---|
| 1. | – | Public Record Office Copy of Trust Deed. 27th December 1856. County Records Office, Hereford. |
| 2. | – | Letter from the National Society, Great Peter Street, London. S.W.1. 31st October, 1966. |
| 3. | – | Lascelles Directory of Hereford. 1851. p. 225. Hereford County Library. |
| 4. | – | Information taken from some copy forms amongst old documents in the parish chest of Llanwarne Church. |
| 5. | – | Letter from National Society. Reference 2. |
| 6. | – | Log Book 15th January 1872. Hereford County Record Office. |
| 7. | – | Log Book 26th April 1872. Hereford County Record Office. |
| 8. | Rev. N. Dredge. | MSS Notes. |
| 9. | – | Log Book 5th February 1886. |
| 10. | – | Log Book 14th December, 1868. |
| 11. | – | Log Book 1st March, 1880. |
| 12. | – | Log Book 16th June 1868. 20th May 1874. |
| 13. | – | Log Book 24th October 1874. |
| 14. | – | Log Book 27th March 1875. |
| 15. | – | Log Book, 9th August 1877. |
| 16. | – | Letter National Society. 21st November, 1966. |
| 17. | – | Figures calculated from School Fees Book, 1877 to 1891. County Records Office, Hereford. |
| 18. | – | Log Book 30th March 1883. |
| 19. | – | Log Book 29th April 1881. 15th July 1881. |
| 20. | – | Copy of letter dated 16th July 1883. H.C.R.O. |

21. – Herefordshire County Council. Abstract of Accounts. 16th November 1892. Hereford County Library.

22. – Log Book 19th June, 1893.

23. – Parish Council Minute Book 1886 to 1913. Meeting 8th February 1886 and 24th January, 1898.

24. – Log Book 3rd June 1881.

25. – Inspector's Reports, 26th July 1895, 31st July 1896, June 1900, June 1901, July 1903.

26. – Minutes of the Technical Instruction Committee, Herefordshire County Council. 13th October 1900 and 12th October 1901.

27. – Minutes of Technical Instruction Committee. 1895, 1896 and 1901.

28. – Minutes of Herefordshire County Council. 7th February 1903.

29. – Log Book 7th October, 1904.

30. – Log Book 11th May 1909.

31. – Log Book 16th September 1909.

32. – Log Book 26th September 1910.

33. – Log Book 7th May 1917.

34. – Log Book 11th March 1941.

35. – Log Book 27th March 1943.

36. – Log Book 19th June 1944.

37. – Log Book 17th April 1942.

# Chapter Eighteen

## THE VILLAGE HALL

The Village Hall was built and opened in 1929. A newspaper cutting at that time states –[1]

*"It was in 1925 that the men of Orcop decided that a Village Hall was desirable and they set about the task of raising the £500 necessary. Nine months later they had raised the handsome (?) sum of £2.6.6. and their womenfolk decided that things were not moving as fast as they might be. And so on Thursday afternoon it was the Orcop Women's Institute which claimed the credit for the fine hall which was then opened. In two years, under the leadership of Mrs Ord Capper the sum of £200 had been raised, most of this necessarily coming from outside the parish, but through the efforts of Mrs Capper, the President, and her fellow members of the Institute. It was women's work, but they did not forget the unsuccessful men, providing for them a skittle alley!*

*The Women's Institute, however, only claimed credit for their achievement, the hall, they handed over on Thursday to the newly formed Orcop Social Service Council, which will represent every aspect of the village life."*

***Orcop Village Hall***

Mrs Capper and her family lived just outside Orcop parish at the Northgate, although in the Rent Roll of the Mynde Estate dated 1674, this land appears to be part of Orcop parish. They were very interested in Orcop affairs, both Mrs Capper and her husband were managers of the School, and the family graves are in Orcop churchyard, with a wall plaque in the Church. Through her varied contacts she contracted for labour to dig the foundations of the hall, and supplied her own workmen who did much towards its actual construction. She died in 1935, and a plaque in the hall pays tribute to the many good works she carried out to benefit Orcop.

The Hall at that time was one of the biggest of the surrounding villages, and was used regularly by organisations in the village, and outside it. There was still a deficit of £300 to be found after its opening, but by 1934 this had been reduced to £32 which sum was soon accounted for by a Gymkhana and Sports.[2]

*W.I. Outing, 1930's*

The Hall was used by the County Council for cookery classes for the school and for adults. It was also used as an extra classroom during the war years for children from Bootle evacuated to the country. In the 1930s there were such organisations as the Girl Guides, British Legion, Football Club and the Womens Institute, in addition to the Church and Chapels which used it for their various functions. The winter programme from September to April in those days would consist of fortnightly dances, together with regular whist drives.[3] Every year either a Gymkhana and Sports, or Carnival, was held which attracted many entries and was always well attended. With the decline in population which will be seen later, the advent of television, mechanised transport and the consequent availability of other entertainment, the programme of the hall has now changed from that of providing entertainment for the whole village to that of the occasional whist drive, Womens Institute meeting and Anniversary party, which is attended by the supporters of the various organisations running them. It is noticeable that at the present time the whist drives which are held are supported, not so much by the Orcop people as by people from other villages who attend all local drives in this and neighbouring halls. The success of any dance which is run now is highly problematical, in fact, the last few have resulted in a loss since the Hall Committee cannot afford the high fees charged by the more popular music groups catering mainly for the younger element; the older people still prefer "old fashioned" music. In short, in common with many small village hall committees, it is no longer possible to run a regular programme of events and be sure of support. Outside pressures and attractions draw the young people from the village, while the older people tend to stay at home, content with television. The maintenance and running costs of a Village Hall are all that the committee can hope to cover. This observation is made from wide experience after over 10 years work as Secretary of the Orcop

Village Hall Committee. Those 10 years saw a gradual decline in support for village activities no matter what new idea was tried. I think this pattern is fairly general in most small villages, and even in many of the larger ones. Affluence has brought apathy towards such activities, and the ease of travel today has taken away the incentive to gather together for making one's own entertainment.

*W.I. A Meeting in 1962.*

The village hall was lit first by oil lamps, and then in 1956 by bottled gas; its heating consisted of an old slow combustion stove in one corner of the hall. Under the scheme inaugurated by the Carnegie United Kingdom Trust the Hall Committee applied for and received grants totalling £210 with which they installed electric lighting and heating, a new stage and curtains and re-decorated the hall. The decoration of the hall was done by the committee, the men working evenings under the leadership of my husband, the village schoolmaster, and the women in the afternoons with me. This was in 1960, and in 1961 another grant enabled the committee to purchase a new piano to replace the original one which was in a very poor state while in 1964 a grant was received from the Ministry of Education which enabled the installation of flush toilets, sink units, fitted cupboards and a collapsible counter in the kitchen. I well remember at the time how ironic it seemed that it was possible to get a grant from the Ministry of Education to install these necessities in the Village Hall while it was not possible to get the same consideration for the School and the School House in which we lived. The committee had also previously installed oil fired radiators to boost the heating of the electric over-head heaters which obviated the genuine complaint that in the past the hall was cold. During the years 1961 to 1966 £850 was spent on the hall, nearly half of this sum being raised by activities organised by the Committee. Much of this sum was raised by the running of Tombola, Orcop being the first village south of Hereford to start this.

One was not allowed at that time to give cash prizes so I had the weekly task of purchasing 21 prizes on the princely budget of £10, (a fair sum in those days). The prizes for the first session were given by the Committee, and since the arrival of mains electricity was imminent, the big prize was a one bar electric fire which cost £1.00. The Hall was always packed to capacity, but after 2 years other villages on main road bus routes offered far greater incentives, including money, and soon took away this source of income.

**ORCOP**

**Carnival and Athletic Sports**

on

**Saturday, July 12th**

Commencing 2 pm promptly
in the

SPORTS MEADOW

(by kind permission of E: Sayce, Esq)

---

**Admission:**

**Adults 1/6 Children 3d.**

---

**DANCE**

**8 pm to midnight. Admission 2/6**

---

Hon. Sec. Mrs W. Morgan, School House, Orcop

***Programme for Village Sports Day, in the late 1940's***

Film shows were part of the winter entertainment, but were always rather fraught with anxiety. Since we had no electricity, the firm from Hereford, from whom we hired the films provided all the equipment plus generator. We were not able to afford the newest releases, so the films were very ancient, often the generator broke down, we never made much profit, but at least, we tried. The Davies family of Wyeval were always most generous in their support of our activities.

All these improvements made the village hall into a very pleasant building, so much so, that on one occasion a few years ago, I was asked by the Director of the Herefordshire Community Council to show a visiting member of the National Council of Social Service the improvements that had been made. This gentleman lived in Yorkshire and was touring the Midlands visiting old and new village halls, and investigating the work done by the local Community Councils. Some while later the Committee were asked by the Community Council if they would act as hosts to the First Area Village Halls Conference to be held in Herefordshire since they had taken advantage of every opportunity offered to improve their village hall. This took place in March 1964, and was reported on by the local B.B.C. representative who attended in their Country Magazine programme. The following extract is taken from the 37th Annual Report of the Herefordshire Community Council.

**VILLAGE HALLS ADVISORY COMMITTEE**

Mr. A. P. Whitehead, M.B.E., M.C. (Chairman)

| | |
|---|---|
| Mr. R. E. H. Baily, C.B.E. | Mr. W. Peach |
| Rt. Rev. K. G. Bevan | Mr. J. Speight |
| Mr. P. A. B. Elkin | Mr. W. Usher |
| Mrs. E. D. Elliott | Mr. J. J. Walsh |
| Mr. H. W. G. Hawkes | Mr. E. Wall |

together with one representative from each Village Hall Committee affiliated to the Council.

The first few months of 1964 were notable for the opening of three new village halls in the county—there are photographs on the outside and inside front cover—and for the holding of the county's first Village Halls Representatives' Conference. The very fact of three new openings might be thought to offer a hopeful response to the question present in many minds at the Conference, namely, "Can the village hall really survive the revolution that is so rapidly changing the leisure patterns and way of life of the country dweller?" Orcop Village Hall was chosen for the meeting place of the Conference for two reasons. Few communities in the county seemed to have less grounds for optimism about the probable future degree of support for using and running the village hall, and few village hall committees have been so active in taking advantage of every conceivable source of grant-aid to improve their building and make it attractive to use. The drift of population from Orcop during the recent inter-censal period has been fairly severe—around 9 per cent—and the parson and the squire, who left some years ago, are shortly to be followed by the village schoolmaster. However, as the population decline in the three parishes where new halls were opened in 1964—Whitney-on-Wye, Whitbourne and Gorsley—has been no less great, the optimistic tone of the Conference was perhaps justifiable. The real message of the Conference was: Make your hall attractive, encourage a fuller and more purposeful use of it, and persuade your local authorities to do their bit on the financial side.

The conference proved very successful, and since then similar gatherings have been held in different parts of the county for the purpose of helping village hall committees to gain advice from experts, and help and ideas for the running of their activities from other committee members.

The Hall is not ideally situated since it was decided to build between the two ends of the parish; this meant that transport was really necessary to enable people to attend since it was approximately 2 miles from both Orcop or Garway Hills. Until the last 5 years or so, it was always possible to fill a coach run by two of the local bus proprietors, but with the dwindling population and easy ownership of private vehicles, the bus did not pay for itself, and this had to be abandoned. Consequently, one feels that had the hall been placed on Orcop Hill instead of between the two ends perhaps functions would be better supported in the present day. Compromise is rarely a success.

So today the hall stands for the most part unused, and yet for its age and layout it is an excellent building, well maintained, but a worry to its committee who still endeavour to serve the community by providing some type of cultural entertainment, and also to cover the normal running costs which have to be met every year. The Women's Institute, which used to hold an annual concert attracting so many people that they were standing in the kitchen, still meets every month, and also makes a donation to the upkeep of the hall in addition to the small rental they pay, whenever their funds will allow. The Welfare Committee which was set up in the early 1960s to cater mainly for the needs of the older parishioners endeavoured to help also, and gave a grant of £10 towards the new piano, but they found it difficult to get support in the village sufficient for their running costs and held some of their events in a bigger hall on a main bus route. This latter committee has now disbanded in favour of a Darby and Joan Club which is held fortnightly at the Fountain Inn at Orcop Hill because of the difficulty in obtaining transport to the village hall.

# Chapter Eighteen

## REFERENCES


1. – The Hereford Times. October 1929.
2. – The Hereford Times. 6th June, 1934.
3. – Orcop Social Service Committee. Minute Book. 1935 to 1946.

# Chapter Nineteen

## FOLK LORE AND SUPERSTITION

There are many legends and superstitions attaching to Orcop and to the adjacent Mynde ground as already mentioned on page 27. The Mynde Wood, which lies below Saddlebow Hill in Orcop is variously referred to as the Fairy Ring, and Poor Man's Wood. It is from a spring in this wood that the water supply of the Mynde stems, and it has long been tradition that in a clearing hereabouts was a place of sacrifice. Local people say that a curse will fall on any family occupying the Mynde if the wood is felled here; another version is that the owner of the Mynde, or his heir, will die within the year. Others say the curse only operates if a certain tree is interfered with; yet others hold, that if the wych elms and wych hazels are left untouched the curse will cease to be effective. Another explanation is that the curse was the penalty incurred by the owners of the Mynde for taking away the wood from the poor of the parish, to whom it had been bequeathed, and that the ban was laid upon the Mynde by the Catholic priests before the Reformation. No record exists to show that there ever was such a charity either in Much Dewchurch or Orcop. Other traditions attaching to the Mynde are that if a bough falls from a certain tree near the house, it portends the immediate death of the owner, and that if some apple trees in the garden bloom twice in the season, there will be a death in the household.[1] The Symons family who occupied the Mynde from 1726 until 1948 certainly suffered much bereavement which may have given rise to many of the old legends, although no doubt, many of the deaths of their heirs at an early age was due to weakly constitutions since there was much intermarriage in the family. This fear of cutting down timber in the Mynde Wood was a very real one within recent years; Brigadier A.F.L.Clive of Perrystone, Upton Bishop, told me that some years ago when it had been contemplated, his uncle, Captain Clive, had considered the possibility of employing Irish workmen who would have no knowledge of local superstition!

Another superstition concerns the luckless Robert Pye who was murdered by his neighbour, Charles Bodenham, (see page 70). It is said that on moonlight nights near the old Bryngwyn House at Much Dewchurch, two shadowy figures can be seen struggling near the big walnut tree which still stands there today.

There are birch woods in Orcop, and local people, as they have done for many years, still make besoms. It is unlucky to make a besom in the Christmas period, from 25th December to January 6th, or again in May. It is also considered unlucky to burn elder wood. Both these superstitions were told to me by Mr and Mrs George Meadmore, descendants of a long line of Meadmores or Medmores who are mentioned in Church documents as far back as 1709, (see page 163). These superstitions are still followed today.

It is also said that there will be nine witches from the bottom of Orcop to the end of Garway Hill as long as water runs in the Garron. The yew tree in the churchyard was also presumed to be the place where an ox or ram was roasted whole, and the people sat round to eat it.[2]

An old lady who had refused to pay to Orcop charities the rent of one acre of land which had been left as a charge on her farm, died and was buried at Orcop, (see page 155). In those days it was the custom to use a fine shroud, with an embroidered edge which was left hanging out under the lid of the coffin which was carried round the chancel before setting it down. At this old lady's funeral as the coffin reached the communion rails, the shroud ripped from end to end and hung down round the coffin. This was supposed to have been a judgement because she had robbed the poor.[3]

Orcop also possesses one of the many Holy Thorn trees to be found in Britain which legend says sprung up wherever Joseph of Arimathea placed his staff, made of the wood of Christ's cross. The tree blooms on twelfth night, and each year sees a few visitors at midnight. Old Christmas Eve 1950 saw B.B.C. cameras appear at Orcop to televise the event, but unfortunately this was never done because due to an oversight it was forgotten that electricity was not available. One of the former headmasters of Orcop School, Kenneth Nuttall, who has since become one of the leading writers of plays for children, has published a book of four plays for Christmas, one of which is entitled "The Holy Thorn".[4] Mr Nuttall with whom I have been in touch tells me that 30 years ago, when he lived at Orcop, there was still much ignorance and superstition. The Powell family who have lived nearby for many years recall that once they received a letter from America addressed to the "Mayor of Orcop" asking for the history of the Holy Thorn, (see photograph on page 279.

Orcop is the butt of many a derogatory joke due to its comparative geographic isolation. In the winter it is common practice to say "Orcop, God help us", and in the summer, "Orcop, where do you think?" I have also heard the village referred to as "Orcop, where the sun never sets", and "Orcop, where the treacle mines are". To my mind with the advent of the motor car, Orcop is no more isolated than many other similarly placed villages, and it is certainly one of the loveliest spots in the whole of the country as well as in the county of Hereford, particularly when viewed from Saddlebow and Garway Hills, (see page 195 and 14).

This feeling was obviously shared by office based members of the local education office whose visits surprisingly coincided with the finest spring and summer days. We, who lived there, saw beauty throughout the year, but the self same office personnel forgot that such a place as Orcop existed in the winter months.

With regard to the saying "Orcop, God help us", there are two derivations which are very interesting. The first concerns an old man who used to come to the Savings Bank in Hereford, and when asked from whence he came, would reply "Orcop, God help us", in the winter, but when asked in the summer, would reply "From Orcop, the Lord be praised".[5] Another suggestion which was made to me recently by Mr Frederick Sharpe who has just completed part of his work on the church bells of Hereford, came from the fact that the bells of Orcop Church were originally only three in number, the two later bells being added in 1731 and 1907. He said it was not uncommon in the 17th century for the churches in neighbouring villages to peal their bells in a sequence with each church having its own line of verse. This was the custom in his own village in Oxfordshire, and the mention of "God help us" convinced him that this was where the saying had originated. I have not been able to find any corroboration for this in neighbouring villages, but it is an interesting and charming supposition.

Orcop has also had the reputation of being very jealous of newcomers who ventured to court local girls at dances, and there is the tale of several lads who were chased for miles, one of whom was supposed to have been run to death, for poaching on the preserves of the local boys. It is possible that this could have stemmed from the following old 18th century Herefordshire folk song.[6]

***Gritton of Garway or the Murdered Man's Lament.***

*I was a wrestler bold and strong as any man might be,*
*In England's land there was no man could wrestle long with me,*
*Fair play I loved and threw him down without an angry look,*
*And now in lamentation these things I sorely book.*

*To Garway's cruel feast I went, it was a hapless night,*
*I bring my God to witness I did not wish to fight,*
*But Orcop's men are ignorant and savage to degree,*
*And nothing less would do but they must have the life from me.*

*Two seconds, they were false and pretended friendship there,*
*Oh, of such hollow friendship, I bid you all beware,*
*For long I was a fighting till I was out of breath,*
*When they held my hands behind me, and I was beat to death.*

A more recent version, written by an unnamed local man many years ago, was given to me, and runs as follows:-

***The Retreat from Orcop Dance.***

*Come all you great old soldiers,*
*Who fought the foe in France,*
*And listen to the story,*
*Of the retreat from Orcop dance.*

*The great retreat from Mons you fought,*
*Your glory to enhance,*
*But our boys greater wonders wrought,*
*In the retreat from Orcop dance.*

*Outnumbered by a thousand foes,*
*With never a backward glance,*
*They fled; on bruised and bleeding toes,*
*In the retreat from Orcop Dance.*

*No more they roam round Orcop Hill,*
*And round those damsels prance,*
*For you can bet they had their fill,*
*In the retreat from Orcop dance.*

***1966. The Holy Thorn beside the ruined forge on Stars' Pitch.***

The writer and artist, David Jones, (1895-1974) frequently visited Wales in the 1920's and 1930's, and possibly visited Orcop at the same time since he writes of the Holy Thorn in his poem Mabinog's Liturgy, a short extract of which follows.

*In the middle silences of this night's course, the blackthorn*
*blows white on Orcop Hill.*
*They do say that on this night*
  *in the warm byres*
*shippons, hoggots and out-barns of Britain*
*in the closes and the pannage-runs and on the sweet*
          *lawns of Britain*
*the breathing animals-all*
          *do kneel.*

# Chapter Nineteen

## References


| | | |
|---|---|---|
| 1 | Hubert Reade. | Woolhope Club Transactions. 26th July 1928. p. 156. |
| 2. | E.M. Leather. | Folk Lore of Herefordshire. 1912. p. 157. |

Mrs. E.M. Leather's husband was F.H. Leather, a Hereford Solicitor, who later served in the Army Service Corps of the 53rd Welsh Division as a Colonel. He employed Austin Dredge, the only son of the Rev. Norris Dredge, Vicar of Orcop from 1893 to 1909, who served with him in Egypt.

| | | |
|---|---|---|
| 3. | E.M. Leather. | p. 125. Also mentioned in the Rev. N. Dredge's old notes. |
| 4. | K. Nuttall. | Four Plays for Christmas. Longmans. 1966. The Holy Thorn. |
| 5. | E.M. Leather. | p. 254. |
| 6. | – | Pilley Collection, 2137. Hereford City Library. Also old manuscript undated Hereford County Records Office. |

# Chapter Twenty

## THE VILLAGE IN 1967

Orcop, in 1967, had changed little with regard to its landscape and buildings from the Orcop of 1867, but the whole tenor of life now after two World Wars, the break up of the large Mynde Estate in 1916, the coming of the motor car, mechanisation of agriculture, installing of main electricity and closure of the village school, is different. The village which once had a thriving communal life is now practically devoid of it.

First of all, a look at the Census figures from 1801 to 1961 which show in the latter decades, steady de-population; this has been a feature of the more remote rural areas of the county, but the Dore and Bredwardine and Wigmore areas have been regarded as the worst hit by emigration to the towns and "key" villages of Herefordshire.

| ***Year*** | ***Country*** | ***County*** | ***Orcop*** |
|---|---|---|---|
| 1801 | 8,893,000 | 88,000 | 356 |
| 1811 | 10,164,000 | 94,000 | 407 |
| 1821 | 12,000,000 | 103,000 | – |
| 1831 | 13,897,000 | 111,000 | 560 |
| 1841 | 15,914,000 | 113,000 | 570 |
| 1851 | 17,928,000 | 115,000 | 631 |
| 1861 | 20,066,000 | 124,000 | 583 |
| 1871 | 22,712,000 | 125,000 | 637 |
| 1881 | 25,974,000 | 121,000 | 554 |
| 1891 | 29,003,000 | 116,000 | 474 |
| 1901 | 32,528,000 | 114,000 | 461 |
| 1911 | 36,070,000 | 114,000 | 396 |
| 1921 | 37,887,000 | 113,000 | 468 |
| 1931 | 39,952,000 | 112,000 | 406 |
| 1951 | 43,758,000 | 127,000 | 438 |
| 1961 | – | 131,000 | 387[1] |

Since 1961 the population has dropped still further, probably to about 340 or thereabouts. The population in 1811 was 407, and in common with the rest of the country, a rising birth rate, coupled with a decreasing mortality rate, led to an increase in population. The completion of enclosure of common lands in Orcop in 1824 led to the establishment of larger farming units which necessitated the employment of more agricultural workers for the extra work involved. The property owners were also more exacting in the standards of husbandry required from their tenants as will have been seen from the wording of the tenancy agreements of this time. The 1851 Census shows that many varied crafts were being carried on in the village. Orcop had –

| | |
|---|---|
| *2 blacksmiths* | *28 farmers (5 to 173 acres)* |
| *2 shopkeepers* | *1 miller* |
| *9 dressmakers* | *1 machine maker* |
| *2 innkeepers* | *2 laundresses* |
| *1 plasterer* | *11 masons* |
| *2 tailors* | *4 shoemakers or cordwainers* |
| *7 carpenters* | *1 straw bonnet maker* |
| *27 house servants* | *1 lath cleaver* |
| *2 sawyers* | *2 woodmen* |
| *2 waggoners* | *2 coopers* |
| *1 besom maker* | *1 basket maker* |
| *1 white hoop maker* | |

Today there is a retired dressmaker who works as a favour, two innkeepers and two shopkeepers, but the rest of the population is engaged in agriculture or work in Hereford as office workers, machine operators in engineering factories, shop works, or on forestry work. Of the 631 persons resident in Orcop in 1851, 116 were agricultural labourers.[2] Today, only one farm employs an agricultural worker full time, a teenager who is not resident, and who, coming from a well to-do family, is preparing the way for his own entry into farm management.

From 1871 to 1911, the village, and the surrounding area of the Hundred of Wormelow, suffered from a continual flow of rural emigration. A comment written in 1912 says –[3]

> *"The story of Wormelow is a record of many centuries of rural prosperity and social wellbeing which has been lost in thirty years. Cardiff, Bristol, Birmingham, London, the Colonies and the States have drawn off the life-blood of South West Herefordshire."*

There was a slight upward trend between 1911 and 1921 which could be accounted for by the selling up of the Mynde Estate in 1916. Many of the farms and smallholdings in Orcop were included in this sale, and tenants had the opportunity to buy, while others went to newcomers to the district. The owning of one's holding encouraged settlement, and the raising of large families.

The impact of mechanisation was making itself felt in farming methods when I first went to live in Orcop in 1955. The changes have already been detailed in a previous chapter. Many men sought employment in Hereford when the big Henry

Wiggin factory was built, and earned far more than they could have done in agriculture, working for a farmer, and also reduced their working time from often 7 days to 5 days per week. If unmarried, they married town girls who were not prepared to live in the country without modern amenities. Orcop girls went to work in shops and offices, and also decided when married, to settle for council or private housing in Hereford or its nearby villages. Twelve years ago a number of people living in Orcop, who were not Herefordshire born, gave freely of their services to village activities, and having purchased properties relatively cheaply were prepared to wait for the coming of electricity and a good water supply. When these necessities were denied them year after year, and having also to contend with harsh winters, when the village was cut off from transport to work etc., it necessitated their moving away into Hereford, consequently their voluntary services were lost. Orcop's population consists mainly of families who have intermarried, and who have been resident for the last 30 to 40 years and more. I well remember the remark made to my husband when he was appointed as headmaster of the village school by one of the school managers, whose family had lived in the village for several generations, and who died last year. "Kick one's backside and they all feel it"! Several families have roots which extend back to the 17th and 18th centuries. The young people who have married and stayed in the village are few, as are those who wished to remain in agriculture and have their own smallholdings, or work their smallholdings in conjunction with a larger farm belonging to their parents.

The cause for the decline and gradual disintegration of Orcop rests mainly on the past lack of amenities, which, in turn, means that homes are sub-standard, and however much attention is given to alterations, such improvements can only be of a short term nature, together with mechanisation of farming and new trends in farming. The location of the village away from a main road, although amongst some of the most beautiful scenery in Herefordshire, is such that it suffers serious disadvantages in attracting newcomers. It is a scattered community, set in a valley amongst hills which causes travelling to be difficult and dangerous when snow comes. Its very beauty has helped to quicken its decline, since the County Planning Authority will not permit building having scheduled the area as one of great scenic beauty. While agreeing this to be the case, surely development could take place without disfiguring the landscape? Land has been available for sale, but permission has been refused time and time again on the same false pretext. Farmers are permitted to put up huge barns of galvanised metal which, although necessary, are an eyesore, and certainly do not blend with the landscape, but anything connected with agriculture escapes censure.

The first official bus service to run through Orcop was run by the Wye Valley Motors of Hereford in 1927. This service still runs today, and although the service is infrequent, it is a daily service which many of the small Herefordshire villages do not have. My husband, when first living in Orcop, often gave lifts in the car to people waiting at the roadside for the bus to Hereford, without realising that he was coming dangerously close to helping the bus service to go out of existence, there being few enough passengers to make the service pay. Prior to this several people in the village acted as carriers, driving to Ross and Hereford with passengers, collecting parcels, or fetching specific items for customers whom they charged so much per article. Mr Sid Wright, the founder of the well-known greengrocery business in Hereford was a great lover of Orcop, having spent his holidays at a farm on the Saddlebow when he was a child. He used to write short articles for the "Hereford Times" entitled "Shop Talks", and I think the following extract gives an excellent pen picture of Orcop at the turn of the century.[4]

> *"We went to Cox's, the Red Lion, to meet the Orcop Carrier. What a job it was getting the passengers together with their innumerable parcels. We always seemed to be one short, and it was 4 before we were jogging along over Wye Bridge. A Herefordshire carrier's brake is so made that the passengers sit along both sides, and all the parcels are on the floor in the middle, and there is no protection from the weather.*
>
> *After a halt at the Angel Inn (Grafton), for delivery of parcels and a drop of refreshment for several thirsty passengers, the lissom ones had to get out and walk up Callow Pitch. All along the road stops were made to deliver parcels, and it was nearly 7 when we arrived at the Wormelow Tump Inn. Here there were a lot of folks gathered to receive their parcels of groceries, and of course, it was simpler to sort them out if we all got out, which we did. It must have been half an hour later before the carrier had rounded the last one up, and got us all safe again on the brake.*
>
> *Then we came to the foot of Lyston Lane, (the lane leading from the main Hereford to Monmouth road to Orcop), and we all had to get out again, except old Mrs Barrell. We seemed a merry company as we climbed up the mile long lane to the top. Outside Mrs Cowley's shop at Catch Corner, what a lively to-do-ment. It was nearly dark. Orcopians from the high road and the low road were there to claim their parcels which had to be found by the light of the lantern for it was 9 p.m."*

Mrs Cowley was the daughter of Mr Charles Burleigh (see page 230); the top road is the road over the Saddlebow, and the low road the road from Orcop Green to Baggywlydiart.

The first Post Office was opened at Orcop in October 1880.[5] Previous to this letters were received through Ross, left at the Post Office at St. Weonards and sent from there to the residents by messenger who received a small payment for each. The first telephone was probably installed about 1925 when the St. Weonards Telephone Exchange which serves Orcop was opened, and the only telephone kiosk in the village was erected in front of the then Post Office, Charles Burleigh's house, Ebenezer House, on Orcop Hill, just before 1960.

Electricity came to the village early in 1961, although many farmers prior to this had bought their own generators. Water was brought to the lower part of the village in 1963, including the school and the village hall, but because it involved pumping to get it taken up to the main village on Orcop Hill, the scheme went no further. As I complete this story (April 1967), I am glad to say that another scheme has been almost completed which will bring water to most of the Orcop Hill end of the parish, unfortunately leaving Garway Hill and parts of Saddlebow still without a main supply. This has been the result of much work on behalf of the Womens' Institute, letters to the Press, and an interview which several ladies and myself had with the Member of Parliament for South Herefordshire, and the Chief Engineer of the Herefordshire Water Board. Unfortunately, all these things have come too late to save the drift of population from the village, and unless the County Planning Authorities are prepared to relax their restrictions on development, it is difficult to see what the future holds for Orcop. The village has an ageing population, some remote cottages which fall empty are sold to professional people from Cardiff and Birmingham who renovate them, and use them for weekend retreats. This applies more to the Garway Hill end of the parish which is even further from the main roads. The village is now without a resident squire, vicar, schoolmaster or policeman, and there is no doubt that the community that has such people as these working among them has a great advantage because leadership is there, and a feeling of community. Mr George Sayce of the Brooklands Farm is a member of the Parish Council, the village's representative on the Dore and Bredwardine Rural District Council, (soon to be its Vice-Chairman), and lately a member of the County Planning Committee; he realises only too well what is happening to the village, and is doing all he can to speak for the small remote parishes, but planning authorities, education officials, and providers of public services are all governed by hard facts and figures, by statistics that are calculated from forms, and the amount of money allocated has to be spent where it can be of benefit to most people.

*Orcop Post Office. Post Mistress, Mrs Fanny Harris prior to and during World War I*

This is a time of great change, not least in the county of Herefordshire, and the tendency to amalgamate and combine into bigger units at the expense of the smaller ones is here to stay. I hope that in the years to come Orcop will once again attract newcomers to settle there so that the village can expand economically, and culturally, without any detriment to its undoubted scenic advantages. Lastly, I hope that this story will have helped in some small way to record the life of a village that has all too often been regarded both as "the back of beyond", and as being devoid of any historical past.

*April, 1967.*

# Chapter Twenty

## References


| | | |
|---|---|---|
| 1. | B.R. Mitchell and Phyllis Deane. | Abstract of British Historical Statistics. p. 6. |
| 2. | – | 1851 Census Returns. Public Record Office. |
| 3. | J.H. Matthews. | Preface. |
| 4. | S.Wright. | "Shop Talks". Hereford. 1941. p. 108. Hereford City Library. Local Collection |
| 5. | – | Post Office Records. London. Minute No. 6775. Vol. 203. |

# Chapter Twenty One

## Postscript 1992

Some twenty five years have passed since this story was written, and in my conclusion I expressed some anxiety as to Orcop's future. The closure of the village school was felt by many to be a body blow to the parish since it had been the focus of interest for all generations providing the unifying bond needed in such a scattered community.

There were several factors which influenced the decision of the Local Education Authority to sanction the closure, one of which was the decrease in the number of children attending. The population decline continued throughout the 1960's, the Census figure of 387 in 1961 dropping steeply to 290 by 1971. It is heartening to discover that there is a slight upsurge from 303 in 1981 to 334 in the latest 1991 Census.

Although the development plan for the future of south west Herefordshire in no way projects any far-reaching changes for the area, housing development is encouraged within the confines of the village, although building in the scattered parts of the parish is far less favourably looked upon. Planning is only granted for someone whose special personal circumstances warrant departing from the norm, or for an agricultural worker. Nevertheless, there have been 21 bungalows and 13 houses erected in recent years, plus another 13 houses which are modern conversions of old buildings, some of which are holiday homes. The great majority are occupied by local folk of all ages, among them retired farmers who have passed on their farms to their children. Regrettably "starter homes" at a reasonable cost for young people are still lacking, as in so many rural areas.

Over the last few years, the village has to a certain extent followed the pattern of many others throughout the country. Farming has followed the relentless trend of smaller units being amalgamated into large holdings, while the introduction of more and more sophisticated machinery in turn leads to less labour being required. The voice of the "lowing herd" of Gray's Elegy, "winding slowly o'er the lea", is fast becoming a thing of the past. Dairying with its ritual of morning and evening milking has been drastically reduced as a result of the Common Market Agricultural Policy with far more land being used for arable and pasture. The poultry packing business at the Ynys farm has now given way to less intensive turkey rearing for Sun Valley, a large producer in Hereford, (Photograph p. 216).

There remains only one Public house now, the Fountain, the grounds of which are most attractively landscaped and should certainly persuade the tourist to stop for a while to enjoy the beauty of the area. The New Inn at Baggylydiart has become a private residence, together with the shop at Garway Hill and the post office and shop at Orcop Hill.

The surgery which was held on a rota basis in a private house on Garway Hill has long gone, while the daily bus service has been severely cut back to three days a week and is currently under further review.

The oldest institutions, the Church and School, which stand close together, overlooking the remains of the old motte and bailey, remain to all intents and purposes, as solid and enduring as ever.

The Church still retains its loyal followers of yesteryear, and boasts larger congregations strengthened by newcomers who have been happily absorbed into its religious life. Plans are well advanced for the full scale restoration of the roof which will display its fine timbered beams to full advantage. Much more responsibility rests with the laity since the Vicar now has the care of five parishes instead of two as in the past, and they appear to accept this most cheerfully. Far closer contact is kept with the chapels, united services being held at regular intervals.

For many years the school was used as storage premises for the sale of Government surplus stores, but has recently been converted into two dwellings. The business now operates close by, and attracts many buyers to the village. The building retains its attractive facade, and other original features, while the hedge dividing school and graveyard no longer exists which gives the impression of a well tended and open garden cemetery. The old school bell still hangs underneath the eaves, and the ancient oak tree in the playground continues to take pride of place against the backdrop of Orcop Hill. When meeting past pupils they often mention the happy memories they have of lessons taken outside under its spreading branches on warm summer days.

The pendulum of change which years ago took people out of the village for their leisure activities has now swung steadily back in favour of rural village halls, due in some measure to the tougher laws on drinking and driving. This has not escaped the notice of the Parish Council and Sports Committee who are actively working and promoting fund raising activities for a new Village Hall; the present one which had its first renovation in 1960 with much help from the Carnegie United Kingdom Trust, has since had a partial re-build in brick to provide much improved kitchen and toilet facilities. Several large scale "fun days" have yielded several thousands of pounds for local activities. This seems an excellent successor to the old style Sports Days that were held before and after the war years of 1939 to 1945. The Parish Council has also worked hard to ensure that 16 ancient footpaths have been re-opened, complete with stiles and signposts.

The Women's Institute, whose members so long ago rolled up their sleeves, and buckled down to ensuring that the village had its own hall, celebrated its Diamond Jubilee in 1983. Its membership is smaller than it was, but it still remains true to its original image, that of catering for the social and educational needs of country women and is always ready to participate in community events when required.

Perhaps the most encouraging revival is that of the Youth Club which, having faded away many years ago, is now flourishing with a firm membership of 60, and boasts a trophy winning Girls' Football team. It became apparent to several folk who were Orcop born and bred, that when children are sent away from their environment to be educated, they tend to lose their sense of identity with that environment. Youngsters from the Orcop Hill area went to neighbouring St. Weonards, and then to Ross-on-Wye. Those from Garway Hill went to adjacent Garway, and to Kingstone Secondary School, some 6 miles west from Hereford. They were growing up seldom meeting each other, and sadly lacking the contacts they would normally have enjoyed. I venture to suggest that quality of life needs to be included in the equation of planning and economics, particularly with regard to the young.

It is fast becoming commonplace through the marvels of modern technology for the professional worker to use home as his or her work base. This increasing trend has reached Orcop and there are several newcomers now who do this with obvious advantages to all. This prevents the village becoming a commuter-cum-dormitory village leading to a closer yet wider based community which is able to enlarge its horizons beyond its agricultural tradition. What could be better than to live and work in such tranquil surroundings? Surely the best of both worlds!

Having written of the Orcop of today, it is fascinating to tell of further discoveries of Stone and Bronze Age axe heads in excellent condition on Hendre and White House farms, both in the proximity of the Garron Brook. These have been duly recorded, and much interest is being shown in the formation of a Local History Group. There have also been recent finds of flints on Garway Hill/Garway boundary which have led skilled local archaeologists to offer their expertise with a view to planned digs and recording. It seems highly probable that Orcop still has a few more secrets to be unearthed, perhaps literally!

So one feels that all is going well for Orcop these days; there is an air of optimism and enthusiasm abroad which augurs well for the years ahead. When one returns to see old friends and acquaintances, it is as if the years between have never been, and Orcopians are as welcoming and friendly as they always were.

This final chapter would not be complete without a mention of those who contributed so much to this village story in their many different ways, but who have now passed from our midst. Their knowledge, interest and encouragement was always so freely given, and I hold them all in most affectionate remembrance.

*W.I. Diamond Jubilee, 1983. Sandra James, Hereford Times.*

# Map

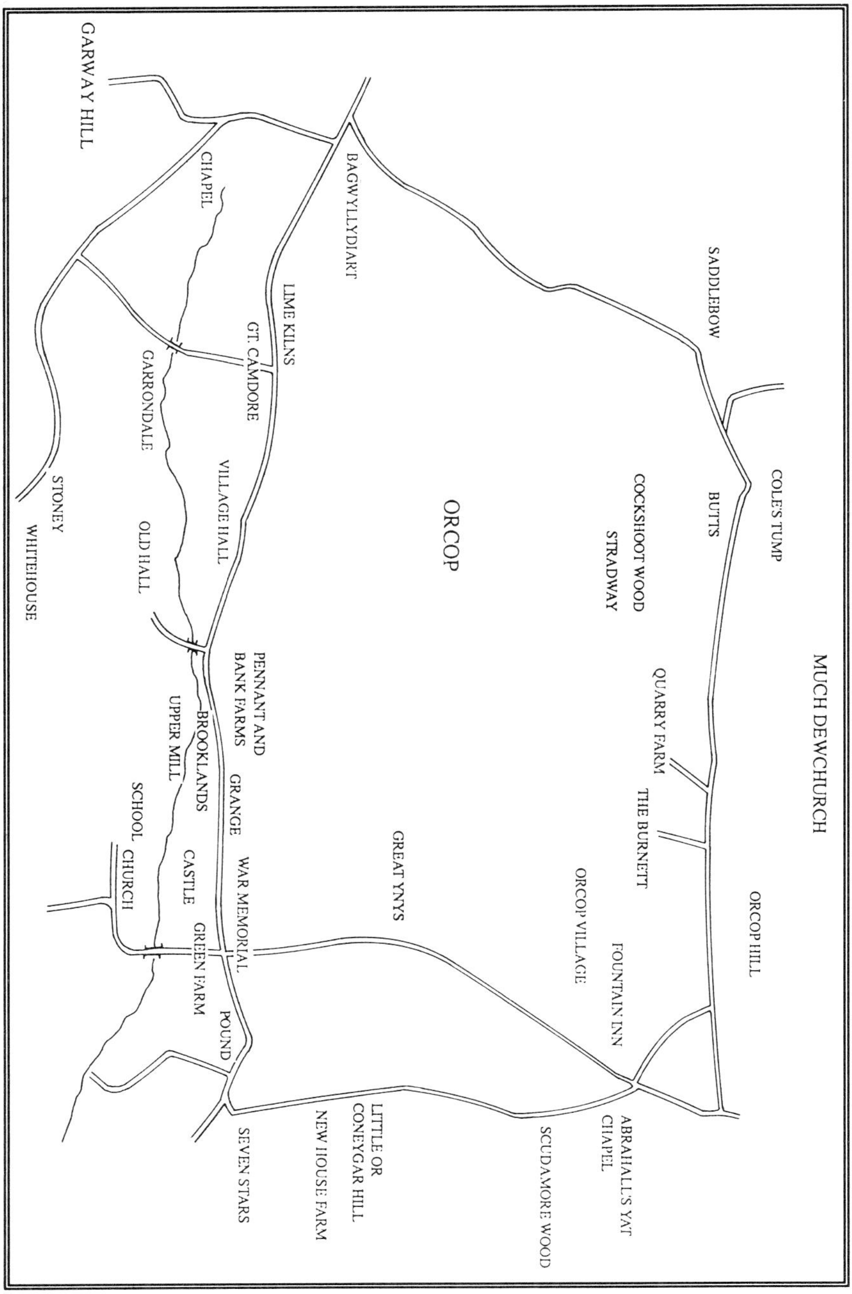
GARWAY HILL
CHAPEL
BAGWYLLYDIART
LIME KILNS
GT. CAMDORE
GARRONDALE
STONEY
WHITEHOUSE
VILLAGE HALL
OLD HALL
ORCOP
SADDLEBOW
COLE'S TUMP
BUTTS
COCKSHOOT WOOD
STRADWAY
MUCH DEWCHURCH
QUARRY FARM
THE BURNETT
ORCOP VILLAGE
ORCOP HILL
FOUNTAIN INN
PENNANT AND
BANK FARMS
UPPER MILL
BROOKLANDS
GRANGE
SCHOOL
CHURCH
CASTLE
WAR MEMORIAL
GREAT YNYS
GREEN FARM
POUND
SEVEN STARS
NEW HOUSE FARM
LITTLE OR
CONEYGAR HILL
SCUDAMORE WOOD
ABRAHALL'S YAT
CHAPEL

# Glossary of Terms

| | |
|---|---|
| ***amerce*** | to punish with a fine |
| ***andirons*** | trivets for supporting wood in fireplace |
| ***bruche*** | spit |
| ***cite*** | kite (bird classed as vermin) from the Anglo Saxon 'cyta' |
| ***cop*** | hill (Welsh) |
| ***copyhold*** | tenancy established by holding a copy of entry in court roll |
| ***court baron*** | a manorial court having jurisdiction over copyhold matters |
| ***cratch*** | grated crib, often suspended from ceiling for hanging of bacon. |
| ***cub*** | a pen for animals |
| ***demesne*** | 'ancient demesne' as in this book was land held by the Crown in 1066. |
| ***deodand*** | any personal chattel which is the immediate cause of the death of a human being, had to be forfeited for pious or charitable use. |
| ***distress*** | to distrain, to seize for debt. |
| ***doom*** | an inferior manor |
| ***doomsman*** | a judge in a Court of a manor of ancient demesne. |
| ***fealty*** | to owe allegiance to a superior |
| ***fumage*** | hearth tax |
| ***fitch-hog, fitchock*** | a pole cat |
| ***geld*** | a tax |
| ***gavelkind*** | tenure by which land is partitioned in equal portions among the family. |
| ***heinfare*** | illegally leaving the service of one's lord (Welsh) |
| ***heriot*** | fine payable to the lord on the death of a tenant, a type of death duty. |
| ***leat or leet*** | a watercourse to or from a mill |

***leet*** — court which had jurisdiction over inferior manors, often the Hundred Court.

***messuage*** — a dwelling house with outbuildings and garden, larger than a cottage.

***moiety*** — one of two equal parts, a share.

***mungcorn*** — mixture of wheat, rye and barley, planted at the same time to produce one crop.

***murage*** — money paid for keeping the walls of medieval towns in repair.

***portage*** — carrying tax or payment, toll.

***present*** — to be called before a court.

***primogeniture*** — seniority by birth among children, the right to real property belongs to eldest son.

***repleveyed*** — to take back what has been distrained upon

giving security to try the right at law.

***rent-chief*** — a small payment made to the lord by the

freeholder by which he went free of any other service to the lord.

***rent-quit*** — another name for chief rent.

***sergeantry*** — service by a knight.

***socage*** — a tenure of lands by certain and determinate service.

***suit and service*** — attendance at court and personal attendance due from a tenant to his lord, a formula in describing certain forms of tenure.

***suit of court*** — attendance by a tenant at the court of his lord.

***seise, seised of*** — possessed of (usually at death).

***thrave*** — twenty four sheaves of grain forming two stooks.

***Tithe map and Schedule*** — Maps were drawn of all parishes when tithes were commuted into a rent charge. The schedule named and numbered all land owners, tenants, farms, dwellings, fields etc. (Tithe Act 1836).

***tump*** — a mound or low hill.

***urchin*** — a hedgehog.

***wayne*** — a farm wagon.

# Bibliography

## PRIMARY SOURCES


***Private Collection, Mr F.J. George. Much Dewchurch.***

Rental Books of the Mynde Estate 1843 to 1870.
Book of Repairs to Farms 1895 to 1904.
Book of Cottage Agreements.
Book of Farm Agreements.
Folder containing copies of 25 Courts Baron 1737 to 1809.

Two books containing Estate Accounts and miscellaneous correspondence, accounts etc. This has now been deposited with the National Library of Wales.

***Deeds and documents of local landowners.***

Church cottage.
Great Camdore.
Springfield.
Pigeon House.
Hawthorn Well.
New House Farm.
Rose Cottage.
Orcop Baptist Chapel.

***Manuscript notes of the Rev. Norris Dredge, Vicar of Orcop, 1893 to 1909.***

***Minute Books and Accounts of the Orcop Village Hall.***

***Parish Minute Book 1888 to 1913.***

***Public Record Office, London.***

1851 Census Returns of all Churches and Chapels, H.O.129.
1851 Census Returns of population of Orcop.

***National Library of Wales, Aberystwyth.***

The Mynde Collection.
Ancient Charters prior to 1200, Ed. Pipe Roll Society 1888.
Calendar of Inquisitions Post Mortem, Henry VII. Vol.11.
Hereford Probate Records, Index from 1711 to 1817.
Calendar of Patent Rolls. 1552 and 1553.

***Parish Records. Now deposited with Hereford C.R.O.***

Parish Registers of Orcop Church, Register of Births, Marriages and Deaths 1672 to 1795.

Register of Birth, Marriages and Deaths 1796 to 1812.
Book of Banns 1824 to 1894.
Register of Marriages May 1755 to October 1811.
Register of Marriages 1813-1837.
Register of Baptisms 1813-1863.
Register of Burials, 1813-1889.
Settlement papers, Bastardy Bonds, Removal Orders, Examination Certificates.

Plans of Church renovations 1860.
Much Dewchurch Parish Registers 1558 to 1903.
Miscellaneous documents and Tithe Map of Llanwarne in Llanwarne Parish Chest.

Trust Deed of Orcop School.
Correspondence regarding the renovation of Orcop Church bells.

***Hereford County Records Office.***

Dore Poor Law Union Minute Books 1839/1842, 1842/47.
Vagrants Admission Register 1887-1888.
Admission Register 1875-1877.
Quarter Sessions Order Books 1733-1762.
Quarter Session Rolls 1740, 1744, 1746, 1751, 1754, 1778, 1800, 1805, 1875 to 1888.

Orcop School Log Books 1864 to 1964
Rolls of Courts Baron and Courts Leet 1806-1905 for the Manor and Hundred of Wormelow.

Archenfield Magazines 1888 to 1896.
List of Voters in the Hundred of Wormelow, 1st November 1835.
Perambulation of the Manor of Wormelow 1639. Manuscript.
Orcop School Fees Book 1877 to 1891.
Herefordshire County Council Minutes, 1895-1903.
Correspondence of Orcop School Board, Inspector's Reports, Grant forms.

Pugh's Hereford Journal, 1774 to 1790.
Harleian Manuscript 6726, 6766.
Register of Papist Estates.
Land Tax Returns.
Orcop Enclosure Award 1824.

***Hereford Diocesan Office.***

Orcop Tithe Award and Tithe Map. 1843.
Much Dewchurch Tithe Award and Tithe Map.
Bishop's Registers 1650 to 1965.

***Hereford Cathedral Archives.***

Parish Register Transcripts 1661 until 1800.
Articles of Presentment and Visitations, 1660 to 1686, from 1701 to 1736, 1762-1769, 1780-83, 1819-21 and 1860-1904.

***Hereford City Library.***

Account of Papists, Local Collection Deed Boxes.
Local Collection of Wills.
Registers of the Cantilupe Society, 1275 to 1535. Pub 1906 to 1921.
Calendar of Domestic State Papers 1581 to 1590.
Hill Manuscript.
Historical Manuscripts Commission, Harley Papers.
Brydges Collection.
Hopton Collection.
Pilley Collection.
Webb Manuscript.
Wormelow Manuscripts A and B.
Analytical Digest of Reports made by the Commissioners of Enquiry into Charities 1841.

Hereford Patrons and Incumbents, W.E.A. Cooke. Manuscript.
Herefordshire Antiquities, 20 Vols. (Including Bird's Visitation to Churches 1845).

Local Collection Deed Boxes.
Llyfr Baglan. J. Williams. London 1910 Edition.
Collection of Water Colours.
Collection of Negative Plates.

# Secondary Sources

## Books


| | |
|---|---|
| ***ANDERSON M.*** | Looking for History in British Churches. Edinburgh. 1951. |
| ***AYLMER G.E.*** | The King's Servants, The Civil Service of Charles I, 1625-1642. London. 1961. |
| ***BAKER C.H. and I.*** | Life and Circumstances of James, 1st Duke of Chandos, 1949. |
| ***BANNISTER A.*** | The History of Ewyas Harold. Hereford 1902. |
| ***BANNISTER A.*** | Herefordshire Place Names. Hereford 1916. |
| ***BANNISTER A.*** | Herefordshire and its Place in English History. Hereford 1912. |
| ***BARLEY M.W.*** | The English Farmhouse and Cottage..London 1961. |
| ***BENNETT H.S.*** | Life on the English manor..Cambridge 1960. |
| ***BOX S.*** | The Good Old Days, Then and Now. Hereford 1954. |
| ***CORBETT W.*** | Rural Rides 2 Vols. Everyman 1957. |
| ***CAM H.*** | The Hundred and Hundred Rolls. London 1930. |
| ***CHALKLIN C.W.*** | Seventeenth Century Kent. London 1965. |
| ***CORNWALL*** | How to Read Old Title Deeds. Birmingham 1964. |
| ***DUGDALE W.*** | Monastican Anglicanum. 8 Vols. London 1823. |
| ***DUNCUMB J.*** | History of Herefordshire. 7 Volumes. Wrote 1 and 2 only. Vol 1. Pub. Hfd.1804. |
| ***DUNCUMB J.*** | Agriculture of the County of Hereford. London 1813. |
| ***EKWALL E.*** | Oxford Dictionary of English Place Names. Oxford 1964 Ed. |
| ***ECTON J.*** | Thesaurus Rerum Ecclesiasticum. (Hereford Cathedral Library). |
| ***ERNLE LORD.*** | English Farming, Past and Present. 6th Ed. London 1961. |
| ***EVANS G.E.*** | Ask the Fellows who cut the Hay. London 1956. Faber and Faber Ltd. |
| ***FINDBERG J.*** | Exploring Villages. London 1958. |

***FLETCHER H.L.V.*** Herefordshire. London 1948.

***GALBRAITH V.H. and J. Tait (eds)*** Herefordshire Domesday. London 1950.

***GORGES R.*** The story of a family through 11 Centuries. U.S.A. 1944.

***GRAY H.L.*** English Field Systems. London 1959. First Ed. 1915.

***GOMME E.E.C.*** Anglo-Saxon Chronicle. 1909.

***HAMMOND J.L. and B.*** Village Labourer 1760-1832. London 1932.

***HAVERGAL F.T.*** Herefordshire Words and Phrases. Walsall 1887.

***HONE N.J.*** The English Village Community. (Hereford College Library).

***HOSKINS W.G.*** Local History in England. London 1959.

***HUTCHINSON C.J.*** Herefordshire Biographies. Hereford 1890.

***JEKYLL and JONES.*** Old English Household Life. London 1939

***KEETON G.W.*** The Norman Conquest and the Common Law. London 1966. A and C. Black.

***LEATHER E.M.*** Folk Lore of Herefordshire. Hereford 1912.

***MITCHELL B.R. and DEANE Phyllis.*** Abstract of British Historical Statistics. Cambridge, 1962.

***MARGARY I.D.*** Roman Roads in Britain. 2 Vols. London 1957.

***MATTHEWS J.H.*** History of Herefordshire. 7 Vols. Wrote Volume 5. Hereford 1912.

***MUNTHE M.*** Hellens.London 1957.

***OMAN C.*** English Church Plate 597-1830. London 1957.

***PEVESNER N.*** Herefordshire. London 1963.

***PUGH R.B.*** How to write a Parish History. London 1954. First Ed. 1889.

***ROBINSON J.*** Manors and Mansions of Herefordshire. Hereford 1873.

***ROBINSON J.*** Herefordshire Castles and their Lords. Hereford 1869.

***SEATON D.*** History of the Deanery of Archenfield. Hereford 1903.

***SMITH A.H.*** English Place Name Elements. 2 Vols. Cambridge 1956.

***STRONG G.*** Heraldry of Herefordshire. London 1848.

***SYSON L.*** British Water Mills. London 1965.

***TATE J.*** The Parish Chest. Cambridge 1960 Ed.

***WATKINS A.*** The Old Straight Track. London 1925.

***WATKINS A.*** Standing Crosses of Herefordshire. London 1930.

***WATKINS M.G.*** History of Herefordshire. 7 Vols. Volume 4. Hereford 1897.

***WRIGHT S.*** Shop Talks. Hereford 1941.

***WEST J.*** Village Records. London 1962.

***The Dictionary of National Biography.***

***Geiriadur Mawr, Welsh-English Dictionary.***

***Oxford English Dictionary.***

***Victoria County History of Herefordshire.***

# PERIODICALS


| | |
|---|---|
| ***BANNISTER A.*** | 'Parish Life in the 14th Century' English National History Review 1927. |
| ***JACKSON J.N.*** | 'Historical Geography of Herefordshire from Saxon Times to the Act of Union 1536. Woolhope Naturalists' Field Club of Herefordshire. Centenary Volume 1954. |
| ***MORGAN F.C.*** | 'A Report on the Cruck Buildings of Herefordshire.' Woolhope Naturalists' Field Club. 1938. Vol. 1936/7/8. Hereford 1940. |
| ***RODD, Rennell of*** | 'The Domesday Manors in the Hundreds of Hezetre and Elsedune in Herefordshire.' Woolhope Naturalists' Field Club. Centenary Volume 1954. |
| ***READE H.*** | 'Ghosts of Much Dewchurch.' Woolhope Naturalists' Field Club. Volume 1927/8/9 Hereford 1931. |
| ***READE H.*** | 'Sir Walter Pye's Monument in St.David's Church, Much Dewchurch.' Woolhope Naturalists' Field Club. Vol.1927/8/9. Hereford 1931. |
| ***READE H.*** | 'Welsh and English Place Names of Herefordshire.' Woolhope Naturalists' Field Club. 1921/23. |
| – | 'Herefordshire Midwives.' Woolhope Naturalists' Field Club. 1958/60. |
| – | Report on latest archaeological finds presented to Hereford museum. Woolhope Naturalists' Field Club, 1963. Part III. |


# TRADE DIRECTORIES


| | |
|---|---|
| ***1851*** | Lascelles Directory of Herefordshire. |
| ***1856*** | Post Office Directory of Hereford, Worcester, Bath and Bristol. |
| ***1862*** | Morris & Co. Directory of Herefordshire and Monmouthshire. |
| ***1868*** | Littlebury's Observer of Herefordshire. |
| ***1871*** | Jakeman and Carver's Directory of Herefordshire. |
| ***1890*** | Jakeman and Carver's Directory of Herefordshire. |
| ***1902*** | Jakeman and Carver's Directory of Herefordshire. |
| ***1941*** | Jakeman and Carver's Directory of Herefordshire. |

# List of Photographs, Illustrations & Maps


| | *Page No.* |
|---|---|
| Map to show position of Herefordshire. | 16 |
| Geological map of Herefordshire. | 17 |
| Map of Herefordshire showing positon of Orcop in Archefield. | 18 |
| Map of Herefordshire South West. | 19 |
| The position of Orcop in relation to other villages. | 21 |
| A view of Orcop from Stars' Pitch. | 22 |
| Map of the "gap" at Wormelow. | 25 |
| Coles Tump. | 26 |
| Late Neolithic Axe. | 27 |
| Family Tree of the King of Gwent and Ergyng. | 31 |
| Map of the Roman Occupation in the vicinity of Orcop. | 33 |
| Plan of the Manor of Wormelow in 1639. | 42 |
| Orcop Castle Mound. | 47 |
| Copy of Sheriff's Account dated 1172. | 48 |
| Mynde 88, 1390. Grant of messuage. | 49 |
| Part of the Baskerville family tree. | 52 |
| Coat of Arms of the Hoskyns family of Harewood. | 53 |
| Coat of Arms of the Baskerville family of Eardisley Castle. | 54 |
| Sir Humphrey Baskervile tombstone. | 55 |
| Coat of Arms of the Pyes of Much Dewchurch. | 56 |
| Coat of Arms of the Symons of Much Dewchurch. | 56 |
| The Mynde, 1992. | 57 |
| Part of the Pye family tree. | 61 |
| Tomb of Sir Walter Pye in the parish church. | 63 |
| Portrait of Sir Walter Pye. | 66 |
| The village Pound. | 77 |
| Bridge over the Garron. | 78 |
| Part of court roll 1674. | 80 |
| Tomb of Thomas Abrahall. | 83 |
| Map of Bank Farm. | 86 |
| Bridle Way, Bank Farm. | 86 |

Court roll 1737. 97

List of Chief Rents, 1700-1720. 98

Inventory of Mary Rodd. 99

Inventory of Thomas Abrahall, 1736. 100

Lower Mill Farm. 113

Line drawing of Lower Mill. 114

Mill stones and leat, Upper Mill. 115

Reclaimed mill stones, Upper Mill. 116

Dovecot and farm wagon, Lower Mill. 117

Mill stones, Lower Mill. 118

Line drawing of mill stone. 120

Drawing of mill mechanism. 121

Orcop Church, 1820. 124

Orcop Church and interior. 125

Line drawing of Bible Box. 126

Preaching Cross. 127

The Rev. Norris Dredge. 129

Seal of Llanthony Prima. 133

The Church of Orcop. 134

Aerial view of Church and School. 137

The Vicarage. 137

Church Cottage. 141

Church wall. 142

The Grange. 151

Charity Board. 154

The Lower Butts. 161

Settlement Certificate, 1720. 162

Settlement Certificate, 1709. 163

Abbeydore Workhouse. 168

The Meadmore family. 172

Stradway Farm. 173

Maps of Stradway Farm. 174

Old Hall farm. 177

Brick oven, line drawing. 179

The Burnet Farm. 180

Quarry Farm. 182

| | |
|---|---|
| Quarry Farm. | 183 |
| The Bank Farm. | 185 |
| Plan of Bank Farm. | 186 |
| Roof timbers at Pennant Farm, line drawing. | 187 |
| The Pennant Farm. | 188 |
| Abraham Baker's grave. | 190 |
| The Green Farm. | 193 |
| War memorial. | 194 |
| View from Orcop Hill. | 195 |
| Map of Orcop Enclosure Award. | 199 |
| The Moat Farm. | 201 |
| Holly Cottage and Rose Cottage. | 202 |
| Stoney Farm. | 203 |
| Poolfields Farm. | 204 |
| New House Farm. | 205 |
| Stradway Farm. | 206 |
| Butter churn and wagon, Garrondale Farm. | 207 |
| Seed drill, Stradway Farm. | 208 |
| Seed sowing. | 209 |
| The New Inn, Baggwyllydiart. | 210 |
| Cruck beams, line drawings. | 211 |
| Little Stradway and Newcastle Farms. | 212 |
| The Meadows and Ebenezer House. | 213 |
| Yew Tree Cottage, and cottage built by John Scudamore. | 214 |
| Cave Cottage and Green Lane. | 215 |
| The Ynys Farm. | 216 |
| The Copywell. | 217 |
| Camdore farm. | 218 |
| Whites Barn and Camdore. | 219 |
| The Lyons. | 220 |
| Meadmore gravestone. | 221 |
| Plan of "Ye Butts". | 221 |
| Land usage, Brooklands farm. | 222 |
| Brooklands Farm and council houses. | 223 |
| Baptist Chapel. | 227 |
| Grave of John Hayes Predgen. | 228 |

| | |
|---|---|
| Orcop Chapel. | 230 |
| Garway Hill Chapel. | 233 |
| Preachers' Plan. | 234 |
| Wedding group, Garway Hill. | 235 |
| Chapel Anniversary, Garway Hill. | 237 |
| Seven Stars Inn. | 249 |
| Seabourne Cottage and the Fountain Inn. | 250 |
| The Globe Inn. | 251 |
| Pupil teacher training agreement. | 252 |
| Robert Davies and class. | 254 |
| Sir James Rankin. | 256 |
| The Jenkins family. | 257 |
| The Coleman family | 258 |
| Playground scene. | 259 |
| Ring-a-ring o' roses. | 260 |
| Snow scene and school centenary. | 261 |
| Centenary tea party. | 262 |
| Orcop School and school house. | 263 |
| Carol Service Programme. | 265 |
| The Village Hall. | 269 |
| W.I. Outing. | 270 |
| W.I. Meeting. | 271 |
| Sports programme. | 272 |
| The Holy Thorn. | 279 |
| Orcop Post Office. | 285 |
| W.I. Diamond Jubilee. | 290 |
| Map of Orcop. | 291 |